LOVE AWAITS

COURTNEY LONG

foreword by maria jones

BANTAM BOOKS

new york   toronto   london

sydney   auckland

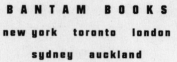

dearest brothers,

Love Awaits,

Much Peace, Your Sisters

AFRICAN AMERICAN WOMEN
TALK ABOUT SEX, LOVE,
AND LIFE

LOVE AWAITS

PUBLISHING HISTORY

Bantam hardcover edition / February 1995
Bantam trade paperback edition / March 1996

ISBN 0-553-37559-8

Published simultaneously in the United States and Canada

Bantam Books are published by Bantam Books, a division of Bantam Doubleday Dell
Publishing Group, Inc. Its trademark, consisting of the words "Bantam Books" and
the portrayal of a rooster, is Registered in U.S. Patent and Trademark Office and in
other countries. Marca Registrada. Bantam Books, 1540 Broadway, New York, New
York 10036.

PRINTED IN THE UNITED STATES OF AMERICA

BVG   10 9 8 7 6 5 4 3 2

for
the
heart
mind
and
soul

brothers

these offset page alignments of LOVE AWAITS
representative of our current state
as a Black mass:
no unity,
order,
cohesion.

Contents

foreword

We must appreciate the artistic and literary gifts that generations of Black people have left behind for us. Without proper reward or recognition, they have bestowed a legacy that gives us tremendous insight into the way we lived, thought and socialized. Through their creations, we are able to review what was once important to us and, especially, be shown whom and how we loved.

If I play the record "A Night in Tunisia," I am there in Harlem, New York, at Minton's Playhouse right in the middle of everything. I'm sitting at a table or maybe standing among the crowd straining to get a better glimpse of Dizzy and Bird because genius is at work. I would both joyously and painfully be partaking of the true-to-life interpretation of the day's goings-on. If I read a novel by James Baldwin or a poem by Langston Hughes, I am in the 50's, sitting on a stoop, talking and laughing with my husband, enjoying a warm summer's evening, watching our children play safely in the street. Yes, I would be in love and my family intact because this is the 1950's and approximately 75 percent of Black households were headed by married couples.

The artistic offerings of the past give us clues to the political climate of the Black community. In the late 60's Black people came into a political and cultural consciousness that is clearly evident in the James Brown anthem "Say It Loud (I'm Black and I'm Proud)." If we did not have our own artistic images and scholarly words to draw from, history would be left in the hands of the Daniel Patrick Moynihans, with their biased depictions of our reality.

During the 1970's Black people struggled together. For the most part, Black Americans were poor. There was no overall dramatic increase in our general wealth, but it's important to make clear that although there was no general increase in wealth, the black family remained intact with household numbers increasing from 4.3 million in 1960 to 6.7 million by 1978.

Yet today, no increase in general wealth is the inadequate reason given for why family households are no longer intact. In our art and in our soulful music of that time, the ways of Black folks were again reflected. The O'Jays sang to us about the importance of the family unit with their cut "Family Reunion." The popular Temptations tune "Just My Imagination" shows marriage and family as the ultimate dream come true. As a child of the 70's, I remember many family picnics. I remember hearing Earth, Wind and Fire songs at those various picnics and how much the music would ignite the spirit of love in all of us. Looking back, I see how the Black woman was very highly respected. Song after song spoke about the love and reverence the Black man had for his Black woman. Stevie Wonder worshipped his "Golden Lady." The Commodores and Lionel Richie paid us women homage with their ballads "Three Times a Lady" and "Lady." We must praise our artists for capturing the images, chords, colors and lyrics of the Black experience. We must praise them for maintaining the love that Black Americans held for one another and celebrating the beauty we see in one another. These are my memories of yesterday.

Today there is Hip-Hop, the ruling cultural art form in today's America, the current mode of expression that young brothers and sisters have created in order to convey their everyday realities across these United States in crowded cities in the East, wide open plains in the West, dirt roads down south, secluded suburbs of the North. Today, through Hip-Hop, the poor and privileged alike are realizing that all Black people are oppressed. The angry, confused and frantic state of Black America finds its way in the music of Black youth. "It's All About Me," "Me, Myself, and I," "Money and the Power," "A Nigga witta Gun" are a few examples of Black music echoing what and how we see, as well as what and how we feel.

In 1995, 56 percent of America's Black households will be headed by single women. The Black woman is working more than ever before because she is alone more than ever before, partly because the Black man is unemployed and incarcerated in larger numbers than ever before. Almost 50 percent of all U.S. inmates are Black men. Tragically, the family unity experienced during the 70's is gone with the wind. The class levels within the Black community widened as middle-income Blacks became wealthier and working-class Blacks became poorer. During the Reagan-Bush years, the stability of the Black family became severely disrupted as more and more Black men found themselves indefinitely jobless. Divisions in the community and family were created at all levels. Black men's and women's relations fell apart and instead of "Fight[ing] the Power" as Public Enemy urged, Black men and women began fighting each other. "What Have You Done for Me Lately?" and "Ain't Nothing Going on but the Rent" could be

heard on the Black formatted radio stations. Movies like *The Color Purple* and books such as *Disappearing Acts,* where female characters appear to triumph victoriously over male characters, were hailed as outstanding artistic works. Black men punched back with songs like "Gold Digger," "Bitches Ain't Shit but Hos and Tricks" and "You Down with O.P.P."— Other People's Pussy or Penis or Property. Black women's defensive and reactionary comebacks, "niggers ain't shit" and "all men are dogs" scream out as the coined and minted clichés of choice. But in calmer and more sincere tones, what are Black women really feeling behind those clichés? What do we women truly feel, what are we crying out, shouting, whispering? If love were not behind our anger and sadness, would we have these outbursts or defensive comebacks. If we go beyond the anger, the attention-grabbing three minutes of hype, we would uncover the heart of the matter, something that says, "I'm this angry because I love and care about my brother so much. I hate to see him do wrong and I hate to see him do wrong by me. Something has to happen to reunite us."

LOVE AWAITS strives to be that something. A start. A sincere communication. Its goal is to foster a simple understanding among young African American men and African American women.

LOVE AWAITS contains more than twenty personal accounts. In their stories, some women tell of only positive encounters with their Black brothers while others have only been hurt. Every experience in between exists in this collection with many varying perspectives that mirror our present-day realities. All these women are consistent, however, in their striving toward something better.

Due to the candid and informal approach, the familiar lingo of the Black community and its cultural youth, it is easy to visualize and feel each scenario and situation, living with these women their tremendous hurt and pain, love and humor, confusion and despair, hope and inspiration. A generation poised at this twenty-first-century threshold and preparing a way for the next, we strive to understand whether we are to live or die in frustration, love or hate in dejection or mourn or celebrate in jubilation.

peace and love,

Maria Jones

Introduction

Started 10/24/01

Between commercials and naps, Nana would pace herself as if addressing a standing-room-only crowd. Even though I was only a wounded audience of one, seeking insight and comfort, her grandeur would not waver. "If you reward a Black man for a job half done, a job half-assed completed, it's guaranteed each subsequent job will be as half-assed, as half-completed, and you better believe he'll still come 'round look'n for his reward."

This is how Nana, my grandmother, would interpret the relationships brothers have come to have with their Afri-sisters. She would explain, citing as examples uncles, cousins, friends, and relatives, that however half-assed a young man may have been taught to perceive and step to a young sister, if in those first steps he's rewarded with sex, well, then it's almost guaranteed each subsequent step will be as half-assed, as tired. And you'd better believe the young buck will come back again and again look'n for his reward, as well as continuing the same exhibition well into adulthood as an old stag. He will still come around as if he'd been rewarded like a mouse or guinea pig for learning his assigned maze.

For too many brothers and sisters there still exists this big Black chasm between the Black men and his maze, the Black woman. We see it most in this on-go'n "NIGGA BITCH, DOG-HO" phenomenon. It's a void, as dark as the Mother Land and as unknown to us, and we walk around it, skirting and sidestepping its edges, singing and echoing into it this familiar refrain that half of us are searching to know the other half, while the other maintains an elusive stance. I'm constantly asked, "What's the problem, Black man, why the distance and why the resistance? Why's the study of your heart such a mystery? And why are they mysterious to your Black sister? Should not the nagg'n, why-you-all-the-time-sweat'n-me, pain-in-the-ass, get-off-my-already-bent-back be recognized as a true concern that says, "I only wish to help relieve and soothe this pain, because this tired and spent back is the very same as mine."

I'm asked is it really too deep to see, the true love behind the rage of a mother's ass-whipp'n; a grandmother's reprimand of, "You should have known better," the irate concern of your woman's, "Where were you?" Can we not recognize a Black woman's interest in her man's future, survival and well being?

And now, after another relationship full of heartache and whys, and only intending to solicit sympathy, I am hit with the unflattering recognition of the half-assed Black man. I see it's a time not for comfort but for resolution, a time for dialogue, exchange and personal introspection. With Nana's words in my ears and the many more harmful witnessings of all my brothers and sisters and their perpetual dissolutions in my eyes, it became way past resolution time for me to jump in the chasm, break out of the maze, start some forthright exchanges to help us come together.

Our rich heritage of intricate polyrhythms would help us break out of the simple, little two-step, the repeated auditioning of the same trite and tired moves, again and again for our Afri-sisters, *dearest brothers,* LOVE AWAITS, *much peace, your sisters* is personal. Either I was under my own sustained disillusion or these one on one sit-downs, speaking directly with my Afri-sister, seemed to allow for seriousness and get-down-to-business-only dialogue. This book began as self-inquiry. It's not meant to serve as prototype for relationships for my Afri-brothers. Here is what my Afri-sister thinks and feels and sees. Hopefully it can help us rectify our dealings with one another. The reader should know that some of these women have chosen to use pseudonyms and to change certain identifying details to protect their own and others' privacy. These adopted names are Assata, Hanaan, Phrencess, Coco, Lisa, Donyale, Freda, Water, Vanessa, Tracy, Nikki and Eunice.

Check'n to see if any ill-fitted mimicry of arabesques and jetés has been assimilated while my butt should have been learning the Watusi, I venture.

—Courtney

II

lesSon 1
as We lay

a ssata

assata, 21

motor city

revolutionist

Brothers and sisters are in a state of emergency. We are in a state of mass confusion. There is no other way to describe it: in a state of emergency and confused within that state. There's no other way to describe what we are, how we've become, what we've been turned into. Confused, backward, disrespectful of ourselves and everything around us. This is how we are as individual Black men and women, and this is certainly how we treat each other.

We are in trouble and we seem to not know or we just don't give a damn. I feel I must not give a damn because we don't have enough, if any, positive images try'n to correct this shit. One or two figures or so-called spokespersons are not enough for the millions of lost, backward, miseducated dying spiritually as well as physically Blacks in this country. Everybody has been bought off. Everybody. From politician to artist and everybody in between. Everybody is too busy worry'n about their next album. Will it go gold, will it cross over, am I number one this week, what do I have to do? Do I need more weave down my ass? Do I need to grab my dick, my blunt, my gat more in my next video? We've all been bought. And the "in betweeners," the audience, the consumers, are the ones who are most thoroughly seduced and entertained by much of this bullshit.

First, I blame the so-called experienced adults. The parents of this confused generation. Obviously, they're just as confused. What were the late 60's all about? "We shall overcome." What did they pass on? What was the early 70's "Black Power," "Black Is Beautiful" rhetoric all about? Screamed by our parents. Like the line from that movie, "They all got government jobs. They went down to the build'n to take it over, and they were giv'n out job applications that day." Silenced. Bought off. They quickly shut the fuck up. Now their children are runn'n around in igno-

rant bliss. At times, talk'n the same confused bullshit. One summer it's all
about dreads and braids, then it's bald heads and short naturals. Then
another summer it's permed blowouts and weaves. We are so confused.
Our culture is a fad. It's style that's in one season and out the next.

Yeah, we got some mayors. We have some puppets. Powerless and
ineffective. Look what happened with that massacre in Philadelphia. They
ain't brief of tell the mayor shit, then bombed the MOVE people, men,
women and children to their deaths. A whole city block, to their deaths,
just like that. The mayor couldn't and I mean couldn't do shit.

You get this situation in Waco, Texas, a white man say'n he's Jesus, he's
already killed four federal agents, FEDERAL, mind you, you kill a federal
agent, you're supposed to die immediately and ten times over. This country goes crazy when one of their police officers is killed, and this man kills
four federal agents and they get this hundred-day standoff shit. This "We
don't want any more bloodshed" shit. If they were Black, as they were with
the MOVE organization, that compound would have been a park'n lot, day
one. Fuck Black women and children. That place would have gone off like
Hiroshima, another place of color. An already defeated and defenseless
people of color, bombed for good measure. Just to see the effects of an
A-Bomb. So what does that say? "We don't give a fuck about you so you
shouldn't give a fuck about yourselves. We treat you like shit so you
should treat yourselves like shit."

Then we have Freaknic in Atlanta every year. This past one I attended. A
total waste of time. I drove ten hours with my girlfriends to be around all
these lost, confused and directionless people. I drove to see a bunch of
college kids act'n like children. There is a way to have fun and have a good
time, and there is a way to show disrespect and disregard for ourselves. I'd
like to say we have officially mastered disrespect and ignorance. We have
elevated it to a fine art. Can't nobody touch us on ignorance and stupidity.

**I mean, we've taken ignorance and ran the fuck'n Boston. We've
mastered it all on our own because I no longer totally support
"Whitey made us this way." Yes, he has but, I've said, fuck it, I
know I'm beautiful, I care about myself, the Black man and the
Black woman are beautiful. I care about them. I act accordingly. I
want only the best for us and I treat my people and myself with
optimum respect. So, what's up? Yes, whitey got us started in a
backward direction, but instead of us turn'n it around, we've said,
"No, let me show you how ignorant I can really be." I have no
excuse for so-called traditionally Black-college-educated young**

adults, having been taught in historical perspective of how we've been treated and somewhat freed, and we turn around and continue the self-degrading traditions on our own. I have no patience for so-called educated people who should know better.

I would like to be able to say that the planning of our downfall is more covert than it appears. That what's being done is so deep, so ingeniously executed that no way could we see it coming and the desired results are in effect: we stay at each others' throats, we stay at the bottom, we continue to hate ourselves, but you know what, the shit ain't covert. It's no secret.

It's right there in our face. We're told time and time again, "NIGGER, you ain't shit." And the tragedy is we refuse to hear it. We hear something and how do we respond? We say, "OK, thank you." Shit we should be against, we embrace. The 40-ounce malt liquor. "Here, nigger who ain't shit. Go drink this poison. Now go disrespect yourself and your bitches." And our response. "OK, thank you. Got any more."

If you have to ask well what else, and what am I talk'n about, then that right there shows your level of ignorance.

Either we've been that psychologically fucked up, that mentally worked over, that the effects are just too deep for everyone to say, "I ain't go'n for it." Either we've been that collectively damaged or we're just that collectively stupid. It must be in our genes.

To paraphrase an argument I once heard, stupidity is the nature of the Black man. Malcolm, King, Du Bois, Clayton Powell were all special cases. They weren't totally genetically Black. Some of them were actually mulatto or octoroon and that's what gave them their intelligence because a purebreed negro is an ignorant, stupid fuck. He's a self-hating, non-progressive idiot. These other so-called Black leaders were just mad that they had those drops of Black blood that made them Black in America and condemned them to second-class citizenry. But they knew they were really white at heart and so they just wanted their white rights, their white equality. They weren't the same as these other negroes. So they felt, OK, since, by complexion, I'm Black, I'm a nigger, OK, let me try to bring this worthless race I'm lumped with along. Let me try to bring them some dignity, pride and self-respect, which they seem to naturally resist. And know'n fully well how self-defeat'n and self-destruct'n the pure negro is, they tried. They went ahead and tried anyway. Like the few that do today, but look at us.

Today they know you can pay negroes to assassinate your ass, as with the case of light-skin, white-blooded, but condemned Black, Malcolm. But he tried anyway. Ignorant negroes were hired to kill him. Malcolm knew he was gonna die because once whitey became involved, the CIA and U.S. government, that's when he knew his time was up. He says, in his autobiography, he knew the extent of what negroes in the Nation could do. As long as they were his only enemy he was alive. So long as they were his only enemy he would have died of natural causes. Check out the autobiography. They rolled alongside Malcolm's car and he bluffed them with a walking stick, a cane. They thought it was a rifle. Whitey would have said fuck that and lit the car up. The government had to step in and say, "Look ignorant negroes, this is how to assassinate, 101." You create this disturbance. You say, "Get your hand out my pocket, nigger." His security will rush the area, then team B will rush the podium and blast his ass. Stupid niggers couldn't even plan an assassination by themselves.

If this makes you angry, good. If you feel I'm defaming Malcolm's image and memory, then you need to get angry. And while you're angry be angry over the current condition of all Black people. And then get up off your ass and do something besides shak'n it at a party.

So, with Freaknic, the name gives it away. It's a place for the ignorant to meet. It's a place for freaks and I shouldn't have been there. I'm just surprised about the large number that was present. This is a Black college function, so now I'm really concerned. I see we'll be go'n through another generation of Blacks go'n in circles.

This was the so-called young, educated, future elite of the Black race. Our future leaders. Lawyers and Politicians, Scientists, Doctors and Activists. I know everybody wasn't an undeclared Liberal Arts major. Trying to make sense of this shit, I thought, maybe this was just a day for everyone to let loose; everyone is really a seriously focused Black person. But then I thought, if you're really serious, even when you let loose you don't let loose like this. Beer, alcohol, marijuana, breast, ass, genitals all out and on display.

A sister had on a big, bold "WILL WORK FOR DICK" T-shirt. This is a college-educated sister just letting loose? Am I overreacting or are they overreacting? This is the future? This is a role model? This is a future mother? A woman who will one day raise a son, a daughter, and she has "WILL WORK FOR DICK" written across her chest.

Did her mother do any march'n as a young sister? Did her mother have a Black pride poster in her daughter's room? Or was that her mother's hand-me-down T-shirt? I only hope the sister wasn't a so-called college-educated sister. Then she'd have an excuse. But college or no college, this should not be our mentality. But this was a college event and she was not an isolated case. She was consistent with the rest of the madness. I was the one out of place. I was the fuck'n square. This brother called me bitch after I stopped him from feel'n my ass. He looked at me like I had the problem. Like, don't you know where you are? Like, baby this is Freaknic, this shit is allowed.

Guys would chant in unison, "Pop that choochie." On cue, sisters would stop, spread 'em, bend over and pop.

There was a danc'n area where they were a hair line away from actually fuck'n. Sisters ripp'n off bikini tops, if not the brothers, and go'n for it.

We're in the most racist state in the Union, Georgia. You have this many Blacks together and all we could do is pop choochie, get high and do everything else disrespectful to ourselves. If white people were there, look'n at us, they'd say, "I told you so. This is why we have to keep them out of our neighborhoods, jobs and schools. This is why we must jail them, lynch them and keep them in ghettoes." And I would have been hard pressed to argue differently. In the face of conscious choice, what is my defense?

If someone said, "Hey, y'all let's go march on the Capitol and show unity and protest against the State's flag," the response would have been, "Why, what's wrong with it?"

I just don't know. Again, I'd like to think we're more than that, but just to show you what I mean, let someone read this and watch how many run to the next Freaknic. Forget about look'n for the next protest rally. It's all about the next Freaknic, the next party, and when that becomes our sole focus, I worry. We just don't get it.

The next time I see a news report talk'n about us as animals, I can't so quick jump to our defense. I'll have Freaknic in my fuck'n head to think about thanks to thousands of college-educated niggers. I can't say it was a small, isolated incident, Freaknic draws thousands. This is an event that draws Black college students from all over. You already have those that are in Georgia. You have North Carolina right next door. I heard "Ain't no party like a H.U. party." Were they talk'n about Howard University in Washington, D.C., or Hampton University in Virginia? I was so hurt to see so many of us do'n the party and bullshit theme, when we can't organize to ten people to march against discrimination, I could have cried right there. No way can you love your people, care about your people so much, witness them degrade themselves, while they believe they're just party'n, and not hurt.

I often look back on slavery as the last time when we had the most unity and the most sense since be'n here in America. We were slaves and it was sobering. We knew we were slaves. We knew we were viewed as worthless chattel, but we knew better. We stayed united and resisted. There were insurrections, rebellions and runaways. We stood by each other. The man loved his woman. If she was sold, he begged to be sold with her. He escaped to find his family. After emancipation, we searched like mad to find each other. Today, a brother gets with a sister and after three months, he wants out. Today, the Black woman is a bitch. Can you picture a slave woman being called a bitch by a slave man? We heard the white man describe the Black woman in this way and now we're mocking him like trained parrots. When are we gonna speak in our own voice?

Was slavery better for us? While we were slaves, we knew we had no one but each other. We were together like we've never been, but once freed, we lost our fuck'n minds. We became free to try and prove that we were just like our masters and we just totally lost our minds. We wanted to integrate and be like them so bad we adopted all their ill traits. We're talk'n about a people that stole, enslaved, raped, killed, divided and totally denigrated a whole people and we're breaking our necks to mimic their styles, values, morals and way of life. Pleading that we're just like them. We have to have lost our fuck'n minds. We've proven we're just like them all right, and then we've gone beyond. They did it to another race. We're do'n to ourselves. Which is worse? Steal'n from, killing, raping, totally disrespecting a stranger, or killing, raping and disrespecting your very own mother?

I'd like to personally address one of our adopted ills, rape. When does a brother know he's fuck'n raping someone? When does he feel it's rape? I have to ask because I seriously think brothers don't know they're actually raping someone in many instances. Is it part of the sickness we've learned? Like "Although she said 'no,' she really means 'yes,' she really wants it."

This is an incident that to me sounds like a rape. If you can picture it, it should look like a rape. I was taught if it walks like a duck, looks like a duck and quacks like a duck, it's a duck. But for some of us, for too many of us, rape is not rape. NO means YES. I'M NOT READY means IN A MINUTE. STOP means GO AHEAD and GET OFF ME means DON'T STOP.

I was seventeen. The situation was I had a crush on a friend of the family's son. He was twenty. One day some friends and I went over to his house. We were all upstairs in the living room with his mother and after a while I went downstairs to see him and say hi. His room was in the back of the basement. He wasn't doing anything but watching TV. I entered and sat next to him and before I knew it we had started kissing. It then got to the point where he was like, "OK, let's do this." I was like, "No." I thought with his mother be'n upstairs the situation wasn't serious. I didn't feel the need to go screaming and running upstairs. He made a suggestion and I said, "No." That should have been the end of it. I felt safe being there because his mother was upstairs and they were friends of the family.

He kept say'n, "Come on, come on," and he kept press'n me. Why I didn't leave at that point I don't know. I guess because I liked him, and I actually didn't want him mad at me by me leaving. I thought he would eventually stop pressing me and we could just chill. But he kept pressing and feeling and holding on to me so when I actually tried to get up, he was holding me down. He keep say'n come on, grinding on me and for some reason, I think to stop him from continuing, in my mind, the picture of consensual sex was better than what he was do'n and I said, "Well, just use a condom." He had one right there, he put it on and then the situation became real. I went back to saying no. Please don't. NO. I really don't want to do this. He was like, "But you already said yes, and I got this condom on." Then I thought if I'd just lie there, not move or anything, he'd realize I really didn't want to do this, and he wouldn't go any further. Of course he didn't see it that way. He sees it as consent. Tears are streaming down my face, I'm whimpering, and he's raping me. I'm thinking scream, but I'm also thinking it'll soon all be over. I'm also thinking if I scream they'll say, "Well, what were you do'n down there? Why did you come over here? Why didn't you come back upstairs? How did you get in this position?" It was obvious I had a crush on him. I did but I never wanted this to happen. It's fucked up. I was also think'n, well, at least he has on a condom, it's not like he's really touching me. My mind was just out there. Then he pulls out, says he can't come with the condom on, takes it off and goes back in. At this point, I was no longer there. Then a friend of his knocks on his door, he jumps up yell'n, "Hold on, hold on." I immediately run into the bathroom. I hear him and his boy talking, I get myself together, come out and start to leave. He has the nerve to whisper to me to stay so we could finish and so he could get his nut. With that, I knew he didn't feel he had raped me. I just ran upstairs say'n, "Are you guys ready? Let's go." They didn't notice anything wrong. He came upstairs and I just rushed out the door. He yells behind me, "I'll call you later."

At my best friend's house I tell her, "Mike raped me." She says let's tell, but I felt it was my word against his. I just wanted to forget about it. She asked why didn't I scream since they were upstairs? I said, I felt I had a lot to do with it. I shouldn't have been down there and I didn't tell my mother where I was go'n.

The next day it must have been written on my face more than I thought. I was at my friend's house when her mother mentioned his name and I just spat out, "I hate him." My friend's mother looked at me and said, "What did he do to you?" I said he didn't do anything. I just wanted to forget about the whole thing.

He was murdered a year later, stabbed to death over some bullshit. Part of me felt, "Payback is a bitch," and part of me felt bad because I was wishing for his death and part of me was thinking what if he really didn't rape me. I did say, "Use a condom." But I also said, "No."

Now, whenever I say no, I get genuinely scared. I think the guy will then start, "Well, come on, what's up? Why are you here? Why'd you let me kiss you?" When I have sex with someone, I make sure I want to have sex with that person. I don't let myself get into any situation where the guy would be able to ask, suggest or hint at hav'n sex if that's not what I want. I can't let it be any other way, because I know if I'm kiss'n someone and he suggests sex and I say, "No," I'll become terrified. I'll think now what is he gonna do? Am I about to be raped? If I say, "No," and he says "Come on, why not?" do I immediately start screaming my head off. Do I yell rape and start fight'n and kick'n? The brother may be like, what the hell is her problem? He may have no intention of ever forcing himself on anyone. He just wants to see if he can talk or reason his way into some sex, as brothers will do. How's he to know I was once raped? But I feel, he really doesn't have to. All men should respect a woman's no, and with no questions asked. I mean, you can ask why not, I do feel you are entitled to some type of answer if it appears things could have gone that way, but that answer should be totally respected. Don't start with the "But come on, I want you, relax" routine. You were told no, accept it.

The first time my boyfriend and I got into the situation of sex and I said, "No," I started to freak. I was like, "Please don't touch me." He wasn't even press'n it, and I'm go'n on and on about not being ready for this. He was cool, whenever you're ready, but why are you tripp'n? That's how fucked up you can become. A friend of mine at work is the same way. She was once raped and now she doesn't even like to kiss on a date because of what it may lead to.

How one can find pleasure in hump'n a dry, motionless body is beyond me. They say rape is a power and control thing. It's not sexual. To me that's white psychology. A brother is try'n to get some ass. He told me to stay so he could come. That's not power or control. The brother just wanted to get his nut off. Had he become physical and hit me, it would have been so he can get in and get his nut. It wouldn't have been so he could exert his power. I don't know about other men, but I do know that Black men just wanna fuck. They hold their manhood in their pants and nothing else. Now, you can break that down any way you want: Mandingo, breeder, whatever, Black men are obsessed with gett'n with as much pussy as they can. With no correct upbringing, sex and pleasure is all society teaches them.

Women are raped all the time. School, street, Freaknic. I just know many women were raped that night in Atlanta. You can't tell me, with all that male aggressiveness, all that drink'n, that no one was forcibly taken. Somebody has a story to tell. Then again, if every sister was like, "Will Work For Dick," no one was forced into anything.

The view that "OK, I took the sister out to dinner, spent x amount on her, that entitles me to some ass" is crazy. It could be one hundred dollars or one dollar, a man will expect something for it. To think a woman's body is worth that little, to think you can put a price on a woman is crazy. That goes back to some slave shit that we've internalized.

One of my roommates is dat'n this guy. The brother is a dealer. She hasn't even hugged the muthafucka and he's bought her this five-hundred-dollar linen suit. He's spent big money on her. Dinners, movies, the whole nine. Now in his mind she's obligated like a muthafucka to fuck him. Like Richard Pryor said, "Somebody's fuck'n. Well, wake up your mama." He'll be like, wake up one of your roommates if she refuses.

Homeboy can say, "Let me take you out. Wear the linen suit I bought you." When they get back to the crib and he wants to get busy, and she's like, "No," he can be like, "Well, take off that fuck'n suit I bought and walk your ass home." Now she's either gonna go home fucked but with clothes on, or she's gonna go home unfucked and without clothes.

I told her she shouldn't be accept'n shit like that. She doesn't know him. I don't even think she knows his last name. Maybe she's already resigned herself to fuck'n the brother. It is like that. A linen suit for some sex ain't no thang.

I want to be made love to. I don't remember if Mike even looked at me. Did he see the tears? Did he just not give a fuck? He just pulled up the skirt and pulled down the stockings. It was that cold. That's why when I do make love, I want to be caressed, I want to be held, I want to be kissed. I don't want anything that even resembles a hurried rushed. Nothing cold and insensitive.

In the words of one of my roommates, "Foreplay is all that," foreplay and afterplay. Foreplay demonstrates the expression of love. It shows how much you care about the person beyond just want'n to stick it in. It tells me you love my whole body and you'd like to kiss and caress every part of it. Foreplay sets the tone and mood of how the sex will be. It can be slow and thoroughly passionate or intense and thoroughly passionate. With foreplay, a woman can climax way before the actual point of insertion. The same with afterplay. We can climax again through just you hold'n and caressing and kissing us. Our bodies are that sensitive. It's that charged and alive and if you continue to just caress us instead of just roll'n off, you can bring us to another climax, if you really cared about our satisfaction. Because of how brothers engage in sex, sisters have to get into this race to see who comes first. We know once you come, it's practically over for us. We have to wait a good half hour till you're ready again, if you haven't fallen asleep.

Brothers, if you know you're a two-minute brother, please take the time out for foreplay. Satisfy your woman. You have to remember we're multi-orgasmic. If your woman hasn't come once, let alone at all, then you have an unhappy sister.

Brothers need to reverse the situation. If you were multiorgasmic, would you be satisfied with com'n only once? Then what makes you think we are? If I weren't multiorgasmic and men were, I'd kiss them softly from head to toe. Massag'n all body parts along the way. I'd release all your body tension, relax you and hold you close to me. We'd roll over, on each other, back and forth, staring into each other's eyes and we'd slowly kiss one another. I'd make sure you got yours, several times.

Women would like to do this anyway, but brothers always have to take charge. Get on top and stay on top. Stay that way through the whole session.

Foreplay and afterplay will make you a much better lover. It separates the man from the boy.

A friend of mine used to be a call girl. Now, within relationships and sex, she never kisses. To me, kissing is so intimate, I can't imagine mak'n love without kissing. It says a whole lot. Where you're kissed, where you kiss them. How they kiss you. How you kiss them. She's like, "Fuck that, I'll never let a guy kiss me." I was like, "What? I'd rather kiss than have sex." She says, "Fuck that, just fuck me." To her, sex isn't intimate. It never became a process of making love. It was just wham, bam, thank you mam. I need scented candles, music, soft blankets and all that.

You want every time to be a special moment. You want him to feel that it's special. I mean, sometimes it may be all about let's just rip off our clothes and pound each other like wild animals, but that's still out of passionate intensity, not cold and indifference.

I'm not into that S&M shit. Right now it's all about the soft intimacy. Not whips, chains and weapons. Let your body be the whip. You really have to trust a person to be tied up and shit. Some sisters will let a guy handcuff them on the second date. You don't know what the fuck he has in his closet. A chain saw or what? His boys wait'n to jump out with video cameras and you're cuffed to a fuck'n bed? Fuck that.

I'm into soft passion and I think that's because I was once hooked up. This one guy said to me, "I want to make you happy. What can I do for you? What do you like?" I was like, "Uh?" I was so used to clothes off, a little kissing, a little one, two, three, I was bugg'n. I was like, "Oh, this is live." He was, "Is this OK? Are you enjoy'n this?" He was so attentive and mak'n sure I was gett'n big-time pleasure. His pleasure was me receiving mine. He was tell'n me I was so beautiful and that this is what he wanted to do for me. Now, how many times does that happen to a sister? Oh, he's made it hard for everybody else. A standard has been set. If I had never had that experience, as most sisters haven't, I would still be settling for what I thought was good sex. Think'n I'm satisfied and that men can't do no better. Men can do better. Much better. You just have to let them know 'cause if you don't, they'll do that two-minute shit on you in a minute.

I like to play this little dance game. Two summers ago I went to this striptease where a friend of mine stripped. After watch'n her, I said, well, damn, I can do that. Guys were really gett'n turned on and getting excited. After that, I would give this little show for my boyfriend and it would really work. He'd be turned on and ready to go. But then again, it doesn't take much for men to get in the mood, but I enjoy doing it for him. That's about as deviant as I get. I have girlfriends who have told me how live it is to be handcuffed and have a guy perform oral sex on you but why do I have to be handcuffed? Lovemak'n with free hands, oral sex with free hands, allow'n me to touch, feel and explore you as you give your pleasure is the ultimate to me. Leather, suede, pumps, wear'n them in bed, that's not me. Those acts aren't spiritual for me, so I can especially not do it. That's another man's culture. Fuck someone say'n buy this and mak'n a capitalistic buck off of my intimacy. Invad'n my bedroom, tell'n me how to make love. Fuck that.

Some people's interpretation of S&M is to urinate on you, spit on you, burn you, cut you, and all this other mutilation shit. If a guy says are you down for some S&M, you need to really ask questions, not to bust grooves, but you don't know what's go'n on in some minds. If you have the personality that goes for the unexpected shit and anything goes, don't ask shit.

The striptease that I perform for my boyfriend isn't exploitive and demoralizing of self because it's private, personal and mutual. I don't worry about how I'm viewed because he knows my mind. He knows that I'm just hav'n fun with him. I'm entertaining myself as well as him. He knows not to view me as only an object here solely for his pleasure. If a woman is do'n something like that for a man and she's disrespected because of it, then we have a problem.

I'm concerned about AIDS in our communities and especially on college campuses. I was at a college health center and I couldn't believe the number of students that has herpes and chlamydia. If you're catch'n herpes and chlamydia from unprotected sex, what's stopping you from catch'n AIDS? I want to have healthy children. Shit, I want to have children. We need to understand that this AIDS shit was man-made. Extermination and population control, and we're steady fuck'n and steady dying.

We need to get that shit out our head, that "it won't happen to me." I think by now we all personally know at least one person who has died of AIDS. Your ass could be next. People will not use a condom to literally save their life. But it's all consistent with the rest of our bullshit.

I was walk'n by this school yard on my way home and two little girls were teasing and taunting a third little girl who was with them. They were chanting, "Karen is a virgin, Karen is a virgin." Karen screamed back, "NO I'M NOT A VIRGIN! NO I'M NOT!" These three girls had to be no older than eight or nine. I'll give them the benefit of the doubt and say nine. I couldn't believe my ears. It took me till eighteen to have consensual sex, and these girls were nine years old. It took me two years after that before I knew what I was do'n. What do these girls think they're do'n?

Aside from their bodies not be'n ready, where, what, who are these girls' parents? Where are they hav'n sex? Who are they hav'n it with? Nine-year-old boys who don't know what they're do'n? We have pushed our children into this hurry-up adulthood until childhood no longer exists. It exists from age one to age five. That's childhood. Then, by age six you should have some well-versed notion of sex, if not already hav'n it. What is that?

I thought you'd be teased if your friends found out you gave it up to a boy at age thirteen. You'd be a slut, you'll feel ashamed and you'd try to deny it. This girl was be'n teased for be'n a virgin, and she was defend'n herself, declar'n she wasn't. And if that girl really was a virgin, I'm sure, thanks to her girlfriends, she went and took care of it. Just so she won't be teased anymore she went and had sex. Will Work For Dick and nine-year-old Karen, the accused virgin, are our future.

What can I say? What can I really say? Black brothers and sisters, y'all love each other. From now on, y'all treat each other with respect. Y'all do that for me, OK? I don't mean to be a cynic, but sometimes you get to talk'n about our plight and you end up say'n fuck it. If we want to be ignorant asses while be'n exploited, killed, discriminated against, what can I say? What can I do? If you don't give a fuck, what can I say? I want you to give a fuck? Will you do it? Are you down for change or are you down for a big ass and that's it? Do we want to wake up and realize our lust and desires have been exploited and taken advantage of? That we've been neutralized to the point of be'n ineffective and powerless, or do we want to take back control of ourselves? The thing is we think we have control of ourselves when we don't.

Do we think we naturally like malt liquor and that we drink it of our own free will, or is it because so many fuck'n commercials and billboards are in our neighborhoods that we can't resist? Do we know malt liquor is garbage? Do we care that it has the highest alcohol content of all other beers, and its quality is the most inferior compared to all other beers? Have we ever seen a white man in a malt liquor commercial? He's drink'n Amstel Premium. He doesn't drink that malt shit. We're sold it because it's known that our ignorant ass will consume it, no questions asked. Market it with a half-clothed woman and there we are. Say it's Magnum Power, play'n on our quest to be so hard and there we are. St. Ides with a rapper's endorsement. Slave and slave massa. St. Ides get rich and what do we get? Drunk, ignorant, punk niggas.

The only thing I'd like to say is for those who are do'n the right thing, those who love their culture, color, brothers and sisters, is to keep the faith. But don't be selfish with your enlightened freedom. Help correct the brother and next sister. Don't be discouraged. Raise your children to know better and one day we'll erase the ignorance.

After five hundred years I believe we should know something. We have to know something's up. We all should know by now that we're meant to remain slaves. How can you live in this country for two minutes and not know? We've all heard of Rodney King, Yusuf Hawkins, Michael Stewart, Eleanor Bumpurs, Latasha Harlins. If not them, Malcolm, Martin, Marcus, Medgar. If you wish to remain ignorant, don't give a fuck, will continue, by choice, to disrespect yourself, your people and your culture, then fuck you, too. You can stay behind while the rest of us move on.

Finished
10/24/01

K y r a

kyra, 21

nation's murder capital, SE

realist

What sisters are identify'n with in Terry McMillan's book is the reality of relationships with Black men. That's the thing that's grabb'n sisters. If you look at the Black woman today, most are single, divorced, have no man, have the child but they don't have the man, are lonely and are lonely with an attitude. The Black woman is either educated and feels that her choices are very limited, or the woman is uneducated and feels that her choices are just limited. Among the Black man, you got 40 percent that are in jail or under court supervision, or will end up dead by age twenty-five. You got 20 percent, maybe more, that are gay, and I say more because you got all these closeted bisexual muthafuckers who are marrying women and leading double sex lives. You got another 30 percent, maybe more, that are abusers, drug users, fools, liars and cheats, niggas you just don't want to get with if you have any sense, and about 10 percent that are college educated with successful professional careers or are professional career athletes. Five percent of which are go'n to marry a white girl. That leaves 5 percent for all the sane and single Black women in this country. That's 5 percent of men for about 50 percent of women who got their shit together and are looking for a man to complement their lives.

This is why women become so possessive and petty over men. When you have one, it's like, "Goddamn, I think I have one of the decent five percent, you better step off." You don't want to fuck that up, you don't want some other bitch com'n along threaten'n and want'n what you have, fuck'n up your program. It's like, "You better go find your own." Then when you do go off to find your own you're tak'n your chances. You're almost tak'n your life in your hands. How do you know you're not gett'n one of the fool 30 percent.

You have to look at statistics. For anyone that does hook up, get mar-

ried or otherwise, it becomes just a matter of time before you find yourself
in the middle of a breakup or divorce.

Now we get into the whys and wherefores. Black men and Black
women simply do not understand each other. And more than that, we do
not understand ourselves. We are confused and we are confused some
more. We are some of the most confused individuals on the face of the
earth. But it comes with sympathy and understand'n because I don't altogether blame us. You can't once you're given a history lesson. You begin to
see the patterns and results. It's a shame we all can't realize this.

You have to understand that we were brought and born into this system
of confusion. Like it or not, this is what we must realize. Our problem is
we seem to have grown to like it. We love to moan and groan about our
misery more than we love try'n to do something about it. If we're not
moan'n and groan'n, you have those who act as if the shit never happened.
I'm talk'n about slavery. That taboo and forbidden word. What we don't
like to talk about. That's in the past now. Leave it there. But the shit
happened.

And it continues to happen. We can't ignore it. We can't ignore that the
state we are now in is a direct result of what we've been through since be'n
brought to this bitch. The percentage that's in jail or on drugs or will abuse
you, all this confusion is a result of us be'n made to be confused. I don't
want to get into "whitey this and whitey that," but I want to make sure and
clear for those that don't know, yes, we are still slaves. That is until we free
our minds, become self-sufficient and independent.

What gets me is when people say, "well, it was that way in the 60's,
we've made a remarkable change since then, we've come so far." That's
bullshit. We haven't made shit. We're worse off if anything. We can see
that, so what the fuck are these people talk'n about? We're lost and groping
for answers.

With Terry McMillan, we can see that people are read'n her shit, still
try'n to figure out what the answer is. The thing is, the answer ain't there.
Waiting to Exhale, it's just another book. More talk about how fucked up
the situation is, and that's all we do. Talk and write about how fucked up
things are until we're blue in the face. Now, what the fuck is the answer is
what I'm say'n. Let's analyze this shit. The hows and whys shit is fucked
up, and once we're finished analyzing, we need to change this shit. We
should have finished analyzing a long time ago. My parents and grandparents were analyzing. Du Bois and Frederick Douglass were analyzing shit.
The Urban League, the NAACP, Nation of Islam. How much more
analyz'n we got to do? Look, we're victims of racism. We're hated and

despised, now let's get our shit together and unify. Let's be about seriously try'n to make a change, creat'n our own independence, and then racism can't touch us.

So we continue to look to analyze. The second part of the problem lies in the shit we embrace to try and find an answer. Shahrazad Ali, OK. Can we burn this garbage? I haven't seen as many women with a Maya Angelou book. An Alice Walker book. Toni Morrison. Sonia Sanchez. Nikki Giovanni. Audre Lorde. Itabari Njeri. All these other authors who have serious literary works out there. I haven't seen sisters runn'n to bookstores to get their books. So that says we ain't try'n to seriously solve shit. We go for the mindless sensationalism. The Black Man's Guide. I give us credit for look'n, that does say we are search'n for an answer, but I don't give us credit for pass'n the word, "Don't bother. It's a farce." Let's be a bit more intelligent in our search.

Observations on *Waiting to Exhale:* The writing is not hard to figure out. It's not at all too abstruse for anyone to follow. It's simplistic. I dare say it's for the majority of the simple-minded people we are. You can understand her if you're eight years old. You don't have to exercise thought, just go, "yeah, girl, unh-huh, I hear ya." Well, I say enough of that bullshit.

They say she's a great storyteller, but I don't even see that. Not when what you're read'n is the shit you and your girls just got off the phone about. No good niggas and some more no good niggas. Shit you and your girls bitch about on the daily.

My thing is, there isn't any insight. No answers to all this shit. Just more bitch'n and moan'n. I'm tired of hear'n myself bitch. I don't want to read it. At first I read it think'n I'd learn a thing or two about these, now officially, "no-good-trifling-ass-niggas," but no such luck.

What also gets me is that the women in the book were dumb. To be in their mid-thirties, they were plain out dumb. Ever since sixteen to eighteen, I was like fuck it. I ain't cry'n no more. I've done cried my last cry. I've cried my last tear over some boy. I went through this shit already.

I do not understand these girls today who are go'n through it at age twenty-one, twenty-two, twenty-five. They're cry'n and droll'n, whin'n about, "Oh, I can't deal. I'm just so hurt inside." They go on and on and on. "I can't live without him. I can't go nooo moooore!" I be like fuck that. I'm dish'n out the papers. You're fired, you're fired and you're fired. Fuck you, fuck you and fuck you. Sisters, get a life.

So the book didn't tell me anything I didn't already know. As far as how men are, I mean, shit, give me a break. It's amaz'n how you can be that old and not know the basic shit about a man. From age sixteen you should know most of this shit. If not most, more than half, and if you don't, then you better ask somebody because something is terribly wrong.

The character Robin, tak'n Russell back fifty times, I'm like, "What the fuck?" I had to say, OK, fiction. I don't think they were *"sistuhs."* I got the impression that most of them grew up in these families where your mom and dad both helped you with your homework, you never missed a meal and everything was hunky-dory. As a result, you grow up not know'n shit about deal'n with your everyday Black man and you become the one that takes a nigga back fifty times. Whereas, if you're from the city: New York. D.C. Chicago. If you have any sense, sistuhs will go, "unh-unh, this ain't happen'n." They'd tell the muthafucker in a minute, "get the fuck outta my life, and if you come back you're gonna get fucked up by my new man."

Ain't no second chances. And these women were giving these men second, third, fifth, sixth chances. What the fuck is wrong? These are mid-thirty, push'n-forty-year-old women in this book. And we're read'n this look'n for answers? No wonder we're still analyzing shit. We'll live by the book's example and keep tak'n these no-good niggas back and back and back. What we need to do is read about a sister reject'n the nigga if he's no good and gett'n her life together. If niggas don't wanna do right, fuck em. I'll try to tell him I love him, I want this to work, but if he's gonna fuck up again and again, then why should I continue to be a part of it?

I know women will be women. We are loving. We are caring. We are nurturing. We are forgiving and no matter how strong we want to be, how powerful we must be in a situation, we all possess a weak spot. We all will give in to a nigga and let him have his way. Especially know'n how persistent niggas can be. So I'm not totally unsympathetic. *Exhale's* women weren't complete idiots. They were *push'n* complete idiots, especially at their ages and for the amount of shit they were go'n through but not complete. You'd expect a little more. We need correctives written about. We need the positive stories that exist written about to act as a source of inspiration. To show that there is hope. If all I see is the bullshit, I'm gonna take that in and put the bullshit in the relationship where it may not have ever been called for.

When I say you should know something by age sixteen, hopefully at least by eighteen, I wonder if that's grow'n up too fast. Did I grow up too fast? Are the majority of sisters out here grow'n up too fast? It makes you think and wonder how should we be. But whatever, this is reality. This is the situation, and we have to roll with it. Listen up and learn fast, or you will be caught out there.

I think we need to stop play'n these fuck'n games. We need to be straight up, no ifs ands or buts. If you wanna fuck, say you wanna fuck. If you just wanna go out, say you just wanna go out. Stop play'n these fuck'n games. As a result of games, people get hurt. I mean, Black men in general play these little games. It's like, y'all almost dehumanize us. You definitely insult our intelligence. Like we can't think. Like we don't know the shit you're pull'n has been done to someone else, and by now your shit is stale. You've ran it so much, it lacks luster. We can see you're just going through the motions. All the "I really care about you. You're the only one. I love you." Stop it.

The same shit you try pull'n on us we know has been pulled on our girlfriend up the block. And the pathetic thing is, you think you look so good do'n it, and you really look like fools, and we're only humor'n you. Girls will go back to each other and say, "Do you know what that nigga said," and we'll laugh our ass off. And what's more pathetic is we'll go right on and give you some play anyway. We both need to wake the fuck up. I'm serious. Maybe if we stopped giv'n you the play, you'd stop with the games.

See, when it comes to meeting a man, we know within the first five seconds whether we're gonna give him some or not. And it's not based on all the bullshit you run down. We know whether we're gonna give you some or play you like a song. And when you get somewhere, you go away think'n it was because of your pathetic rap, but it wasn't.

We need to just act real, cut the bullshit, and sisters need to stop all the humor'n and patroniz'n. When we act real we don't have to worry about keep'n up this false front. We know Miss America doesn't keep up that crazy, rehearsed smile, twenty-four–seven. Get real, be real and stay real.

We do end up letting down the false image we project once we're in the relationship anyway, so why not do that from jump? With the false image and then later on the real you, we're now like who the fuck is this person? I thought you were all about this and that. Boom, end of relationship. That's not the time to drop the false image. There was never really a time to put one up in the first place. You tell me you're try'n to start your own business, you have all these contacts, and a year later you're still living at home with your mother. And do we learn from our mistakes? No, we go to the next person talk'n the same trash.

Brothers want to pop shit about "Oh, y'all just don't understand what we go through as Black men." More bullshit! We have given birth to Black men. We have raised you. We have taken care of you. We have marched, fought, suffered, gone to jail and died for you. For you and right alongside of you. We have done all we can for you, so I don't think it's a matter of not understanding.

I'll tell you, the misunderstanding is with these girls out here having sons and they're so goddamn ignorant, they don't know how to raise a son into understanding himself as a man. He doesn't understand himself because his young mother doesn't really understand herself, nor does she understand the boy with whom she had the baby because he's nowhere around. So there's the answer to a man's "Y'all don't understand."

We understand quite well. We understand we noticed our father's absence. We understand we watched you hurt us. We understand we raised your child without you there and we understand our children will go through the same thing because at this point it's gotten to be no big deal.

Then you have these women who are will'n to raise a son by themselves because they claim they can teach him to grow up to respect women. Bullshit. Right after you say what you have to say to him, he still has to go outside and walk those streets by himself. You can't hold his hand twenty-four–seven. It's nothing a woman can do or say by her lonesome that's gonna make a boy turn out to be the overall best he can be. The presence of a man is needed in order to make a difference. The streets have more of an influence than Mommy try'n to do her part after work. I know, I have brothers.

Men, at a certain age, I guess around thirteen to sixteen, realize these GI Joe dolls ain't mak'n it, and these Nintendo, Sega and Game Boys are like boring. They're gonna discover that they want some pussy.

Moms can take him back to his Kings and his great ancestors, his Queens and show him all kinds of respect that existed for the Black woman, but that don't mean shit when he gets out there in the streets. Ain't nothing ancient and Egyptian walk'n around in the ghetto, so all that great shit is just a picture in the mind. Reality is the projects and all that you see in it.

He ain't gonna be with moms once the door slams behind him. He's gonna be with his boys, and his boys are gonna be like, "You punk-ass-nigga, what you talk'n about? You better get you some pussy." You know what I'm say'n, that is the reality. That is what he's gonna go through. He needs a man there whipp'n his ass at every wrong turn and then maybe Egypt will stick. Egypt will be the welcomed alternative. Those principles will stick because he knows anything against them will get his ass whipped.

So when sisters say, "All I want are boys, so I can teach them how to respect and treat women," I'm like the best of luck to you.

A lot of guys around here come from single mothers and they play the role like, "Yeah, I know how to treat a woman." They say the right things, do a couple of the appropriate things and in the end will dog you just as bad as the next nigga. A dis is a dis. I don't care if you say, "Bitch, I'm tired of your ass," or, "I need time to myself," a dis is a dis. Being used is being used.

There are men who will say, "How can you say my mother didn't do a good job with me, look at me, I turned out great." Yeah, according to you, but I don't sleep with you. Most of the time niggas don't even know how screwed up they are. How sexist, disrespectful and fucked up they may be. You could be a spoiled brat who's used to hav'n everything done for yourself. Meals cooked, clothes cleaned, and as long as he's with the fool who'll do everything and anything for him and not complain, he just may be the greatest. He's great for that sister. But we're soon back to the same old problems. How do you think her son is gonna turn out?

You take a woman who's been raised to make sure she caters to every one of her man's needs, expect'n nothing in return, then you'll never know how fucked up you both are. But I guess if that's OK for the two of you, then who am I to intervene?

But if a man gets someone different, someone who likes be'n catered to just as much as she caters, now we have another problem.

I'll tell ya, I don't wanna raise no boy by myself. I can't. I know I can't. Just like most women who might not admit the shit, but I'm too soft for one. If he does something, I'll be like, "Oh, God, I know I wanna beat the shit outta him, but I can't." Plus I know after a certain age I won't be able to keep beat'n on him. He needs a man. He needs his father is what he needs. He needs a man there to whip his ass and help discipline him so that the shit be'n said will sink in. I'm sorry, if I can't have my husband around, I don't want a son.

Grow'n up in the city, I've seen what sons be'n brought up without fathers have done. Hell no, I don't want to raise a son without his father. If I had to raise a son alone, say his father died, that's the only way I'd do it. Other than that I'd make his ass come get his son and take care of his child. Spend quality time with his child. If the father couldn't be there, I'd definitely, definitely get my son into a program where he would have a male mentor and be around men he could look up to. Decent, self-sufficient, self-knowing men. Men who can lead him in a positive direction. I would get him into a Big Brother program. I would involve him with as many programs as possible. As many to keep him from look'n toward the streets. I'd rather have a program child than a street child. I'd rather have a program child with the exposure and aspiration of mak'n something positive of himself than a street kid with the aspirations of becoming a drug dealer, a hustler, a child himself mak'n babies himself, all over the ghetto.

When do we break that cycle? Parents need to take some initiative and show some concern in their child's life. This lett'n him play in front of the build'n is not the answer. These parents know what's go'n on in front of these buildings, and yet they still let their children play there.

Then when he comes upstairs call'n his sister a "bitch-ass-trick," Mother doesn't know whether to laugh or say, "Who taught you that?" When he comes in high, or he's started sell'n, mothers want a cut. So somebody tell me what's the answer?

I've seen little girls go runn'n to their mother cry'n about some girl who was bother'n them, and the mother's response was "Go kick the bitch's ass, and you better not come back here cry'n or I'll kick your ass."

We need to straighten out these parents first. Because however the parent, there goes the child. It's as if we need to get the parents in a program, not the child. If the parents knew how to parent, you wouldn't need the child in any specially designed program.

If my son came to me say'n he was having trouble adapting to his manhood, I wouldn't know what to tell him. All I can do is say I love you, you are somebody and I believe in you. All I could do is put my trust in him. I couldn't tell him anything com'n from the experience and knowledge of a man because I'm not a man. I couldn't say, "Look here, son, this is what you gotta do. This, that and the other." I couldn't say anything that he could really relate to as if com'n from a man. I could play it off, but he can walk away say'n, "But she's a woman, she really don't understand." A man tell'n his son to respect women has a lot more weight than a woman tell'n him the same thing. Coming from a woman it seems like a selfish statement, because as a woman I would benefit. If a man said it, the child can't see the selfish angle and he'd want to know why. He'll then be able to learn how the woman and the man will benefit when there's mutual respect.

My son might not even ask me shit because he'll feel I'm a woman and I'm not qualified to answer. He'll then make the decision on his own, or go ask one of his boys. Either choice will get you fucked-up results. And my answer could be the same exact thing a male figure would say, but the fact that it's com'n from a woman makes my shit null and void. There are just some things a woman cannot tell a boy. You can try all fuck'n day, but it's just like knock'n on a wall, it's not gonna penetrate.

The opposite is true, too. There are some things a man knows he can't explain to a little girl.

All a man knows about a woman is the sex he's been trying to get all his life. So what does a man really know to teach a little girl? All I see him say'n is "watch out for them little boys." As a young brother, do you really feel confident to raise a girl without the mother? Say she flipped the script and left you with the child. I know the first thing you would do is run to your mother.

On TV we see "Go ask your mother," or "Go ask your father." In our case we have only one choice. "Should I go ask my mother?" Or we can say, "Should I go ask my grandmother?" A father needs to be there can be a father's choice.

Now, if you asked how would I raise my daughter, the answer would be different. Cuz, see, I know. I've walked in these womanly shoes. I know our psychology. I know our feelings, our emotions and our desires. I could tell her the shit I've been through and what I don't want her to go through, and what she won't go through if I have anything to do about it.

I could tell her women set the standards as to how relationships will go. As to the way we allow ourselves to be treated by men. So with a daughter, I'm more comfortable. I'll let her know that she sets the rules and regulations. She won't be like these silly little girls learn'n and tak'n their cues from fiction novels.

The problem today is all my efforts can still be wiped out by the lack of parenting by these other parents. Let's say my husband and I tell our son to do this and do that. Treat a young lady with all this respect and that respect. He goes out there and all these little skank girls will totally destroy all our efforts. They're act'n like hot little mamas in constant heat. They act in direct opposition to how I'm trying to discipline my son. You can teach, but it needs reinforcement. These girls are not the reinforcement. He'll come home, "But, Ma, she put her titty in my mouth and she sucked my thing, what else could I do?"

We wear these hoochie-coochie, ass-tight shorts. We can't wait till the summer so we can show our ass. As if our ass defined us as a person. For some of these sisters it does, and for most of these brothers they'll react accordingly: They'll view those tight shorts, with the piece of ass hang'n out as defining the way we can be treated. And then we wanna bitch and complain when we're gett'n dogged. Well, if you go out there display'n your shit, you're gonna get dogged. It's like a male friend of mine said to me, "If you're gonna put your shit on display, I'm gonna treat it like a display item. I'm gonna use it, abuse it and throw the shit away when I'm finished." We get what we ask for.

It's sad. I don't have to show my ass to get what I want. And again, look at the parents. They're dress'n their daughters the same way they dress themselves: tight, lewd and in trendy name brands.

The older parents have become too comfortable. They weren't comfortable back in the 60's, but now they are and look at their children. Our generation is fucked up. They're like, "OK, now we have this nice house in the suburbs, we have this nice luxury car, we can live like whitey, and our kids are not gonna have to struggle." Fuck that. The struggle continues. It never stopped. It's no such thing as Blacks be'n comfortable and a period when we're not gonna have to fight. We're never gonna stop fighting. That's evident. As long as there's a white man on the face of this earth who's in control, wants to stay in control and not share the wealth, we will be some fight'n to survive muthafuckers.

It seems like our parents just gave the fuck up. I mean, look at these kids. All my male friends that I went to high school with are in jail, dead or just drifting.

And you mean to tell me not one of their parents were aware of the 60's and what it was supposed to mean for their children. It wasn't so their children can walk the streets without a fuck'n thing to do. Or was the 60's parents who burnt Watts in protest the same as the 90's parents in L.A. Out there gett'n a TV and VCR. More shit to show how simple we are. Entertainment shit to show that all we need to be is entertained. Parents out there exploit'n injustice in the name of a VCR. They should have marched to Simi Valley and burnt down the fuck'n courthouse, not your own neighborhood.

Even if the parents didn't end up with a suburban home, wasn't the point to teach their children about Black pride and unity? But look at us now. It's a fuck'n shame. As they were struggl'n and fight'n and march'n and shit, they needed to let their children know exactly what they were do'n and why they were do'n it. They needed to teach them about whitey and about be'n a nigga in the eyes of whitey, and about be'n a proud Black child. Not about be'n a nigga to each other, your woman, your man, and to yourself, which is what we are teaching by our actions. Nor should we be teach'n them to be little Black-white Oreos.

There was an episode on *Fresh Prince of Bel-Air* where something happened and the parents went into tell'n Will and the rest of 'em about their civil rights involvement. That shit should have been told to them day one in the crib, and every day after that as a fuck'n bedtime story.

Look at Hilary on *Fresh Prince*. Her fuck'n priorities and values. Carlton, what the fuck does he represent? I see a dark-skin white boy. Values, belief system, culture, dress and all that shit. And the fat fuck'n father. He's so comfortable he's become a fat comfortable fuck. He represents fat comfortable America. You gotta check out the symbolism, but there it is again, we don't think.

There's now a Holocaust museum. You think bus loads of Jewish schoolchildren won't be up in that joint. We better get our shit together.

A lot of kids go to Black University and it's "I'm a business major, I have to go to class. I graduate and I get a high-profile job." That is all. Can't really blame 'em. That's what they're taught. Not about now go back to your community. All these professional Blacks you see in these high Presidential Administrative positions, or big hospitals that we don't go to, or whatever, we only see them on TV, why aren't they back in the community where we can see them? Why not where they came from, in a small office, work'n day in and day out with their people, for the betterment of their people? Why, because the pursuit of the American dream says fuck that. Take that distant position so you can get you that Lexus or BMW, the Black Man's Wish.

I know you're not gonna get out there and have your own shit right away. You're gonna have to work for white America somewhere along the line. But damn, at least teach us the skill and motivation to want our own. So that when we are work'n for white America, we'll know the shit won't be forever. We'll have plans, ambition and dreams of sett'n up our own shit, just like them.

We can hire our own dumb-ass son-in-laws, and sons and nephews and daughters, just as they do. Instead, we sit around twiddl'n our thumbs, look'n at a glass ceiling, and think'n about how we're gonna spend our check Friday and Saturday night. Which club and which outfit are we sport'n?

We don't think past our toes. And that's why he, the white man, can do to us whatever the fuck he wants to do to us because we refuse to think. We refuse to step over the bullshit placed before us.

"I got a house. I got a car. I'm liv'n large. I'm happy." The thought isn't "I got a house, I got a car. Got a nice family. Now, what can I do to enhance my people's way of living? What can I do to put back and give back?" We don't think like that. We get our shit, and we're out. We don't think about start'n a Little League baseball club for the guys in the city.

Maybe commit five, six, ten hours a week to a community center. Take a
few more kids out on a weekend camping trip, along with your son.

You know what I'm say'n, we're some comfortable muthafuckers. It's
ridiculous. That's why we don't know or respect each other now. We're
jealous of each other, we hate each other. There's inner turmoil and confusion. And if we don't change, we'll find ourselves go'n back to be'n physical slaves. The older generation can't stand talk'n about slavery. "Why are
you so angry?" "Why not have fun and go listen to that Rap music you
like?" Little do they know how angry and rebellious Rap is, all they know
is Hammer. But now when white parents, who monitor what their children are do'n, say wait a minute, what are these rappers say'n, now we
have parental advisory explicit lyrics stickers. Now here comes the Black
parents with "Yeah, listen to what they're say'n." But that's back to the
stupidity of today's parents and older generation. They didn't know shit
before and it's their very own children, but now you have Black Reverends
steamrolling Rap tapes and CDs. Where were they day one?

This past presidential election. This Bush-Quayle shit. This Clinton-Gore
shit. The lesser to two evils. We just refuse to be aware. Clinton ran his
campaign call'n Bush's Haitian-refugee policy "immoral" and "cruel." Now
Clinton has taken up where Bush left off. Yet, the Caucasian-look'n Cuban
refugees, and every other Caucasian refugee has no problem gett'n into the
land of the free and home of the brave. We refuse to be aware.

Like we refuse to be aware that there has been a Black woman candidate
on that ballot for the past several elections, Lenora Fulani. But people
don't know who she is, and don't give a fuck. She gets only 0.3 percent of
the vote, whereas a fuck like Ross Perot can come in, pay off his constitu-
ents and be a factor in this bullshit. He can go before the Black community
and say, "you people" and we provide the forum for him to say this. We
support a man who certainly does not have our best interest at heart, and
we don't know who Lenora Fulani is, but we can sing every lyric to Janet's
latest single.

Fulani and Perot. They both have the same zero percent chance of
winning, but who do we choose to support? Massa. We totally ignore one
of our own in order to side with, and snuggle with the rich ol' southern-
drawl'n-massa mentality. We're just stupid, stupid, stupid. I can't believe
us sometimes. Our so-called leaders and church leaders giv'n Perot the
forum to talk down to us. But it makes sense, because if we're still in a
slave mentality, why not give in to the massa mentality? That shit goes
hand in hand.

🅰s far as relationships go, we think even less. Why should we be any different in that arena? We don't think about anything else, why should all of a sudden we decide to love and think about how we relate to each other? We fuck over each other without thought. We fuck anything that wants to fuck without a second thought. We cross color lines without think'n. Or at least on that issue, we think we're gett'n with something better. That's when we apply thought, but then again, we've been told to think that, so we're still not think'n, or we'd know better.

I'm not fuck'n no white man. I don't want to be with no white man. I don't want to even think about the idea of dating a white man. This is the same devil that raped my mother, my grandmother, my great-grand-mother, and will rape me and my daughter if given the chance. Look at the case, I think it was at St. John's where this sister was dating a white boy, she got drunk at his party, and before the night was over she was raped by him *and* his boys. They went to court and all the rapists were acquitted. From coast to coast, no justice. I want to say good for her ass, but that's my sister. We'll just continue to make poor decisions until better in-formed. Now let's see what Reno does about her commitment to bring'n equal justice for minorities. Keep an eye on New York with their new overseer. Black folks' fault again, didn't turn out to vote. Just got so comfortable. We almost deserve whatever happens.

No, I do not ever want any love relationship with any white man. Fuck him. Or what I should say, so as not to sound racist, I'll say I'll always and only love my Black man.

I need my brothers. I need my Black man. Honey, I need my Black man like you just don't know. I don't mind mak'n dinner. I don't mind provid'n for my man. Lov'n. Nurtur'n him. Hav'n his little Black, rusty-butt babies. As long as I know he's on my side, he's respectful of me, and what I do is appreciated and mutual, he can have anything in this world. We can have anything in this world, together.

The Black man needs to understand we're not against him. The media will have you think all of us are. The way they parade Anita Hill, who waits ten years to say, "Oh, he touched me on the ass and told me about Long Dong Silver," you would think the Black woman was on a mission against the Black man. But that was some more of that media bullshit. Like she never in her life dealt with no Black man that made any type of pass at her. I mean, that's a sister and I'm gonna stand behind her, but what was her real motive behind exposing something so commonplace?

Not to excuse his actions, but if you're hit on by thousands of men all your life, why are you gonna single out one nigga ten years later? If you're offended by the shit, raise hell at the time. Be real and say you didn't report it because the shit is so commonplace you're used to it. I'm surprised she remembered so much detail. My ears don't register half the bullshit brothers say on the street, I'm so used to it. It's become like natural environmental sounds. Traffic, car horns, police sirens and a brother's "Yo, baby." Pretty soon you don't hear it all. You just go on about your business. But Anita can quote Clarence word for word.

This shit ten years later is political and personal and payback. Does she really feel he's not fit to be a Supreme Court Judge because he goes around pinch'n asses? Like everyone in politics are Angels. Kennedy was sitt'n up there like "Who am I to judge? Just don't bring up my past. Chappaquiddick, or about my brothers fuck'n Marilyn in the White House."

We don't have any real representatives of the race. I mean, Bush nominated Clarence, how Black at heart can he be?

What a lot of people don't know is he was once married to a Black woman before he married his dream. You see what happens when you marry white. You get a Supreme Court seat. But, yeah, Clarence knows about ass. The sister divorced him and he misses that ass. He saw Anita and said, "Goddamn!" Maybe that's why Anita dropped dime. She knew he divorced a sister, married a white bitch and was like "All this time he's been pinch'n my Black ass, unh-unh, fuck that. I'll wait. However long it takes, I'll come back to haunt his ass. He's a Tom so I'll get him."

Mike Tyson, Michael Jackson, Tupac, I can't take any sides, I wasn't there. With Tyson, I don't know if he did or didn't. I don't know if she freaked him or what. I do know it's some shit that could have been prevented. At two o'clock in the fuck'n morn'n she could have stayed her black ass in her hotel room. Some man calls you up, who has a reputation, and you don't take no friend. I don't give a fuck if it's Jesus Christ, you know what's up if he's call'n you at two A.M., and you're in the bed. I mean, how naive can you be?

Her mother says she's only eighteen and she didn't know. Didn't know what? That he wasn't gonna try to bust them walls? Fuck that, you know something. You know something about a young, healthy, celebrated Black man with a reputation call'n your ass two A.M. in the morn'n. If you don't know shit else, you know what's up in this case. You don't go to some man's hotel room at two o'clock in the morning.

I'm sorry, I try not to take sides, and I still won't, but it's hard to accept that naive role if I had to make a decision. "I didn't know." Tell me anything but that. You're in a worldly beauty pageant, yet you know nothing of the world? You know nothing about Mike Tyson? You don't read newspapers. You don't watch TV? Mike and Robin on Barbara Walters. Mike has been known to go around clubs touch'n everybody on the ass. Between him and Clarence they've grabbed half the nation's ass. If he didn't rape her, he's pay'n for something. I believe in divine justice. Mike is pay'n for something and I hope it turns out for the best for the brother. He's a Black man and I love him unconditionally. He's a victim like all the rest. He was pimped as a boxer and nothing else. Where is the time for social skills and how to treat a woman? But he knows how to bust a nigga upside the head. Now he has to be talked to so he can make a positive change.

Desiree and Mike only highlights the problem we have with each other. We don't know each other and we don't communicate. Did Desiree's mother and father not really tell her how things are out there? About com'n across a brother like Mike Tyson. Know'n that she's go'n out there to participate in a worldly pageant. Were they that "Everything is beautiful, I haven't been to the ghetto in decades, so I don't think about it." Were they think'n "There's no need to alert my daughter to the ghetto mentality and how it can get you raped." The father knew Mike would be there. You don't expect the worst, but you do advise your children when you send them into any type of situation. In the ghetto, wherever you go you're told to "be careful." What did Desiree's parents say, "Have fun"? That's that distant, comfortable, everything-is-fine, Black-upper-class mentality. They better wake up. Because of Hip-Hop there's a mixing of the two. Suburban kids Black or white only want the truth. Not the bullshit their parents are project'n, that everything is peachy keen. They want some culture. Some truth and a real sense of what this country is about. That's what Hip-Hop provides. The truth is all they want and they'll run to it.

Where did Mr. Washington think Mike was from? His neighborhood? Mike is from Bed-Sty, Brooklyn. Do or die, Bed-Sty. I know about it and I'm from D.C. A new position in life really doesn't mean a new attitude. If anything, it means only the chance to magnify your already-fucked-up thoughts. Now the girls are kick'n it to you. Now what is a nigga from Bed-Sty gonna do?

Guys need to be more open and honest with what they don't know. Be it intellectual or sexually speak'n. Don't be afraid or ashamed to ask, especially sexually speak'n. We're not gonna laugh because you may not know how to perform a certain sexual act correctly, or perform it to our satisfaction. It's not like we're gonna laugh and go to our girlfriends and say,

"Girl, let me tell you about this sorry nigga." You may do that with your boys, say shit like "She ain't move her ass enough," but we don't do that. We'd rather talk over our sex life with you, the person we're involved with. Our girlfriends can't help us. They're not in the bed with us. So brothers need to realize runn'n to their boys can't help me. Talk to me about how we can make our lovemak'n and relationship better.

If you don't know something and you're honest with what you don't know, that's makes a girl feel like "Damn, he's special. He's kinda cute. Innocent." He's not think'n he's some hard nigga who knows everything, can't tell him nothing. Women like honest innocence in a man. That turns women on. We don't like a man who thinks he's Mr. Casanova-get-over. He's the Mack, has everything and knows everything. We don't like that shit. You can't talk to that nigga. Men who are man enough to say they don't know are attractive. At least to me. And what you don't know, honey, I'll teach you.

On the for-real tip, Black women are there for Black men. We love you to death. Why else would we keep putt'n up with all your shit? We have a common experience and heritage, we understand what you've gone through, what we've gone through, and I want to come through all this with my Black man. I want us to survive. I want us to return to lov'n each other with a perfect love. One that only we can share. I'm tired of all this instigated negativity. Black men need to know it's all bullshit and stems from someone else's do'n. I just can't say enough how much I love, support, worship and adore my Black man, and I pray for our unity like nobody's business.

Lastly, we need new leaders. New leaders like you don't know. Today's so-called leaders are out of touch and are not representing the dominant thought of their children. In the midst of all this fucked-up activity, I feel we're ready for a serious, positive change. We need only the right voice to start the shit roll'n. In the meantime we'll just party and bullshit. We talk among ourselves about how we wish brothers would change, about how we wish sisters would change, and that shows that the thought and wish is there, but without that dominant strong voice bringing clear that thought, and without a focused agenda, then we'll just go, oh, well, it was a nice thought, and back to the same old and real bullshit.

We sometimes feel we're the only one wishing for change because no one is out there say'n it for the whole. I sometimes think I'm the only one with my thoughts because there's no leader out there say'n the same thing. And if he is, it's watered down. It has no appeal. It's insincere. It's just talk. The perfect political talk. It's mixed in with their own personal political agenda which is personal advancement. But I'm not the only one. Ask your common sister, shit, I'm your common sister, or ask your common nigga on the street, be it hustler or whatever, we all want change. But, hey, if the feeling is no one is gonna change, then I gots to go for mine. I have to push, kill if I have to, hustle and sell this shit because that's all I'm left. Somebody didn't bring a new school program or job program into the ghetto, but somebody did bring the crack, the drugs and the Uzis. Sounds like a plan of genocide to me. What else are we supposed to do with them if I have no choice between that and something different? But despite that, you better believe we're on the verge of someth'n. Good or bad, and good or bad for who I don't know, but something's com'n. Something has to give. That's only the natural course of time and history.

hanaan

hanaan, 19

down south

poli-sci

Within the Nation of Islam women are taught that there are certain duties subscribed to them. The men are also taught that there are certain duties that they ought to perform, and for both sexes they are God-given duties. Within the Nation of Islam there is an emphasis on our nature, the way God made us. We are taught to treat one another according to his and her nature. For those who are not in the Nation of Islam, and do not know themselves, we are to still treat those individuals by their nature, not their condition. We are to still treat those who don't know themselves, all of our brothers and sisters, as the forgotten Kings and Queens they are.

For the purpose of us living this life we have to live, to live it in peace and unity, I feel what is most imperative is that the Black man needs to understand the nature of the Black woman. I feel an understanding on this will help us tremendously, because the problem is simply that we don't know or understand each other. And it's up to the man to understand the woman. The woman, for the most part, already knows, or is trying and willing to know the man. The Black man's setback is that he feels he doesn't need to understand the woman. He's the man in control in this society and so why should he make the effort to understand something that is beneath him, a woman? First of all, this is the white man's way of thinking. The Black man, although a man, is not the one in control. He's not even an equal partner among men. The Black man is powerless in this society, and so he can't afford to not need his Black woman. This is what keeps us apart, and until we understand that we do need each other, and most of all need to seriously understand each other, we will remain apart and forever behind.

By our nature we are Queens. We are warriors. Queen Hatshepsut is an example of the nature, strength and beauty of the Black woman. Read about the Black Queens of antiquity. Those that existed, their accomplishments, and you will gain much respect for the Black woman. Read, learn and know that we were and are more than what you think, believe, have been taught and told.

It needs to be understood that without us there would be no man. We need to know this. We need to know how much we really need each other. A man can go and make ten million dollars a year, but he will never be satisfied unless he has a woman. That is nature. That should tell us something right there. And the motivation behind making the ten million is most likely a woman. To impress her, to wine and dine her, to have her. There may be a whole lot of mistreatment, taking advantage of and wrongdoing within all of this, but the point is that we do live for each other. We need only to correct the way we live for each other. Correct the lack of respect and wrong influence we allow ourselves to adapt.

The same thing for these women out there talking about they can live without a man. That's bull. God didn't make it that way. God made it to be man and woman. A woman is the epitome of rounding out a man's life and vice versa. A woman is all that a man desires to have. He could be the poorest thing on earth, but having a woman by his side will make him feel like a King.

Until Black men realize this he can hang it up.

The Black man will never achieve anything without the love, support and nurturing of a Black woman. Do wrong by a Black woman and you will fail at everything you do.

That's something men need to strongly consider.

Calling our sisters bitches, please, there is no place for it. I mean, I have never in my life heard of such foolishness. Without me you can hang it up completely. If you're a Black man disrespecting a Black woman, hang it up. If you don't respect me, you now have the world and the Black woman against you. But at least I'll pray for you. If your wife or your woman or your girlfriend is not there to comfort you, not there to say, "It's OK, it's gonna be hard, but I'm there for you," you can forget it. Go dig a grave and lie in it. If you disrespect me, I won't be there for you. No self-respecting Black woman would.

Sisters should concentrate their energies on a brother who wants to strive to make a better world for us all. I don't mean to say give up on the brother who doesn't know himself. We need to understand he's been made to not understand himself and made to not live up to his fullest potential.

So we do need to try and help. We need to dialogue and help show that there is a difference. Some people need only to be shown that difference. But if he's beyond help and you've exhausted yourself without any want of change from the brother and he's just beyond help, all you can do is pray for the brother and move on. It's out of your hands. Only God can save him at that point.

If I hear a brother say, "bitch," and I say was that necessary, and he turns to me and says, "what?" I have to make the choice to stand there and try to dialogue with this brother about his attitude. If at the end I'm still a bitch, all I can do is pray and move on.

We need to understand the importance of our roles as individuals. And as either male or female we need to know our nature. If we don't understand this we will never succeed as a race. We will succeed only as individuals who think they are more than they are. We think we shouldn't have to give back to the community. We might do it, but it's only for the sake of good PR. We need to know it's our duty as human beings to give back. In Islam they call it charity. In Christianity they call it giving tithes or paying dues. It is our duty to give back. If you don't naturally feel this, then you are not a human being. You've been made into something else which is against your nature. We need to realize and know ourselves and our roles.

You should never feel the need to distrust me because I am a woman. You should know it's the exact opposite. Black men do not need to be afraid of women who are ahead of them educationally, politically, socially or financially. There is no need to try and pull away, hold back or get jealous and undermine the woman. If you feel that you are not as strong or as positive as this Black woman, then do something positive about it. Make the change in your life.

As I've grown older and have gotten into the dating scene, I've found that it's very hard for me to communicate with these guys. **Thus far, in the area of my peers, I have not met one guy who knew himself as a Black man. That should not be.**

It's hard for me, who didn't grow up in the same environment as most Blacks, and it's hard for those who didn't grow up with the same background as myself to relate to each other. It's hard because I treat the Black man according to his nature and not according to his condition. I treat him with respect and dignity, love and pride, devotion and worship. Now his condition is that he has no sense of self. No self-esteem and no positive motivation. The Black man doesn't have any confidence in himself. He doesn't know where he stands within society, what he should be doing and where he should be headed. He is insecure. My treating someone according to his nature when he is this unfocused creates problems.

Knowing yourself is the basis of being secure. It's the foundation to knowing your future and controlling your destiny. Because I act and treat Black men accordingly, they seem to not know how to act toward that. They don't know how to respond to a Black woman giving them support. It's like they'd rather I curse at them and expect them to fail. They don't understand a woman trying to help them and believing in them. A woman can try and believe in them, believe that they can do better, she'll try to push the man to do better, but from my experience he'll tend to ease out of the relationship. He'll leave. It's sad and it hurts.

In the Nation of Islam we are taught that relationships are the foundation of family and the foundation of unity. A lot of brothers don't look at relationships in that light. They don't take relationships serious. They tend to look at them as just something to do and get into for the moment, to relieve their sex. And much later, after they've slowed down, they'll say, well, let me now marry someone, and even then they'll still play games. Others look at marriage as something that means the end of their life. They see it as meaning they won't have any more freedom, so they won't marry. I'll give that type a little more credit than those that marry and still play games.

When it comes to relationships, most guys tend not to want to get too involved because they feel as if their freedom is being cut off, and you know how touchy we are about freedom. If a man is in a relationship, it's no surprise if he one day up and says he wants out. I know it's understood, or rather misunderstood that to be a man is to have more than one partner, to be very sexually active. To have one woman is seen as cutting off one's manhood. As long as this is believed, our brothers will never rise above themselves. He will rise only with the help of one stable relationship, one stable and strong Black woman.

You see it time and time again. Men losing power and wealth because of their infidelities. No stability. If you have a stable relationship, you'll have stability in your life.

According to the teachings of the Honorable Elijah Muhammad, the original man is the Black man. He is the Asiatic Black man. The original King. The maker, the cream of the planet earth. He is talented. He is strong. He is wise. It is our Black men that built pyramids. It is the Black man who started science. The nature of the Black man is that he is intelligent, but society has projected this image that our Black men are not capable of great accomplishments. From the Nation of Islam I treat the Black man as the creator, the original King. But in this country he is a fallen King, so I push and support him to return to his rightful place.

I'd prefer a Black man be self-employed than work for somebody else. This helps return him to his rightful place. Unless that somebody he's working for is Black, he should be his own man, with his own job, providing for himself and his family. This is the way so many other groups have come here and secured their future. Self-employment is a little store on the corner of your community. Even if you were making more money in a big corporate position, I'd have much more respect for you if you were working for yourself in a corner store in your neighborhood, and employing one or two neighborhood youths.

In order to be a man or woman in this society, you must have economic stability. Your economic stability lies in your being able to control your financial destiny. If you are working for someone who is not of your kind, particularly if he is white, and by their nature, not all of them, but enough, by their nature their interest is not in trying to advance you as an individual, and definitely not your race as a whole, there are limits. There are ceilings that are imposed, and this is no surprise. No one else is surprised except the Black man. Every other group of people knows this about their particular group; they work for their own and become financially independent. The Arab, the Jew, the Asian, the Korean, the East Indians, and meanwhile the Black man cries about discrimination. Every other group recognizes the discrimination, they form their own community, open their own businesses and move right along.

There is but so much that you will be allowed to achieve if you are working for someone who is not looking out for your best interest. In this situation, you do not control your destiny. You can be laid off, your pay cut, you can be fired. If you have your own business, it's you who determines your destiny.

I believe Black women have suffered as a result of the women's liberation movement. I think women should understand that being a woman means having certain duties. Because of the women's movement we all tend to think that if I as a woman cook and clean, then that makes me subservient to men. The way I was brought up was that it is not necessarily my only duty to cook and clean and raise the child, but the thing is, these are duties that are set aside, particularly for a woman, because she is better suited for them. She is better at motherhood. We were chosen to bear children. If we weren't, the man would be the child bearer. The man has a responsibility in raising the child and in cooking and cleaning the house also, but his main job is to provide, and to keep away all enemies. He is physically better suited for that. This is only accepting and living according to our nature. This is what brings about stability.

The Honorable Elijah Muhammad explains it by example of a farmer. A farmer would do anything to take care of his crop because his crop is his family's sustenance. It produces and he must take care of it. Without the farm you can't have anything and the farmer won't be able to produce and provide. He won't be able to operate as a man. In relationship to woman to man, we are your crop. The woman is the man's crop. We are the ones that produce. It is the man's duty to take care and fight off all infirmities and all enemies that come upon us. He is the protector and the provider. The woman's job is to support and help the man. Help him to be able to live and cope in this society that is continuously trying to hold him back. And if a man can't have confidence and sustenance from his wife, then who or what can he depend on?

If we understand that this situation is not aimed at the Black woman, that this plan is against the Black man, if we understand that the Black man is meant to be destroyed, because if he is destroyed, his women who are now defenseless are also destroyed, then we will understand that it is our responsibility to stay by his side and to build confidence in him. If we understand that, then we can understand that it's not about being less than or subservient to the Black man. It's about us doing certain duties to provide for both of our futures. The women's liberation movement has Black women not seeing what their cultural position as a Black woman is.

The women's movement was the white woman's fight against her white man oppressing her. The Black woman and the Black man have longtime been oppressed and will be continue to be oppressed. The Black woman doesn't need to embrace women's lib because she should have already been in another liberation movement. One for her people, and that automatically includes herself. When she focuses on women's lib, she loses focus on her and her Black man's liberation. The Black man isn't the one directly oppressing the Black woman. His treatment of the Black woman is indirect. It's a result of him aping and being taught to mistreat the Black woman. If the Black woman wants her voice heard in the women's lib movement, then she should also be saying to her oppressor, "And while you're at it, liberate my Black man."

The friction and shortcomings I've experienced are because brothers are not doing their part as I do mine. I may be encouraging and pushing, but the brother has already accepted defeat. He's accepted that he can't provide and survive the correct way, like a man should, so his response to me is like, "What are you doing? This sister is too much." That has been my experience, and it's been perceived as me expecting too much of him. Or my standards are too high. When all I'm doing is my part as a Black woman. I expect you to do your part as a Black man. I know it runs deeper than just expecting the Black man to live as he should. I can't automatically expect the Black man to live up to himself, because I see how deeply he has been mentally defeated by the white man's oppression. I know what the white man has done to the Black man. I know what the white man has told the Black man, and what he continues to tell him. Look at the Rodney King case. I as a Black woman can say, "Black man, you are the creator, the King, go and provide for you and your family, you can do anything," but there's another force working against me. He's out there beating and busting the Black man's head and telling him he is nothing, and in this country, they have a four-hundred-year head start over me.

One thing we need to realize is there is a conspiracy against our Black brothers. When you look at it, I don't know how else to term it, but we need to know that something is in effect so that we can counteract. There is one program called Federal Violence Initiative. This is designed to medically drug young Black boys between the ages of kindergarten and elementary school. Their basis comes from so-called scientific reports that says crime is genetic and inherent to Blacks. Therefore, by drugging the genetically violence-prone Black child, his natural habit toward crime and violent activity will be curbed. The government has actually tried to implement this.

To combat pregnancies they're also drugging Black boys so they won't have any sexual desires. We need to understand these initiatives. There is a weed and seed program that is aimed at going into Black communities to weed out what they consider the bad elements, the drug dealers and users, and they're supposed to take the drug money and seed, build and develop what they consider good programs for the community. But we know that's bull because what new programs are in the ghetto? You still have the same burnt-out buildings from the 60's riots. They're taking our Black boys into prisons and what are they doing with them? Are they seeding and rehabilitating them to be better men? Are they really seeding programs in the

Black communities that will eventually prevent the future need to weed out bad elements because everyone will have a purposeful responsibility? What's going on in the jails? Why was there a recent prison uprising in Ohio?

You hear conspiracy, and you say no, not in this day and time. But in State after State, program after program that does not help the real problems, but only add to them, then what else would you call it? Misjudgment? They want more jails built, stiffer jail terms, more death penalties. How about more jobs created?

Even the misguided that are here on this campus, attending class, are not what they should be, or claim to be about. They act too foolish. I can't believe the stupidity of these brothers. They talk much bull. I don't care how much Black power you talk, until you walk what you talk, you are nothing but a fool.

We need to get out and do something in the community besides sell drugs, buy the 40 ounces and make babies that we don't take care of. We need to realize that as a race this country was built on our backs and we deserve a definite part of it. We need to understand that the Constitution refers to us as three-fifths of a person. The Constitution endorsed slavery and "We the people" didn't include we the Black race because we were slaves and specifically singled out to be three-fifths a person.

We have to understand that capitalism is for the advancement of the individual and not the group. We then need to see that this country is selfish, it's not in our best interest, and we need to think in terms of what we as individuals can do to help us as a group. When this society stresses individual success, and we buy into it, literally "buy" into it, that means the race suffers.

If we take the time to try and build unity, and build respect for one another, not only in male-female relationships, but male to male and female to female relationships, then we too can succeed as a group. Until we do this, we will continue to walk around like the misguided fools we are.

My goal is to be a corporate attorney, but I plan to work with Black businesses. That is what I *am* going to do. But I need the Black businesses to work with. But are the schools educating us to get our own business? Even here at a historically African-American college they do not educate you to be an entrepreneur. They'll educate you like crazy to have a successful interview with IBM, but what about when IBM turns me down? I mean, I love this college, I would never trade it for another school because it does instill and promote a sense of pride and self-respect for the race, but they'll more likely teach you to have Black pride while working for a white company. How much pride can you show in that situation? You have to conform to a corporate look, image and attitude. We should be taught to have Black pride while working for self. That will really give you a reason to feel Black pride.

Coming here has also allowed me to see the diversity of Black. I've seen and gotten to know people from the islands, people from the motherland. I've seen Blacks from England, France and every corner of the world. Not only do you learn to be proud of who you are and your culture, but you also learn that you are an individual and your beauty is different from what the western world says is the final word on beauty. Personally, I would never trade Being Black. Even if it meant I would be oppressed for the rest of my life, I have no desire to be any other color.

I've long since realized that there is more racism directed toward Black men than Black women, but, until recently, what I didn't realize was how constant it was. And that men don't tell us how often it comes. I don't understand that and I wish you did come to us. I'll admit I'm very naive to the ways of the world because I was brought up in a very structured society, but it seems to me that the man would want to talk with his woman about his frustrations. Maybe it's because of that difference in how we're brought up.

I mean for me everything was structured. The way I ate was structured. I ate two times a day. I got up at five o'clock in the morning, we said our prayers and we ate breakfast. We had school, we went bicycling, we did our family activities, and we did our homework. Between four and five o'clock we were eating dinner. From six to seven o'clock we had our leisure time, and at eight o'clock we were in the bed. This is how my life was, and it wasn't until I came here that I became a little bit more aware of outside society and how unstructured and undisciplined it is. I see how men who weren't raised in the Nation of Islam or any other structured society are. This, perhaps, should help me to understand why men don't come to us for support, but I still don't understand it. Why can't Black men come to us for support? Is this society, outside the one I was raised, that irresponsible? There should be no reason, no fear why you as a Black man can't come to me a Black woman and talk about your fears, experiences and pitfalls. I know them. I know they exist, so stop trying to hide yourself from me. I want to listen. I want to be there. I want to be a strong woman for a man who is strong enough to talk with me about his troubles. This whole "I am man, I can handle it by myself" is what's destroying us.

My understanding of the purpose of sex is that aside from pleasure its purpose is reproduction. This is something men and women do not understand. Men in particular take sex as a joke. They take it as nothing more than a game and for social pleasure only. They don't have any idea of the responsibility involved. If the woman gets pregnant, his outlook can easily be "I was just there for that moment, I want nothing more to do with you, so I'm out."

We don't put enough emphasis on the importance of sex. Sex is important and it's not a game. Sex is for two people who love each other and understand each other. When you have sex with a woman you are going into a woman, you are entering a woman. She has opened herself up to you, and if you are going into a woman you have to understand what you are going into. It's more than just an opening that brings you pleasure.

I know guys who want only one-night stands. And want them without a condom. You don't know my history. You don't know what I may have. You don't know if I'm a man, a female or both.

People are just too irresponsible when it comes to sex, and the younger the age group, the more irresponsible. With AIDS out here, as well as herpes, gonorrhea and syphilis, you would think the younger generation would especially want to protect themselves because they have their whole life ahead of them. They should feel they have something to live for, that they're too young to die, but they're the most reckless. It's ridiculous. It doesn't make any sense.

We're having babies and don't even understand the importance of what we're having. Because we're reckless we're having babies and raising them wrong. If we understood the importance of our Black babies, maybe we'd be reckless, yet raise our children with more of a focus and purpose, if we were caught out there like that. We'd try to raise the next Malcolm or Martin. Black people are producing at an alarming rate and that's why the United States government has all these initiates aimed at our population control. They understand that if we knew better, we'd continue to produce with the idea of raising a leader, another powerful Black leader like Moses. But we don't see it that way. They do and they fear one day we'll realize we're the majority and in a so-called democratic society that means something. They know that out of all these babies, one of them has got to be our leader who'll turn this thing around. We need to understand the importance of having sex and the importance of reproduction. We need to understand we can't take each other for granted, and we sure shouldn't take the activity of sex for granted.

I wish I could have kept my virginity until I was married. One of the reasons I say that is because every time I was in a relationship my heart was broken. The guys would say, "If you're not with it, forget it," and I would get hurt because I would really like the guy, but I would lose him because I wouldn't sleep with him. My friends would say I can't believe you're almost twenty years old and haven't had sex.

When it did happen, I just wasn't thinking. I wasn't thinking at all. I would prefer to have waited. A woman would respect herself more if she waits, and as a result a man would respect you.

If I had gotten pregnant and he didn't want to marry me, or he didn't want to take on the responsibility of raising his child, I couldn't walk away and say the child isn't mine. I couldn't walk away and say how do I know it's mine? I couldn't do that because I'd be the one carrying it. However, if we were married, I wouldn't have to worry about him denying his child.

I would advise all virgins, all teenagers who are virgins, to keep their virginity until they are married. It is not worth it. If you value the act of sex as something that should exist only between husband and wife, then wait. Don't give in to pressure or self-doubt. If you get pregnant and he doesn't want to take care of it, you are not putting yourself in an advantageous position. And any man who doesn't own up to his responsibility of fatherhood is the epitome of trash.

The Koran, the Bible, any religion will tell you God wants you to give yourself only to your husband after you say, "I do." Now that I've done what I should not have done I'm redressing my lifestyle. I won't be doing what I did in the past because I did feel very badly about it. All my life virtue is what my mother and my father taught me, and when I lost my virginity I felt like I just totally dissed them, and myself as well. I did the worst thing in the world. So now I'm retracting my lifestyle and I keep praying.

Men do not need to call women out of their names. Bitches, to be more exact. It defines your attitude and your behavior. We are the producers of civilization and you can't call me a bitch. That is like calling your mother a bitch. Men need to treat women the way they wish to be treated as human beings. The way they want you to treat their mothers. Or the way they would want to be treated if they were women. Think about it. If you were a woman would you want me to call you bitch? If no, then don't call me a bitch. The woman is the direct reflection of the man, and if you beat me, that means you don't give a shit about yourself. Your behavior would be destructive, and it will continue to be fed by the negative things you say. It will get to the point where you will not recognize your actions as being destructive.

I was once raped. The guy that raped me had no self-confidence. He was light skin and thought that if he was involved with a darker skin Black woman, and I look more native African than an African American mix, he thought he'd appear to be more down. He thought, in the eyes of those on campus, he'd look as if he was down with the Black movement. He's still here on campus and he loves to be seen walking with a darker skin sister. But he is very insecure, he has no self-confidence, he doesn't understand himself. He isn't satisfied with the skin color he is. He hasn't realized that he is still a Black man in any shade he walks in. He needs to understand that his skin didn't become any Blacker while he was raping me.

I've asked myself all the questions and tried to see where I provoked the incident, but I didn't. I must say the way a woman dresses does not provoke a man into doing anything he should not do. Growing up in the Nation of Islam, we are taught to dress a certain way. That is so you don't give the man the chance to use the defense "The way she was dressed said she wanted it." You keep yourself covered so the man won't have an excuse, so when it comes down to it, the bottom line is the man is at total fault.

We need to stop using excuses. If we continue to use excuses we will never succeed. Many of these Black males are not men, and I say "males," because they don't deserve the title of man. Until they stop with the excuses and assume the position of man, they can't be termed as such. You are not a man or you are not a woman until you stop using excuses and take on responsibility.

With this unfortunate incident, there is the tremendous feeling of guilt. That if you know the man then you could be as much at fault. For the longest time I thought it was my fault. I told myself I went to his house, I shouldn't have gone to his house, but that's not it. I understood my intentions when I went to his house. I'm not foul in my language and I never abuse a man. I never call a man out of his name or treat him disrespectfully. I'm not about "If you ain't got any money or a car, then I don't want to be with you." I never provoked him. I always supported and encouraged his potential. Anything he wanted to do, I was there for him. But there was something within him that made him do what he did. It

wasn't a matter of me saying anything, it was just my presence there, and
he felt he had the right to do whatever he wanted. The language he used
toward me, and his lack of knowing himself as a Black man and me as a
Black woman made him do what he did.

It wasn't date rape because at the time it wasn't a date. We were boyfriend and girlfriend, but we had broken up. When I went over to his
house I had called him a week before and told him we needed to talk. I
wanted to talk to him because whenever we would see each other on
campus or in hallways we looked at each other in total disgust. I felt that
was unnecessary and we should not be acting like that toward one another.

I went over to his house for the simple reason of saying we needed to
stop behaving as we were. We were friends, we were lovers, now the least
we can be is humane, we don't have to act as if we are enemies. He didn't
even want to look at me. He didn't want to talk to me or have anything to
do with me. I told him this on the phone, and I told him I was coming
over so we could talk this out face-to-face. He says, "Well, you know if
you're coming over, I want you to stay the night." I told him, "I'm not
going to stay the night." We had broken up, and that was one of the
reasons why we couldn't be together any longer.

I mean this was a longtime friend. He persisted with me spending the
night and said if I wasn't coming over to spend the night then don't come.
He hung up the phone and left it at that. I was fine with it because if some
people are beyond the help and reason you try to extend to them, then
you have to let them go. I didn't expect to talk to him again, but he called
me back the next day and apologized. He asked me to come over. I told
him I was coming over but I was coming to talk. We would talk about
what we felt and I'd hope we could still be friends in the end. He said
come over and we'll talk. He said "we'll sit down and talk it out."

I went. I sat down, started to talk and before I knew it he was on me.
There was no warning, no words, no nothing. I fought and I fought like
crazy. I fought like I had never fought in my life. I had bruises on my leg
and for days my arms were sore. Days later I was over my friend's house
and she noticed I was limping.

When you're with someone you know, at first you don't think they're
serious. When he first jumped on me I didn't think he was serious. I truly
did not believe he would rape me. I was laughing as if this has to be a joke,
but I was pushing him off me. Once I realized he was serious, I kicked and
I screamed and I fought, but it was all in vain.

My mother once told me there is no such thing as date rape and that
was one reason why I thought I provoked it. But I analyzed the situation

over and over again. I replayed it too many times. I thought about it till I'd get headaches. But I know that I made it clear to him, I did not want to have sex with him. That was definitely not my intention in going over there. But I guess by my going there, he read it differently.

I pushed him. I told him to stop. And I do remember I told him, "If you continue with what you're doing this will be a rape." And he said, "Well, if that's what it's gonna be then I'm just gonna have to rape you." Those were his exact words. Despite what I believed from my mother, that's how I knew I was raped. I know it was not my fault. Never did I think this would happen. I make it a conscious effort never to put myself in situations that I believe may be harmful. I think, and have always thought of myself as a careful person. But here I am to say I was raped. Every time I talk about it I get very tense. Even now as we speak, I feel sick. A Black man, my so-called brother, has me like this. That shouldn't be. That just shouldn't be. I'm able to forgive him, but that just shouldn't be.

II

you move there, while i move here

Sahara

sahara, 20

kentucky

arts administration student

Let's begin with what really disappoints me about men. Being a single, somewhat attractive young Black female, I feel qualified to speak on this issue. I feel very capable of speaking on what young Black men need to know because I'm approached by them every day.

What really peeves me is when you're outside, walk'n down the street, or in your car, or at a bus stop, anywhere, supermarket, health clinic's waiting room, theater, church, protest march, anywhere you name it, a guy will see you it's on. "Psssssssst. Pssssssssssssssst." Now, what language is that? You can be half a block away and "pssssssssssssssst!" You can be two feet in front of them as you walk by, "psssssssst." If I'm that close, speak a comprehensible language, not "psssst." I think that's very disrespectful. Pssst is not a language. I don't know what it means. I understand "hello" or "excuse me," not "psssst."

All brothers talk about is wanting respect. GIVE UP THE RESPECT. DON'T DIS ME. Brothers shoot each other for feeling they were disrespected. That's all they want. Almost more than sex. And their first form of communication with a woman is what? Disrespectful. They do the very thing they hate most, to get the very thing they love most. If there's any sense in that, explain it to me. I don't even go psssst to my dog. I call him by his name. I give a dog that much respect. Is it men respect us less than a dog? What woman in her right mind would respond and speak to this person? I keep right on walk'n and don't pay them any mind. That is some nerve. I've just been disrespected by someone who cries for respect at every turn and now I'm supposed to respond in the positive? You'd think Black men would understand about giving up respect. That's totally ill. Like Blacks being racist is ill. You would think we'd understand racism. We don't like it directed at us. We scream and protest for others not to practice it, and then we turn around and discriminate against another race. Black men raving about wanting respect and then disrespecting a Black woman is some ill shit. That's one thing that really ticks me off. It may sound trivial, but if you're called "psssssst" every day it really starts to get on your nerves. After the hundredth time it does start to get under your skin. You feel less than human. You know you have a name that your parents took time to give you. That you take pride in, and it's reduced to "pssst." That's not my name. Ask it, I'll tell you. This is why we catch attitude. It's why I do. Then you call us bitch, we'll say fuck you, we continue the disunity. A guy will say she's a bitch, but what did you first say to her? Was it in any known language? Speak a known language and maybe she won't be a bitch. Even Spanish brothers who try to kick it, I'll say, "No habla español." They spoke a language, and I spoke back. You say, psst, and I can't respond.

Guys are very, very aggressive. They carry their sports, video games and music aggression right over into women. They just can't leave you alone. Let's say you're at a club. Someone comes up to you and says, "Hi." Thank God they do speak in clubs. Pssssst doesn't work well in clubs, but outside, it's pssst. Let's say we respond, but we let the guy know that we're not interested in anything beyond a dance. Why is he still right there, after the dance? We give all this negative body language and mumble all the one-word answers we can think of, we're look'n everywhere but at the guy, absolutely no eye contact, giv'n hints a blind person could see, but he just won't take it. He persists. He asks more questions, and you're still with the one-word answers. You excuse yourself to the bathroom and he's there when you come out. Why? Why and when will this type of man get the picture? That's a club example, but on the street, the aggression is the same. Why can't men just step off? If you see that you're not getting the same energy that you're putting out, just say something sarcastic like, "Well, OK, nice talking with you, I'll give you a call" and walk away.

What's up with, you politely ask a sister to dance and she looks you up and down? All we may wanna do is dance. Is a club not a social place where people go to dance and socialize?

Sometimes when you ask someone to dance, you're the fifth, sixth or tenth person to come up and ask. And not all the ones before you may have asked politely. You come along, and we're in a bad mood. You're looked up and down because, come on, you know the deal, we're check'n you out. We're allowed to pick and choose. You do. If I was a fat, thick glasses, in Sergio Valentes, are you talking to me? Are you even asking me to dance? For fear that I may mistake it as a hi, are you even say'n excuse me in order to get by, or are you just pushing my big ass out the way?

But, we also could be say'n no because of the most common reason: OUR SHOES ARE KILL'N OUR FEET. That doesn't mean we don't want to *sit* somewhere and talk, but y'all will play the hell out of this dance issue. "Then what you here for? Can I ask you later?" Next time ask about sitt'n and talk'n, you'll be surprised. I know I'll say yeah if you're asking in a decent way. Many times it's all in how you present yourself. Most brothers don't know how to take no for an answer. They make the biggest issue out of a dance refusal as if their life depended on it. If you really want to dance, go dance by yourself. You don't need me to help you dance. The dance is just an excuse anyway to try and talk to us, so why not ask if you can talk to us from the start? Games. Chill with that.

Guys who have a whole group of friends they can't go anywhere without is something to address. He'll ask you to come over, you go to his house and there's this whole posse. You thought you'd be alone with your man, but it's you, your man and his boys. He doesn't know how to put his boys second to the relationship. He is too easily influenced by his boys and I'd rather not be in a relationship with a whole posse. I understand about giv'n people their space, but sometimes it's ridiculous. This is about an immature individual who doesn't know how to have a mature relationship. Guys need to grow up. I know women mature faster than boys, but I think twenty-one, twenty-two years old, and you still need your boys around when you ask your lady over is a bit much. You know how to get rid of them only when you want to get off. You get to the house, there's no one there and you know what's up. One day I went to my man's house, and his boys were leaving. After two minutes, I'm on my back being undressed.

I need my space within relationships. Most of the guys I've dealt with never gave me my space, and now that's very important to me within relationships. I think it's important anyway within relationships. People need their room to breathe. If you're in a relationship, it's one on one, it's close, it's intimate, that can tend to make a person feel anxious. You'll go through the anxiety of feeling tied down and trapped. You may feel as if you don't have enough personal freedom. You start to feel the need to break out for self sometimes. If the person interprets this the wrong way, and takes it to mean that you wanna break up, an argument will start, and you will break up. Know'n you have someone who is secure and they don't have to be under you every minute is good to know. It's a comfort. You

won't feel as if you're suffocating. This is something women need to do
because I know how women can be with their men. Men already feel like
they need to be out there try'n to get with every female. If their girlfriend is
smother'n them, they'll try to ease that anxiety by asserting their freedom
and pulling away. They'll feel a stronger need to be out there, and you'll be
the cause. If you give him his space, he'll want to spend more time with
you. Show some independence to a man, and watch how he acts.

I've been in relationships where the guy was always smother'n me with
affection and I couldn't handle it. It was too overwhelming. A rose the first
couple of times is sweet, but a rose every day, every other day, every time
you see me, gets played. I started think'n what is this guy do'n? He didn't
communicate his feelings any other way, and so his flowers became a
nuisance. It seemed as if he were told to do this, and it wasn't from the
heart. Guys need to forget the games they learned. Forget what they think
or believe a girl wants. Act from their heart. His flowers were a mechanical
gesture. Just go'n through motions with no true feelings. It's better when
you say how you feel. I'm think'n, why couldn't he do that? I understood
in the end. He really didn't have feelings for me. Act real. But when it's
real, do it in moderation. Don't smother. Keep it fifty-fifty. You'll save
yourself some money in the process and everything should be fine.

W hat's up with older men, men who are married with families, some
with daughters my age, hitting on younger girls? I know I really don't have
to ask, but if we're address'n ill shit to bring about awareness and change, I
want to bring this up. Aren't these men supposed to be more mature, more
settled, wiser, and they're act'n worse than these young guys out here.
Where does it end? I know their reason, and it's not right. They think
we're dumb and won't be a problem. All we want are material things and
they can get theirs. They're exploiting young women, girls even, don't
sleep, all in exchange to disrespect their wives. Where does it end is my
question?

This man sweated me for six months. I'm taking him for all these
material things, and he's think'n he's gonna get some. Never happened.
Now he knows, not every young woman exchanges sex for material shit.
But where do men draw the line? If you don't respect the institution of
marriage, what do you respect? Am I to expect a lifetime of dogg'n and
cheat'n? I try to tell myself, the way guys act today, they'll grow out of it. I
figured by the time they're thirty, thirty-five, they'd want a serious one on
one and settle down with a wife. By fifty, fifty-five they're totally chill with

whom they're with. But I'm in clubs, on the street, and men who can be my father are hitt'n on me left and right.

I usually don't approach men. If it's someone I know, it becomes a lot easier. I can play around and throw hints to let them know I'm interested. But a stranger, I don't do that. When I know you, I'll flirt a lot, and say something like, "When are we gonna go to bed?"

It would be really nice if more women approached men, but I'm not used to do'n it. I don't know how to go up to a stranger at a club and start yak'n. Maybe I'll work on it.

Cause if you're alone, and you don't have the nerve to speak to the one you like, we're in your face.

You're right.

Guys can stop runn'n lines. I've been lucky lately and haven't had any thrown at me in a long time, but I've heard my share. Honesty is best. It's not hard. Come right out and say you're interested in getting to know me.

So why can't you say something that simple to a stranger you're interested in?

It's not easy for women. We're used to be'n approached. We're used to the customs as they are, but I said I'll work on it. But then, I don't want to be taken as a ho. That's also what's stopping us. But I guess it's all in the approach. How you present yourself and what you have to say.

And what's, what's, *what's!* with, "Yo, come here"? You want to talk to me, you come to me. What's with guys say'n come here when you're the one that wants to talk to me? That says, you must not be serious. I keep on walking and hear "bitch" thrown behind me.

I hate video hos. I hate *those* bitches. They irritate the fuck out of me. They ruin shit for all of us. That image is a pain in my ass. Want'n to fuck anything that paid. That's the image. Wear'n those tight-ass ho dresses. Stuff hang'n all out. Shak'n it. Because of them, I can't wear anything like that, wear it with class, and still not be taken for a promiscuous video ho. In real life, shit don't happen like what you see in a damn video. But a lot of these fools don't know that. They make fiction and fantasy a reality. You have fools out there ask'n, "Are you a gangster bitch?" Like the girl from the video, you need one, and I'm her. We don't know how to separate entertainment, fantasy and fiction, from real life where you work, pay taxes, eat, raise a family and try to contribute to the betterment of the world. We don't know how to laugh and say nice fantasy concept. Trying to live these fantasy videos don't contribute to anything. That's where we go wrong. Wanna be fantasy hard guys and these stupid-ass girls who follow. Because of these videos, every brother who's paid thinks that every female wants him for his shit. They'll think every female is a ho and they'll treat you like one.

Video hos have no morals, no self-respect, they degrade themselves and all women. And they can't even dance! They're up there because they have chest out to here and ass out to here. Real dancers are skin and bones. These fake hos, with their fake ho weaves, are a joke. These are the girls who participate in phat booty contest, encouraging all this shit to continue. Why are they do'n it? Money. Now they're really hos.

My girl, rather, I know a video ho, Monica. She ain't a close friend, I just know her. Her attitude is it's all about gett'n paid. She's actually like, fuck what people think, she has to get paid. She's like, I know I ain't a ho, so fuck what others think. Fuck her, I call her a ho. And if you're living like a video ho, you're a real-life ho. They justify all of what Snoop and Dre say. Video hos in a Luke video, I hate 'em.

There's no need to share your man. I've noticed a lot of that lately.

Women shar'n their man is some more ill shit. This shortage-of-man excuse is not work'n. I'd go to another country. Men will continue to get over and over and over on women, and now it's to the point where we're help'n them. We're lett'n them know we'll willingly share them with another woman. What is that? There is no shortage of men. Women are be'n lied to. A man probably started the lie. There are people of color all over this world, what do you mean there is a man shortage? You better carry your ass across state lines, if not the border. If I can't find my choice in this country, I have no problem traveling to another. I'm an international sister. You can't confine me to this sorry-ass country.

That's something we need to expand upon. Getting to know other cultures. Cultures that are originally a part of ours. In Australia, the Aborigines are of African descent and they were there before the white man. The Caribbean islands, South America, Brazil, we're all over. This man-shar'n because of a bold-faced lie needs to find another excuse. The truth of the matter needs to come out. Somebody just wants to have fun. Somebody wants to ho for life.

We'll remain apart, because if we don't form close relations with one another, which man-shar'n doesn't allow, we'll always be at war with one another. Man-shar'n, how does that even work? You fuck him on weekends and I fuck him on weekdays?

Games are a trip. "I'm not gonna call her for a week, because I want her to call me," what is that? "I'm gonna let her know these other girls are sweat'n me, so she better act right." Why is it so hard for men to express how they really feel, and trust those feelings? Women are not like men. We won't try to take advantage of your feelings. If you tell us you like us and would like to try to make something work between us, we're not going to put you on hold, play you along, sleep with you two or three times, juice you and then kick you to the curb. We'll either let you know we're interested, we already have somebody or we're a dyke. Whatever. It'll be the truth. A man can have a girlfriend, and if you let him know you like him, he'll still try and get with you. The mention of his girlfriend will be the last thing out of his mouth. He'll try to see if he could sleep with you and not let you know what's up.

What disappoints me about sex is when a man makes sure he comes first and then forgets about the person he's with. I hate it. It's like, you know you're gonna get some sex, you get all excited and before you know it, it's over because you were so excited. You act as if it's go'n somewhere. Like you have only two minutes before it evaporates. And you work within those two minutes. No foreplay whatsoever.

This is how I picture perfect sex. He starts kissing me. Lips, neck, face. We slowly take off each other's clothes. We rub and massage each other. We hold each other and kiss body parts. We exchange oral sex. Nothing too intense. Call it oral sex-lite. We do this to get each other sexually aroused. We can kiss or massage more body parts. Soft music is in the background. We go back to oral sex, this time a little more intense. The first time was just a tease. This time is so I can climax. This is because men usually come first. Now it really gets good. For me, it's beautiful, it's so, so beautiful after I've come from oral sex and then you enter me . . . Now that's it. Can't say no mo'.

For me, that's a good sexual session. And to get to that point, you have to slowly go about things. There has to be time for foreplay, and giv'n the woman a chance to get excited. To actually get wet. For men it's very easy to get aroused, but for women it takes time. Men need to learn patience. Then sometimes it depends. If I'm with you for the first time, I'm usually excited and ready to go. But as time goes on, I want us to take more time. Take time and try some new things. You can't keep do'n the same thing because it's gonna get played. Be creative.

Be patient and let the woman have her fun first. You know, ladies first. Men are so easy. It's obvious that you should make sure we come first. Then you can go on with your twelve thrusts.

Men need to be more sensually creative. Start with the feet for a change. Starting with a foot massage can be all that. You tell a man to be creative and the first thing he'll think of is handcuffs. I've been handcuffed one too many times.

One thing women really like after sex is for the two of you to lie there hold'n each other. We can hold each other and talk about it. Talk about how you feel. About how I feel. Talk about how much closer you feel to the person, because you do feel closer each time you make love. And men, please stay awake! You come and then you're out like a light. No afterplay. Women take it as a dis when men fall asleep.

Can we fall asleep hold'n you?

It doesn't count. Well, maybe. That would be sweet to have you fall into a peaceful sleep while in my arms after we've made love. You'd be my little baby and I'll rock you to sleep. But it has to be that beautiful. You can't be all loud, snoring with slob runn'n all out your mouth.

And I don't buy "We're show'n you how good it was by fall'n asleep. If we got up and watched TV, that means it wasn't good."

Men are everything we want you to be while we're hav'n sex. You can say some of the sweetest things during sex. We're like "Wow, did he just say that?" And don't let it be only during sex that I hear "I love you." Usually just as you're com'n. Fuck that. I know sex will make you say some crazy things, but this shouldn't be one of them. I better have heard "I love you" before. Then you can say it all you want during our lovemaking. It's so sweet then. That's when it's good. When that hits my ear, it can actually make me orgasm. And I'm not saying this so some clown can go and do this to some girl he doesn't care about. But women know when it's meant.

Y ou know what's a biiitch?! What's a real bitch. I'll tell you what's a bitch. To have some guy tell you, "I think you need to go get a STD test." That's a bitch. That's why I don't fuck around. That's why I'm always with a condom. Look. One right here. Fuck that. I'm never embarrassing the hell

out of myself again. Nigga told me "I think you should go get a STD test."
I'm like what the fuck?! Yo, he could've said AIDS test. Fuck that I don't
play.

I like men who are into keeping themselves in shape and look'n decent. I
think that's major. I like a man who is well groomed. I like a man who
cares about his looks, has a good haircut and especially has a nice smell. If
he has a certain scent, I can be totally turned on. If it's someone I really
care about, I'd like to go home with his smell on me. It makes me remember our whole evening together.

I like a man who is goal oriented and focused. I like a man who knows
what he really wants out of life and is work'n toward it. I have a goal
myself, and I want someone who also has goals. I love men who are able to
teach me things, and is also open enough to let a woman teach him
something. Don't be caught up in all that macho shit. That's all I ask. And
of course to be true to me. Let me be the only one he's sleeping with.
That's all I ask for. If he's not the type that goes "psssssssst, come here,"
which isn't the type I talk to, things usually go OK. Space, respect, and
communication and commitment, and we're in there.

Coco

coco, 21

seattle

dancer

First, I would like to go through a quick rundown of a few incidents, and maybe, just maybe by recounting them, brothers would actually see how non-progressive and just plain stupid their actions are. Now, mind you, these are all within the past week. It's as if warm weather brings out the rawness in men. Although I can quote year-round occurrences, the warmer the weather, the more frequent and crazier the incidents.

Last week, I'm walking down Fulton Street. I stop to look at some tapes from one of the sidewalk vendors and I ask the man if he had a certain tape. He said he was out of it. I ask him about another one, and he's out of that, too. Another brother is stand'n next to me. He's also looking at the tapes, but is also obviously into my conversation. As I start to walk away, this brother says in a perverted snarl, "He don't have it, but I have those tapes home. How 'bout you come with me and I'll give it to you?"

A few days later, I'm walking downtown, Flatbush, with my girlfriend. A man comes up to us and says, "You two look like gravy and I'm the biscuit to sop you up," and then he makes this sopping sound with his tongue and lips. The statement could have been cute, but he turned it into obscenity.

The next day I'm on a crowded train and this guy is all on my ass. The train sways and he makes a dramatic move on my ass. I felt we had gotten so close I was gonna ask him *his* name.

Last night I was at Honeysuckle's, enjoying my solitude and the glass of wine. All of a sudden, one by one, all of these drinks are being brought to my table. I'm sitt'n there with three drinks in front of me. I asked the waiter who was sending the drinks and he says, "That man over there, and across the room that man over there." I look at each of them, and they're both sitting there with beautiful dates. Both of them. They're not looking in my direction because they have dates, but I'm supposed to somehow slip them my number or something. Or go to the bathroom, they'll excuse themselves and meet me in front of the bathroom. This is how it's supposed to work.

I have the waiter send them back to the table they came from, and if asked, say it's on the house for the two of them being such a beautiful couple, and that the drink is called "beautiful." I was not going to sit there and accept drinks from men who have women with them. She's thinking she's enjoying a nice, private evening with her man, yet he's trying to set something up on the side. Now, what is he doing when she's not there? You can hear the word coming a mile away. Dogs.

Later on, one of them quickly comes over to me, and says, "You know, you're beautiful, but you're a bitch." I'm a bitch? I waved him off, but I wish I had that moment back. I would have gone off. His date would come back, hear what was going on, and he would have seen a bitch. He calls me a bitch because I won't accept his drink while he's sitting there with another woman. Because I won't be the other woman to the one he has. Some muthafuck'n nerve. I handled the situation in a mature manner. I could have told the waiter to say to them, in front of their dates, that "The woman over there says thanks, but no thanks. She's not look'n to be picked up on the DL." I don't do it that way, but yet I'm still a bitch.

The same evening, same club, a brother comes to my table and asks if he can sit down. I say he can. Why did I say yes? He immediately takes my hand and tells me I look like hot cocoa. He says it with the same look the biscuits-and-gravy man had, as if he'd like to drink me. I tell him that's an interesting thing to say because that's my nickname, Coco. He's still holding my hand, and right after my response about my name, he leans forward, sticks out this gross tongue, and gives my hand this big, long cow lick. I got up, went to the bathroom, washed my hand, and left the club. I haven't gone out since. I need a break.

It's amazing how men think something like that, something like what they say and do would encourage a positive response. A positive response that may lead to something positive. It's beyond me. Am I supposed to be attracted to this stuff? Am I to say, "Oh, you're the man for me, where have you been all my life?" Is a hand-licking by a total stranger supposed to be a turn-on? He turned my stomach. Am I supposed to like that? I wonder if that's the first time he's done that? I wonder if he did that to some other girl, and she just fell all over him? Went home with him, and actually slept with him? At one time I thought maybe I was taking these come-ons the wrong way. That no way could men be taking themselves seriously, they're only joking, they're trying to be funny, saying and doing outlandish shit just to break the ice, no way am I supposed to take them serious, but this is not the case. They are serious. There is no punch line. I thought I was the one with no sense of humor and just wasn't gett'n it. At times, I would entertain these men and wait for their real side to come out. Wait for this jerk to settle down. You know, "OK, my name is so-and-so, I do so-and-so for a living, I want to get to know you because I think you're very attractive," but it never happened. The conversations would get more and more outlandish. More bizarre, and I'd have to put it to an end. Now I'm back to dismiss'n them altogether. Unless their initial approach is humane and civilized, I'm not pay'n attention. If you're only joking with a bizarre come-on, I can't take that chance and say, "He's only joking. Let me talk to him." I'd be a fool. If you wanna play a joke, do something like that after you've shown me you have some sense, so I'll know you're joking. You do not do these things as first impressions. I don't know you. And now what I do know of you is that you're on a weekend pass from Bellevue.

Men. Brothers. Black men, please approach a Black woman as if you're approaching your mother.

Expecting that you do have respect for your mother, approach a sister with civilized words and I guarantee you'd get a civilized response. Even if you're let down, it will be in a civilized manner. "Thanks for the compliment, but I'm in love with someone at the moment." We'd even playfully flirt with you, letting you know we appreciate the compliment, and that you find us as attractive, but you give us cause to wanna curse you out. You know, "Look, muthafucka, get out my face." Or I'll ignore your ignorance.

Why can't we have that open, civilized brother-to-sister admiration and support of each other? Not the attitude we get with "psst, com'eh." I don't know if you wanna do me harm, sell me drugs, or ask me for my phone number. "Wait up–wait up–wait up." Let me get this straight, I'm supposed to stop and wait for you?

We're try'n to tell you something by not answering to "yo" and "psst." Pick up the hint. Try something else. Try something civilized. You'd think after years of being ignored you'd get the message.

As ignorant as these incidents may be, that's not to say I'm entirely turned off men, or this accounts for the reason that I'm now single. In fact, I've had nothing but positive and good relationships. The guys that I've dated through come-ons in no way acted like most of these guys. They came on as men who took an interest in me, wanted to get to know me, took a civilized approach and things developed from there. Nothing hard, nothing difficult. It's so easy to meet an available sister. Say hello. Brothers make things difficult for themselves with "pssst." I'd like to believe these guys are not really look'n for anything serious, or they would change their approach, but they get so offended when you ignore them, I believe they really were try'n to start something. But I guess somebody is answering them, or else they wouldn't keep doing it. But I thought more sisters are not responding than are, so that should tell men something.

All the sexual undertones behind come-ons are a turnoff. They're not needed. First of all, I'm offended that all you take me for is something that can only make you come. How else am I to respond to that? I think anyone with any self-respect would be insulted. Second, all that overt sexual suggestion totally destroys the mystery. It destroys the romance. The mysterious exploration that can exist. Women are into the process.

If you're sexy, all you have to say is "hello." Carry on a civil conversation, and let your silent sexuality carry on the undertones. If you're sexy, the last thing you need to do is try to be sexy. A positive and a negative equals a negative. Simple algebra. That kills everything. No one likes arrogance or conceit. If you're displaying chest hairs and all that, you ruined the mystery. If you act as if you aren't even aware of your sexuality, I'll be wondering and taking an interest. Along with listening to you and finding out where your head is. What's in it? Are you brains as well as beauty?

Men need to know they can make themselves beautiful by being brainy. Having good, stimulating conversation. Women are not like men when it comes to looks. Just be neat and clean. Men need that fine ass, chest, full lips for whatever men like full lips for, I'm not speculating. Men are just only led by the body. Women can appreciate a beautiful body, but have a beautiful brain, too.

Finding out that you are more than just your sexuality makes you even more sexy. If you come on with nothing but sex, sex, sex, I don't want to have it. If you play it cool and show off your other talents, now you got me going. You've begun the foreplay. All we need now is a nice romantic evening, and some Luther.

I've never had a bad relationship because I've always made sure I've gotten to know the person first. Is this the person I want to become intimate with? Is this the person I could talk with every day? Could I wake up, roll over and be happy to see him? I'm interested to know what questions brothers ask.

When you date someone you have to realize that you're dating a person who may be coming with a whole lot of baggage. It's important to get to know that baggage. You have to open up that bag and check out what's inside. You have to check out if there's anything that needs to be gotten rid of. If there's any deep, sentimental belongings that will stand in the way of you two? Why is that still in the bag? Is there anything that says he's looking for the same as the last, and you can't be that, you have to be you? You're bringing a whole new person to the relationship. Whole new tastes, likes and dislikes. Everybody has a former love. Now what you need to know is how much of that person still affects them and how may it affect your relationship?

You need to check out if there are any gifts in the bag you'd be happy to keep. I mean, you just need to know what type of baggage this person is coming with. Is the bag empty? Does it appear they're not staying long? You know, "This bag seems awfully light. Not even a toothbrush. Why, baby?"

Relationships are friendships. We befriend people based on how well we connect with their personality. Why not do that to the people with whom we'd like to have an intimate relationship? Don't base it on two dates. Everything is wonderful and roses when you just meet someone, you're both on your best behavior, so you really have to let time go by. That's when the real person surfaces. If you like that person, then you can start making wise judgments.

Sisters are either too eager to get a man, they fool themselves into thinking they can excuse, live with or put up with what they know they'd rather not be dealing with or they believe they're the one he'll outgrow his unwanted behavior with. We think we can be the one to change this brother. Be it running around chasing other girls, hanging out with his boys, drinking too much, spending too much of your money, you name it, we think we can be the one to change him. I say, get you someone you don't have to change. Make it easy on yourself.

To have a "relationship" is to know a number of things. I wouldn't expect anyone to date me and think they were in a relationship until they checked me out and were able to accept my baggage. To know me and be in a relationship with me is to know my background. You'll know my family, you'll know my friends, you'll know the books that have influenced me, you will know a great deal about me, and I you. To know a man is not just to know his body. I don't care how many times you sleep with him. Sisters will sleep with a brother and IMMEDIATELY, IMMEDIATELY, IMMEDIATELY think they're in a relationship. What is that? And I'm not saying don't immediately think you're in a relationship. No, that's not what I'm saying. I'm saying don't immediately sleep with him. Don't do it. If you know what you want but you're not sure what the other person wants, don't do it. If you're about to get into things, ask him, "Are you ready for this?" If he don't understand, clear it up. He may think you mean "Are you ready for this here sex?" Of course he's ready for that. He's been ready. He was ready when he asked you your name. Clear it up, say something that doesn't allow for any misunderstanding. Say, "I want you to know this means I'm ready for total commitment, do you feel the same?" See what he says then.

I understand this ratio thing plays a large part in how women act with men. I don't know whether this ratio thing is true because there *are* actually more women than men, or because we as women have been taught to look for and expect something that doesn't exist. This mythical prince. This IBM, Intelligent Black Man, or BMW, Black Man Working. Of course they should be intelligent and they should be working, but we've gotten carried away with how intelligent we want him and what type of job we want him to have. Legal or otherwise. Many of us go for the drug dealers. What does that say about our morals and values? It says we're willing to accept him so long as he has dollars. So long as he's paid, can do for you and buy you much happiness downtown. If your type is dealing drugs, and he's willing to kill, get rid of another brother over bullshit, don't be surprised when you're dissed and gotten rid of. Don't bitch and cry when he buys a new bitch. Don't be hurt when some other girl gets pregnant, too. Don't complain when you're not the only one he's fucking. Don't cry at his funeral. In a sense, he's already walking around dead. Don't get upset if you're hit by a bullet intended for him. Don't cry if a family member of yours is shot and killed because of him.

His pleasures are base and simple. He'll satisfy them with anyone who is willing. Usually some other girl who wants him because he's making madd money and she wants a part of it.

So ordinary just won't do? So now there's not enough men for women? I personally feel there aren't enough women out there for the average Black man. There aren't enough women who are willing to accept the average hardworking brother. We need to realize we've been taught to expect a myth. And the woman can be the most ordinary, minimum-wage-earning, most average-looking woman around, yet she'll insist on having a prince who's earning top dollar. He has to be Mr. Look-so-fine, Mr. Perfect, Mr. Right, and when we can't find this myth, we say there aren't enough men for women. And don't let the sister go to college and have a little bit of education. Now he has to have a doctorate. Well, she's just excluded a whole segment of available, hardwork'n Black men. And she can be a college dropout, but she's been "exposed." Ain't nothing wrong with wanting a highly educated man, but don't want only a highly educated man. Some of your biggest fools out there have college degrees. Don't let a college degree fool you. Another man can be self-taught. He can have tremendous common knowledge. He can be street smart, while Joe College can be taken for a sucker at every turn.

There are enough men for women. Dozens of them go "psssst" every day on every block. They just need to learn how to talk to a woman. Maybe we can say there aren't enough decent, civil-acting men, but if they all were to get their act together, there would then be too many men. Imagine if every brother that says "pssssssst," started to go "excuse me, sister?" Followed by something decent and respectful. Now there would be too many men for women. We'd be overwhelmed. We'd have three, four and five men. We'd be the ones cheating if all men turned civilized. You all would be irresistible. We would constantly be say'n there aren't enough women for men.

Then there's the comment that sisters are losing too many brothers to white women. This has always been a relevant issue within our community. It's been a relevant issue to me personally. I have one sister-in-law who is white. I have a second brother who's been dating the same white girl for three years. Preference, circumstance or coincidence, I couldn't accurately say.

From a woman's standpoint, as far as the psychology behind white women getting with Black men, I think it may begin with the penis. This isn't the only reason, but this damn sure is where we can start. This reason may have worn itself into a tired cliché but it's so, so valid. We all know that we all live and die for sex. As a woman, if I believe a certain man's performance to be better, I may very well perform my own investigation. Let women hear some shit about Mantaukimo men in bed. See how many women will search themselves out a Mantaukimo. "Girl, you got to get you a TAUK.KI.MO." "Well, where do they hang out?" "Where do most of them live?" "Yeah, well, I think I'm due for a vacation?" If I fall in love with him and want to marry him, can you fault me? If I feel guilty for primarily wanting to get with him only because of his gift, I may marry him to prove myself not shallow. Or he may just very well be the perfect man to marry, outside of the sex. I've had white girls question me, with much interest, about Black men. Questioning me to make sure they weren't going to do something and have it turn out disappointing. The whole Mandingo, strong Buck, well-endowed, taboo, forbidden-fruit syndrome is very valid.

As far as brothers, it's the whole beautiful-white-American-woman complex. I still see this large preference for choosing lighter skin Blacks as a mate. The epitome of beauty and womanhood and refinement is where we can begin with this shit. They too can both grow to have a positive relationship, with love and respect and all that, but they had to have had the psychology that said, "I want a Black man—I want a white woman" to start with. You have to realize people are going outside their twenty-first-century segregated communities and circles to find this member of the opposite race. Why? Myth? Forbidden-fruit syndrome? Not enough Black women? Not enough white men? It begins with that sexual attraction. That's what brings anybody together. Brothers are like "I like how she's look'n over there. Ass, thighs. I gotta go for mine." A brother wanting a white girl, "I like how nice and white she's look'n over there. Milky white, lily white skin. I gotta have that." When it comes to Black and white, the United States takes a funny position.

Moving beyond the sexual psychology, we head into location and job circumstance. I could use my brothers for that. They're in Washington State and Canada. There are no Black women in these areas. There are plenty of Black men, but no Black women. SISTERS GO WEST. GO TO THE PACIFIC NORTHWEST! There's another answer to there not being enough Black men out there. They're in the Pacific Northwest being taken by white women.

Then there are those who know if it's the last thing they do, they're gonna get and marry across color lines. They'll go out of their way, and at any cost. A Black man will get him a white woman, and a white woman will get herself a Black man. And not just regular Black. His color has to be black. I've seen so many white girls with the blackest Black man you've ever seen. YOU NEVER SEE A WHITE GIRL WITH A LIGHT-SKIN BLACK MAN. He must be black Black. It's like black Black is king dick. You can't get no better. And size really doesn't make a difference, well, yeah, it does. Forget I even said that. But this optimum sexual obsession is a trip.

But why can't any woman want optimum sex? What's wrong with white women wanting that same personal satisfaction as Black women if everything isn't a myth?

My initial reason for wanting a Black man is the natural affinity I feel. The common culture and heritage. The shared struggle. It's deeper than know'n I'm getting the best lay God created. White

women don't have that motive. They have only the sexual attraction, the myth. I have a history of loving Black men. I love my father, my grandfather, my brothers. If you want to look at it with a color-blind eye, fine, but this is the United States, it's not that black and white. There existed this Black sexual myth for white women. Black men have been hung because of this myth, so people do *act* on myth. As long as it exists, and in this country it will exist, then I'll continue to question the motives of any white woman with a Black man, and I'll question the Black man's motives as well.

I do believe somewhere people of different races can come together without any preconceived motives, but if a white woman knows U.S. history, somewhere in the back of her mind, just before the brother takes off his clothes, she's anticipating this big, huge black piece of manhood to jump out. She's anticipating the best fuck of her life. You can't help it. That's natural U.S.-bred way of thinking.

That's U.S. history and culture. It can't be helped. If I'm dating a tall Black man, and he has big hands and big feet, I'm thinking "Oh, God, what if it can't fit?" I haven't even seen it, and already I'm praying. Then, as often, he could be regular. But that shows you how we've been trained. And I'm a Black woman with experience. So what is a white woman thinking? We're so caught up in this color thing, it could be regular, but because it's a Black man, our brain is telling us no, despite what you see, it's tremendous. It feels tremendous. We've having the best time of our lives. On this issue, we're crazy, that's all.

Now, as far as *sexuality*, I feel we got it going on. Let's look at diet. Ours is soul food. Most white people's diet is bland. Ours is full of flavor and spice. This comes through in your spirit, your sexuality. Do you want unflavorful bland, or do you want hot, flavorful spice? What's more appealing? What's more satisfying?

I've had one interracial relationship. I had just graduated high school. He was thirty-six, a self-made millionaire. He was retired and he dated only Black women. He said he never, ever dated a white woman. His mother, his friends, his sister, all verified it. He said he finds Black women more appealing and more satisfying. Spiritually and sexually.

Wait, I gotta interrupt.

I know what you're gonna say, but I had just graduated high school. I hadn't formulated U.S. history, myth, racial solidarity, and I'm now sounding double standard and hypocritical, this was a bygone era. So, anyway. We had started out as friends and things progressed. He wanted to step up the relationship. He wanted to take me on a safari to Kenya. He wanted to lavish and spoil me like I've never been. I found out that he did that for every Black woman he's dated. He's taken them to Africa. My mother wouldn't let me go.

But you were eighteen.

But my mother didn't want me to go.

And you didn't go?

Never seen the continent, but I've gotten all this other stuff I don't use. I have a pair of Jet Skis sitting in Seattle collecting dust. I don't know if he was try'n to make up for something with this Black woman thing, guilt complex or what, but, Africa, gifts, this was what he was doing for Black women.

As far as sex, we never had any. We never had full intercourse. He was very much content with just performing oral sex. And as far as the myth goes about men compensating through oral sex for not having a large penis, that wasn't the case. He was in there.

Why was he content with only oral sex?

Well, he knew at the time I was young and I wasn't ready for sex.

Were you a virgin?

No.

Then why was he content with only oral sex?

He also knew that's what I liked. See, that's a difference between Black men and white men. White men will make sure you're satisfied. Black men seem more concerned with their own satisfaction and that's it.

You're tell'n me he had no desire to enter this young, beautiful Black sister? A tight, dancer's body. He loves Black women. He dates only Black women. They're more appealing and satisfying. He has an energetic, fresh-out-of-high-school eighteen-year-old, and he's satisfied with just oral sex?

Well, then fuck it. To tell you the God's honest truth, it wasn't him, it was me. The thought of having sex with him turned me off. I only told him I wasn't ready to have intercourse. It wasn't so much that he was white, but he was white, white. He just wasn't sexually appealing. Had he a tan, and worked out, I may have been attracted. That's why I didn't go on the safari. I didn't want him going to that expense, not saying that means he's entitled to sex, but I didn't want to give the idea that we were becoming a solid couple, and the occasion for intimacy was here with no excuse.

I was grateful he didn't pressure me for anything more. He was very respectful of my wishes, and I really appreciated that. That's what allowed me to really like him. Most guys would have been like, what's up? He felt, when I was ready, I'd let him know.

I was wrong with not being honest, but it was a nice relationship. We had a beautiful friendship. Anything deeper, as far as commitment, I could never really relate to him. He always had. He didn't know what it was to not have. How that shapes your view of things. Even though I enjoyed my time and places spent with him, I still felt this isn't really important to me. He didn't know my culture. We had good conversations, but some of my best conversations are when I'm with Blacks, and we're talk'n about culture, and talk'n Black. I just feel more myself, more natural, relaxed and free.

It wasn't a matter of him reading a few books, seeing a few movies, listening to Jazz or the Blues or Rap to be able to relate. If you're not Black you just don't have that deep connection. We can connect, we did connect on a certain level, but I know of a deeper connection. One that I'm at home with. That's why I cherish Black men.

I'd like to talk about spiritual depth. We as Blacks, because of our spiritual kinship, can't help but have tremendously excellent sex. And I mean with each other. And most of us don't know why. We're oblivious as to why it's so sensational between us. We're also oblivious as to how much better it could be if we were more aware of our spiritual essence and how to channel it. If we were aware of this essence, and approached sex from a totally spiritual level, the spiritual level that it is, we'd blow the roof off. I think even back then that was part of my spirit that I wasn't fully aware of, not being attracted to my friend. It just wasn't there.

Take dance for example. You've seen white people dance, and you know about our rhythm. Put the two together. It looks like the most ill-conceived piece of choreography, ever. I'll go to a Seattle club and it's pathetic. It's funny. People will excuse the rhythm difference, but I take that as a spiritual sign. You may say, just because someone is not in rhythmic sync with you, how can you condemn any potential relationship? To me that rhythmic sync speaks volumes. It goes beyond the dance. It speaks of what is the natural extension of you. Relationships are about perfect unions. I don't want to start off imperfect. I don't want to think, no matter how good this seems, could it have been better, deeper, more spiritual with someone who is my spiritual other? If I can help it, I rather not hook up with someone due to geographics or job circumstance. I want my cultural other.

Video shakers. That's what they are. I'm a dancer. I could never get a job on a video unless they needed a dancer. These sisters are hired for their physical looks, that's all. I'm attractive, but like most dancers my breasts aren't out to here. Beyond that, what does it all mean? The contribution and continuation of sexism. Exactly what needs to be corrected. You can't only fault the sisters. They just wanna have a good time. You can't only fault the brothers, they just wanna have a good time. You fault them both. I'm all for the good time, but it needs to be done where one side isn't look'n as if they're there only to shake, while the other is there to stand and look. One side isn't there only for the gratification of the other, and the other side isn't there only to feel, point at, freak and control the other.

The last thing I'd like to address are hang-ups, sexual and otherwise.

Oral sex: Not enough of it. What's with guys loving to have it done to them but not returning the favor? Black men, we can stand more oral activity.

Anal intercourse: The ass is an erogenous zone. It's a pleasure worth exploring, from what I've heard. If both partners are willing and able, go for it. Men, open up to allowing your partner to play around with and caress your booty. If you like it, it doesn't mean you're gay or have homosexual tendencies. It only means you're finding enjoyment and pleasure in an erogenous zone.

Blow bootie: From what I've heard, despite all my friends claiming they don't blow bootie, I've heard it's a fun, worthwhile experience. It feels good doing it and really feels good having it done to you, from what I've heard.

Bisexuality: If you are, definitely let your *partners* know that you cross. There are too many diseases.

Sisters: The "get what you can while you can" attitude needs to stop. You show no self-respect. The sexual favors in return for money, "I need some shoes, my baby needs a leather coat," is absolutely ridiculous. Sisters need to seriously check out how they're living. I can be poor and struggling but have self-respect, as opposed to poor and struggling and I'm known as a ho. Now I'm poor, struggling and get no respect.

Unity: We have to be responsible for each other. Some do need guidance, advice and help more than others. Those that go around licking people's hands. If they're not gonna take self-inventory and check out their own bag, then we have to do it for them. We have the patience and kindness to let them know what they're do'n wrong.

I truly wish everyone enlightenment on this issue of brothers and sisters
coming together in harmony. If everyone is serious about *wanting* a positive change, we have to be serious about actually *trying* to make a change. I
pray that we will obtain the enlightenment to know what to do, what to
say and how to act.

Peace to my brothers and sisters.

Phrencess

phrencess, 23

clinton hill

sales

Sex is all that, as I'm sure we all know. The mislabeling that women are conservative, take it or leave it, little know-nothings, is just that, a mislabel. To be blunt, it's a lie. Truth be told, women think about it and want it just as much, if not more, than men. Women will tell you what they want most is to be held, they want honesty, communication and love, but they're not really tell'n you all. You're not be'n told what's up. Would you really, only and mostly want to be held? Part of that is a woman tell'n you what she feels she should be tell'n you because it's what she's been told to tell you. It's what she's been told to want as a woman: to be held. Hold me during, hold me after, don't stop hold'n me. The "hold me" really means "just don't bang me." "Don't treat me, and think of me only as a screw doll." That's all valid, but we shouldn't give the false impression that "a hold" is all we crave. A hold is what we want when all you're do'n is stick'n it in and roll'n over. But now we have two problems. When we get down to it, there's a whole 'nother answer. One that goes beyond what we've been told to say.

Good sex is the number one priority. It's at the top of the mental list. Everything else comes after that. Honesty, truthfulness, commitment, that's only after good sex. When you ask a sister what she really wants in a relationship, the first thing that comes to her *mind* is good sex. She may say something else, mainly what we think we should say, but sex is number one. I swear. Trust me, I know what I'm talk'n about. Etiquette holds us back from tell'n you it's sex. It may sound shallow or plastic, but it's really the main concern. Good sex. Isn't it that way for men? You can be honest, but I can't. The first thing you want is a slamm'n body that you'd love to get into and rock. Then you can give her a nice personality. Well, the same thing for women. Let him know how to make love like a

professional, then we hope he's a nice guy. So that is what's most important to us. That's the first thing on our mind. We just have to say other
things. Which are important. They are of concern, but sex rules supreme.

I know sisters are not find'n perfect sexual partners, so I don't see how
they can simply glide right over other issues without stressing the importance of sex, not the way these young men are performing. They're too
selfish, fast, hard, rough and quiet. Sometimes that's just fine, when that's
what you want, but the majority of times we want the opposite. We want it
the way we end up hav'n to show you, if women are that brave. Because
too many women also don't say what they want. But if we did, and if you
responded perfectly, that's when we're like, "Yeah, let this relationship last
forever." That is if we can now be comfortable with the personality. If so,
we're in love.

You can be in a relationship and not agree with him on most things. You
may have your problems. The way you communicate, the way you get
along, but if you have the chemistry when it comes to sex, those problems
become small. That shows you the power and importance of good sex. It'll
have you look'n at real personality problems as small, and they can be
dealt with. When the sex is good, we sometimes take years until we can
break things off due to personality differences. If it wasn't for the sex, the
relationship would have been over a long time ago. You know it should be
over, you know he's totally not right for you, you're not agreeable with
him as a person, he's changed, you changed, and you know the relationship needs to come to an end, but you think about the sex and you're like,
"Damn, I'm gonna miss this boy. I'll end it next month." That's good sex
talk'n. That's the one thing you both don't have a problem with. That's the
one thing that seems to set everything right, and it will have you sing'n a
different tune. You do it, and an hour later you're on each other's nerves
again.

But I'm here to say, when you're not really happy with the rest of the
relationship but the sex is good and you're stick'n with him because it's his
sex, not the sex but his sex, because his sex is all of that, you still have to let
it go. I personally didn't want to see a relationship end because I knew it
was his sex. From all my sexual experiences, I knew that his sex separated
him from the rest. I just knew, no way was I, just like that, gonna go out
and find another brother who could match his sex. I started to rationalize
that no one has a perfect personality, and I would excuse a lot of shit I
shouldn't have. Things had to get really ugly before it ended. But I knew it
was over way before it actually ended.

For any sister to say sex really doesn't matter, she hasn't had a seriously good sexual relationship. When you've had a good sexual relationship, that's all *you* think about. You think about how good it was, how much closer it made you feel to the guy, and you think about when you can have it again. When can we have some more of that good lov'n? The thing is, we don't let you know that. We really don't have to, because the minute we're alone with you, you're all over us. Then we *act* like we're not pressed, and "why is that all *you* think about?" Most times we're accusing you of our own guilt. "Why do you want us only for our bodies?" That's us talk'n. If we feel that's how you feel too, or even more than us, we'd feel better about ourselves. If men acted less pressed, you'll see how much we really desire it. Give us one month. We'd be all over you. If you only knew.

I have two brothers and they tell me how their girlfriends act: unpressed and indifferent. I know both of their girlfriends and no way, no how are they indifferent and unpressed. I'm not indifferent, but I'll never let you know that. I have girlfriends, and you should hear how we talk. Do you think clothes, the way we walk, talk, move, behave means nothing? You don't see the planning, but we see the results. Whether in or out of a relationship, that's what we crave. It's natural. It's biological. Catch a woman around that time of month and she's impossible. But if we're not in a relationship, we don't go out and nail everything we see. That's the difference. Women have more control and discipline. And the scary thing is, it can so easily be turned around. But men have been so thoroughly seduced that I'm not really worried. In addition to the individual woman, commercials and advertising are do'n our job. Men are whipped.

I believe when you meet someone with whom you may have a relationship, you have to get to know this person sexually. Taking for granted all people are basically nice, as they are. There are nuts out there, it goes with the territory, but basically people are nice. Yeah, yeah, we'll enjoy the good things in life, go here, go there, have fun, but, now, what is the real fun? What is the real good thing that life has to offer? That's why the two of you have to know what's sexually up. How is this person in this A-number-one, important area? It's a shame, because of a few nuts, we have to give so much attention to personality clearance before we can give in and do what we want, but I'm coming from the real-life point of view, sex is the first thing we think of.

You have to let each other know what you both like, hate and love because that is what's important. If you don't let each other know, and the sex is bad, the relationship won't work. I have girlfriends who have had to end relationships because the sex wasn't good. That may sound cold, but it wasn't as cut and dry as "You can't fuck, I don't want you anymore." The fact is, if the sex is not good, that places stress on all other aspects of the relationship. Unfulfilled sex leaves you frustrated and edgy. If he jumps on and jumps off, and you're like, "Whoa, wait a minute," and despite try'n to talk about it, he goes on about his business, you know this ain't gonna last. That's an easy case. Now, if the two of you talk it out, and he tries, but for some reason he just can't move his ass right, not all Black men have a good sense of rhythm, he comes too quick, he's on the small side and tries to compensate, but overcompensates, resulting in disaster, the two of you will end up just be'n friends, that's all.

If you have to take your lover A through Z, where to kiss, where to lick, where to suck, where to touch, where to feel, where to rub, where to put things, where not to try to put things, and finally, how to make you come, who the hell wants that? It becomes too technical, and he's only do'n things by instruction, not passion.

I mean, if you actually have to sit down and say, "Look, you're the worst lover I've ever had and you can't seem to learn,"—it doesn't have to be that harsh—but if you have to have a heart to heart, this will put a strain on the relationship. You've now insulted the man's ego. From that point on everything will try to take on a sense of normalcy, but everything has now been tainted. You'll try to act as if the conversation had never taken place, but what do you do when that time comes? That all-important moment. You've taken the most significant aspect of the relationship and placed it on a pedestal. He's thinking, "Well, she told me I don't know how to do this. I need to do that, more of this, less of that," he's broken out in a sweat just thinking of the problem, and fuck it. He wants out. You want out.

What should make a problem better, but it gets worse, is talk'n about it. I don't think all cases are that serious. A word or two can't remedy things and the relationship is saved, but brothers today and their sensitive egos.

Many of you are not mature enough to handle a sister sitt'n you down and say'n to you, your lovemaking needs work. You're insulted, you can't believe it. You think "But I be bang'n like a muthafucka," but that's the problem. It's not how hard you bang. It's how you bang. Take it easy, feel me. I ask myself, what is he feel'n go'n a hundred miles an hour? You exhaust yourself in five minutes and then you can't do nothing more for us. Take it easy. Enjoy the process.

I feel the man's lovemaking is an extension of how he feels, how he'll view the relationship, and how he'll treat the relationship. And more important, how he'll view and treat me. If his sex is fast, insensitive, selfish, not passionate, intense, loving, what does that say about him? If the sex is taken for granted, you're taking me for granted. If I'm just a quick pleasure, deposit box for him, then this is someone I don't need.

I want my lover to make love to me with all the passion, time, respect and love he feels for me. Lovemak'n as an extension of how he feels is what makes for good sex. The sex being perfected is only a simple matter of say'n to him, "I love it when you do this." Or, "I love when you concentrate on this area." Or, "I've discovered through you that I really like this move." When he shows you something you never knew, now, that's deep. That's good communication. Excellent communication is saying, "Don't stop, don't stop. Right there. Yeaaaaaah."

Talk'n about what you like is hard. All of this is new to us. But I think this generation, as with each, is allowed to be more sexually aware and expressive of itself. But it's still new, we still have a long way to go, and we're still not as comfortable and open with it. Sexual conversation can break some people out in cold sweats. When women do try, and we're more always the one who will initiate it, the man will immediately get on the defensive and it's not even about that.

I think men don't see sex as something you talk about, you just do it. Do it and take for granted each time will feel good. Has a man ever had sex he didn't like? I mean really didn't like? Not, "It was OK" or "It could have been better." I mean, really, really didn't like. I don't think that's ever happened. My understanding is, as long as you get it in and come, you've had good sex. And what's more, you'll have the nerve to believe it was good for us.

Sex should become more intense as the relationship grows. Talk'n about how you can best be pleasured and be'n able to have it done is what will help make the relationship grow. It shouldn't go in the opposite direction. The trick is, how do you communicate that without offending?

We may try not to think about the importance of sex within a relationship, but it really can't be downplayed. You really can't get away from it being the foundation on which the relationship will either grow or die. Think about this. What if each time you had sex with a woman, you didn't come? Many, many women go through this, and if she's not suffering from any health problems, ten out of ten times her not reach'n orgasm is because of the man's lack of performance. If you as a man weren't coming, could you just brush that off? Will the love grow deeper? Will the problem first have to be resolved in order for the love to grow? If it couldn't be resolved, will you still want the relationship to last? TV says, "This is the time when I'll love you all the more, honey. So what I can't orgasm, we'll get through it." But remember, that's TV. In real life, I won't be gett'n through it. I know men won't say, "You can't make me come, but that's OK, I'll be with you forever." Get real. It'll be "Next." "See ya." You'll still be friends. If I meet a person and a relationship develops and the sex is bad, then we'll have to be just friends. I'll nip it in the bud right away. Before any deep, deep attachments, before any declarations of undying love, we will just be friends. Ain't noth'n wrong with that. We can always use a friend. Especially Black men and women. Many factors go into a relationship being able to work. Sex is one of them. Sex is not a requisite for friendship.

In actuality I don't sleep with men right away. I may want to, and sex is important, and it is the first thing on your mind, but as I said, because of the nuts out there, we have to go about it with care. If not for the nuts, the sex would come much sooner.

Three weeks to a month if we got something working. If I get the sense you're not a nutcase. For some women three weeks to a month seems too long. It depends on how intensely you two have been seeing each other. Every day for two straight weeks, OK, something's gonna happen. It depends on the intensity of the two individuals, them knowing themselves and how well they click together. But I'll still encourage the sex if you're not too sure about the person, because it's always not until after the sex that people show their true selves. You can be holding back for months, trying to get their personality down, have sex, and now you have a totally new individual. You could have found the real person months ago, after the sex. Look, after a week, if he hasn't killed anybody, said some super-crazy statement, hit you, or is wearing a dress on your date, go on and get the sex out the way.

If you can say although I don't really know him, but he appears sane, and you two are spending time together, go on and have sex. You'll see where he's com'n from much sooner. Did he just want the sex or not? If you spend six months with him, thinking this is a working relationship, you have sex and he leaves, of course you're angry. Acknowledge the sexual attraction, say you'd also like to have a relationship, if that's possible, and work from there. If we can all be honest and say it's just the sex I want right now, we'll save each other a lot of time and heartache. We got it backward. We do it in reverse. We withhold the sex, although that's the first thing we want, and try to have the relationship. Don't we know people will be pleasant just to get the sex. We're believing the relationship is going well, but it's going well so the sex can be gotten. I say, take care of the sex first, if everyone appears sane, then work on the relationship, if that's what the two of you want, after the sex has occurred. Don't waste six months of my time. If we get out the way what we initially feel, work on a relationship, if it don't work out, I'll have no regrets. If we agree we don't want a relationship but the sexual attraction is there and we do it, I'll have no regrets. I'll regret trying to make a relationship work first, not have sex, so now I'm sexually frustrated, nothing works out, and I've wasted months.

You try not to sleep with someone on the first date. But nothing is written in stone. This last relationship, I'll admit I wanted to sleep with him on the first date. He was so sexy, everything was click'n and I just wanted him. But will he think *I'm* the nutcase. Will he think, "Is she some slut?" See, as it is women don't do that. I have that to keep in mind. Although that understanding is against how we feel, I still have to respect it. Until the day comes when it's understood that we're not sluts if we sleep with you on the first date, I'll have to put things in check. But I'll be honest with you on the second or third date. I'll let you know something as soon as I feel safe enough to be alone with you. It's not about knowing your life story, that'll come, I just wanna feel safe with you. I've come to be a very good judge of character. I wasn't always like this, some things make you sensitive to becoming a good judge of character, so unless you can read people well, don't take my word as law. You have to know yourself, and know by what criteria you're able to form opinions about people. But I'm also say'n things that's in accordance with how we think as humans, and if we allowed ourselves to be more honest with who and how we are, maybe things could be better.

When you meet someone, what is it that attracts you? You like how they look. It's the sexual attraction that makes you take interest. It starts right there. You both like how the other is physically looking, and you stand there mak'n small talk, when in the front of your mind you're fantasizing about you and that person going at it like dogs. So what should we really be say'n to each other? We say it months later to each other while in bed, "You know when I first saw you, I wanted you." If you can tell me that in a nice, respectable, honest way when we first meet, I won't be offended. I understand human nature, I understand we can see someone and want them on sight.

Sometimes relationships do develop out of "meant to be one-night stands." That's the exception. The rule is, my rule is, if I'm sexually attracted to you, and I want a relationship with you, and you appear sane and safe, in a short while, say within three weeks, maybe less, I will have sex with you. All the while I'm searching for the deeper person inside to see if I'm attracted to that part of you as well. If I find that to be the case, then we're off to a good start. If not, I'll be honest with myself and go from there. I won't put the relationship on hold, try'n to find out your most deepest secrets before having sex with you. I'm aware, in reality, the relationship doesn't really start, walls don't really come down, relaxation and comfort doesn't really kick in until after the sex. I try to stay grounded in reality.

If the person doesn't want the relationship but wants the sex, I beg the person, please be honest and let me know. If the person don't even want to have sex with me, let me know. If you just wanna be my friend, let me know. Whatever, just let me know.

Right now I'm just gett'n over the fairy tale that most girls are taught. The "being swept off your feet by Prince Charming and living happily ever after" fairy tale. Why do they feed us this? Why not a picture of what really happens for most women? You'll grow up; you'll have your heart broken once or twice; you'll become bitter; you'll become untrusting; at some point you'll get tired of the games and settle for someone who'll do; you'll get married; infidelity may come about on someone or both parts; you'll get a divorce; you may get half; you'll become a sexually free and out-there individual, then you'll live happily ever after.

After a certain age, people, my family expected me to get married. It seemed they thought I would go to college, get a husband, and pick up a degree along the way. Unfortunately, I went to the wrong school for that. I went to the Fashion Institute of Technology, where most of the men are gay. If there were any straight men in the school, they were in the closet. Maybe had I gone to a different school like Hampton or Morgan I may have been married by now. Maybe that's where the fairy tale exists. I would have met Mr. Right at some point and I'd be married. But some of my friends say going somewhere else would have been like being at FIT, only now the majority of men are straight, but you still can't get one to be with you, settle down and be serious. The ratio is like thirteen to one, favor the women, and the guys act like they're in heaven.

One thing I've learned is if there is an abusive relationship, where the man is mistreating the woman, whether it be sleeping with other women, physically harming her, or verbal abuse, it's not only his fault. Somebody will continue to treat you as bad as you allow them to treat you. Somehow we have to accept this. If you're still in it and complaining to yourself, then you have to take the blame. You have to realize there is no excuse for tolerating mistreatment. If you're being abused, you have to find the strength to ask someone for help and get out of the situation. If it can't be worked out, and there is no more relationship to salvage, you have to find some way to get the strength to get out of it. If anything is to be said to your girls, it should be, "My lover mistreated me, and I had to let him go," nothing more. If you're not talking to them for help, then don't say anything.

I realized that there was no one to blame but me for some of the things I put up with as a teenager. There was nothing keeping me from telling this person good-bye, I'm not happy with this. The more I put up with it, the worse things got, and it was all my fault. It was his fault for issuing the mistreatment, but it was my fault for allowing it to continue. I didn't have his baby. It wasn't a marriage situation, and the deep feelings were gone, so what was *my* problem? What's the problem with so many other women?

This is deeper than sex keeping you there. Sex will keep you there when there's a personality difference, and you can put it off till next week, but you know it's over. You wait for things to turn ugly, but you're still having good sex. I'm talking about an abusive relationship, verbally and sexually. There is no good sex. When the relationship becomes more harmful to you than anything. At this point, I think it's insecurity. I was insecure. It's hard to say, just walk away. It's hard to give that advice when I know I couldn't just do that. My mother saved me. And when your mother isn't there to save you, what if the reason you're in an abusive relationship is because there is no family? You may have family around, but what if there is no family? That's when you have to find someone to talk to, anyone. And talk to for help, not complaint. If you're only complaining, that says you don't want help, and people can't do anything for you although they may try. You have to talk of being helped.

Toleration of abuse can be learned from your family. Both of my sisters were in abusive relationships. My mother took care of her abuser until the day he died. And to think she went looking for my sister's abuser with a knife, intending to kill him, but in her own situation she could never defend herself. She wouldn't dare think of picking up a knife. Not in her own house. It blows my mind.

I would prefer if I weren't made any promises within relationships. I don't make them and I don't ask for any. For example: If you tell me that you love me so much that I'm the only woman you want, you just made me a promise. If I find out you've been see'n someone, you've broken your promise. You've lied. I'm hurt and that's the end of the relationship. You can't beg your way back into it or anything. You've killed all trust and respect I had for you. If I can't trust you, I can't have a relationship with you. If you don't claim any devotion and you cheat, I'm hurt, but I'll hurt less. I'll know you didn't promise me anything and, at least, you're not a liar. I'm not immediately ending the relationship. I'll see what's the problem. But if you lie, I can't have a relationship with a liar and a cheat. Staying with you is abuse.

I have a problem with the term "my man." He's my man. I've never used it and never will. The person that I'm with is my lover. A lot of people will hear that and immediately picture a couple in bed, but **when you listen to the term "my lover" and see the depth beyond sex, maybe more people will understand it and use it. I think to have a lover is more than having a boyfriend or a girlfriend.**

It's on a different level. It sounds as if you have someone who loves you and you love them. To me it doesn't sound possessive, which is the second reason I don't use "my man." We have this problem with thinking we own the person we're with when we don't. To say you have "a man," I don't hear the love. I hear only the ownership. "I got me one." Then when the relationship ends, you're more upset over having lost something you believed to be yours. We're more angry than hurt. We're angry because of the loss of ownership. Like, dammit, I lost my purse with all my money in it. We're angry. With the loss of a lover you can only be hurt. So I'll be in a relationship and have a lover.

I think sex when wisely practiced can be very good. It can become beautiful with time as the two of you grow closer and closer. The more you get to know each other, feel better about the other, respect and have an understanding with each other, it can't help but become beautiful. That's a natural progression. When everything you mean to one another is incorporated in sex, it's beautiful.

I think any form of love practiced by Black people is beautiful.

I hope one day there'll be no such thing as a Black sister say'n her Black man abuses her, she realizes it's her fault, and she has to let him go. I hope one day no one can accuse any Black man or woman of abuse or mistreatment. We would only speak in terms of loving each other. I strive to do that now, because despite our faults, we have so many more reasons to love.

l i s a

l i s a ,   2 0

m i d w e s t

a c t o r

I'm tired of be'n looked at as a sex object rather than a human being. That's first and foremost. I want to be taken seriously. I want to be viewed as a full human being. Although, in the back of my mind, I know I can't fully complain. I know that how I projected myself in the past is com'n back to haunt me, and you do reap what you sow. I used to pump, "Look at what I got up here and back here." Now it's payback. What goes around comes around, and here it is.

I've since toned all that down. And, of course, now that I've done that, now that I'm trying to put brains first, all men still see is body first. I've realized brothers don't care how well you cover or disguise your shit, they'll still see only one thing, and act as if you want to screw them just as bad as they want to fuck you. Fuck that, things have changed. It took some doing, because a lot of shit is psychological and that's a bitch to overcome, but when you know you have to do something for your own good, you do it.

I think people who really want to change need to take an inventory with their past. You have to clean house in order to make sure the present and future will be correct. I know every time I talk about certain things from my past with someone, it reminds them of a parallel in their own life and makes them aware of something they need to work on. This helps them move in a more positive direction. Away from what they need to leave and toward where they need to go. Every time I talk about my past, some new revelation comes to me. This helps me and it can help whomever I may be yapping to. It's learning from others' mistakes.

My shit goes all the way back to my child years. Not hav'n a father, my first love, my heart be'n broken, and still haven't fully recovered. My attitude was totally different. Compared to who I am now, my way of thinking has changed drastically since high school.

In a sentence, I used to be a pampered little bitch. Any man I wanted, I had. I made sure they catered to my every need. I knew they really didn't care deeply about me, they were just about gett'n that one thing. In return, I made sure they did what I wanted. When I wanted a man there for something, he was there. Wherever I wanted to go, we went. Whatever I said do, they did. Jump, they would ask how high? All that shit.

Then I had one boyfriend who worshipped me. Truly cared about me. I loved him to death, and he loved me even more. And like the rest, I was gonna make him work and wait for the sex. But once I noticed he truly loved me, and would have waited forever, it was like too deep. I was freaked out and I couldn't have sex with him. The only kind of sex I knew: quick, cold and selfish, I didn't want to experience with him. I don't know why I thought it would be that way, but I did. I didn't want it to be like the only way I knew sex to be. Or maybe I was just afraid it would be different. That we would actually make love, I would really be in love, and be in love with a man. A man whom my mother told me you couldn't love because they were dogs not worthy of any woman's love. To love and make love to my boyfriend, that just seemed too deep and too against what my mother said. I'd go off and have cold sex with other guys instead of try'n to have something real with this guy. But I couldn't continue do'n that to him, so I just let the relationship die.

Then I got to college and I allowed myself to have a relationship. I allowed myself to fall in love, make love and have a full mental and sexual relationship. I wasn't gonna mess up twice. And that shit just blew my mind. It was different. It was deeper. Mak'n love on a regular basis within a relationship and with someone you cared about turned me out.

Although I was hav'n sex prior to mak'n love, it didn't compare. I had never had an orgasm. I didn't know I wasn't com'n until I came for the first time within this new relationship. I had grown comfortable with him, developed deep feelings for him, I was in love with him, and for the first time I had an orgasm. Each time we had sex I was hav'n orgasms. I was bugg'n. We moved in together, did the whole couple thang, and then just like that, he decided he wanted out. Instant heartbreak. I was too crushed. My heart was broken, and since then it became hard for me to open up to guys. I went back to practicing what my mother preached. I went back to how I used to operate, but even harder.

You didn't try to find out why he was out like that?

Yeah I did. It wasn't a real talk, but much later I went back to him and

asked what was up? He told me I wouldn't let him be a man. That's
something that has always stuck in my head. To this day, I don't know
what he actually meant. I've come to the conclusion it wasn't me hold'n
him back, he just wasn't a man. I was raised by a single mother. A strong
Black single mother. She was independent. I was raised to be independent.
I was raised to be strong, just like a man. So how can I not let him be what
he already is, or should have been?

But were you giving him a chance to be an equal? Or were you dominating?
But what is that? I wasn't be'n some subservient little female. Why
couldn't it be a partnership of two individuals who were both strong and
independent? How do you not let a man be a man in a relationship? Either
the brother is a man or he isn't. I don't see any in-between. I'm the type of
person that's gonna push a brother as far as he lets me. I'm gonna take you
this much. And if you go for that, I'm gonna take you this much more. If
you go for that, I'll keep push'n till you put your foot down. If you can't do
that, if you can't put your foot down, then you're not a man.

*But if we're in a relationship, a genuine relationship whereas I care about
you, and I genuinely love you, then I'd want the relationship to work. And work
because I'd believe in the full potential of what we have. I'd believe in and
cherish how special you are to me. I will take a little shit. I will take this much
and that much, not because I'm not a man, but because I love you and I know
that relationships mean compromise and tolerance. And a lot of patience. If
you're tak'n me this much and that much, I'm not think'n you're gam'n and
test'n my manhood. That's some weak shit to be do'n in a relationship. I'd think
you had a small problem, one that I can overlook, but one that I'd hope you'd get
over.*

*If you're do'n what you say you were do'n, I'd think you haven't yet fully
trusted me. I'd think after a while, after you'd see the truth in our relationship,
you'd calm down. If after a reasonable amount of time and effort on my part I
don't see any change, and I can't take it anymore, I'd be like, "Damn. I really
wish this shit could've worked," but I would have to let you go. I'd see us as
incompatible. I wouldn't put any more energy into try'n to change you because I
don't want a person I'd have to change. The same as I don't wanna have to
change for anybody. I wanna find someone with whom we both naturally
harmonize. That's probably what homeboy was do'n and what he meant. I'm
sure, if he really loved you, that things coming to an end was a bitch.*

Damn. . . . Everything you just said I relived. I almost cried. The
tears welled up and were like right there.

I was that selfish. It's that plain and simple. I was like, you let me do it,
I'll do it. . . . I told him what to do, we did it. When and where we'd go,

and we went. I decided when we would have sex, that's when we did it. I was like if you don't have enough pride and self-respect to stand up to me and say, "Look, Lisa," then I'm not gonna give you any pride or respect. He didn't demand any respect, so I didn't give him the respect I thought he didn't deserve.

Love outweighs pride. If you love me, I don't need to demand respect from you. Shit should be unconditional.

And it was easier for me to say, "Damn, I can juice this muthafucka. He doesn't have any spine, so let me take him." You have to look at where I was com'n from. I'm a Black Leo. I'm a Queen. I'm regal. I'm royal and I expect my man to be a King. I'm think'n, it makes me, as a woman, lose a lot of respect for a man who's not gonna stand up for himself and put you in your place.

What did he have to do, beat your ass?

I would have respected him as a man. I'm say'n back then. I probably would have respected him a whole lot more. I can't say I'd see it that way today, especially if I'm not do'n anything to warrant a beat-down, but back then I would have respected him, and I would have stopped with my games.

I understand what you're say'n. Well, it seems after all was said and done, I was the one who ended up really hurt. It was totally my loss. And tonight when I think about it, I'll hurt all over again. Even more so now.

I was young and didn't know shit about men. I'm also a sister, like a lot of sisters out here, who was not raised with a man in the house. So that's something that needs to be understood. That situation will definitely change a woman's perception of men. How she deals with men and how she relates to men. Beyond know'n that all you want is some ass, if I stop there, I know you as a man. But if I'm to give you any more credit, I don't know you. But most men act as if "All you need to know about me being a man is that I require sex and only sex. That makes up my total existence." I swear this is how you act, but I know you have to be a little deeper than that. But this is what women are generally shown from you.

So when you hear that I would have respected the brother for slapp'n me, you have to check out where I'm com'n from. That's why a lot of sisters take abuse. They don't know how a man should really be treat'n them.

I have no idea what to expect from a relationship. A real, post-teenage one. No games, no test'n, no prove your manhood, no ill shit. I realized a

large part of my understand'n of men was from TV. I'm serious. My
mother told me one thing about them, and I let TV fill in the rest. But
that's like white people say'n they know Black people from watch'n TV.
That ain't even half the picture. That ain't any of it.

My mother never brought men around me. I never had a man in the
house. I never had any man to relate to while grow'n up. I never had
anyone to call daddy. All I know comes from TV and another woman's
point of view. And a woman who's been dogged. So you know what's up.
So, here we are and I've never been in a real, honest, no-games relationship. What kind of advice can I give if my relationships are a part of the
ones that need the advice? I have to first sort through my own shit, correct
that, then move on. Then I can offer something.

I guess I can say, if you're starting out in relationships, learn from my
shit. See what your personal agenda is. Does the relationship help? Are
you using the relationship for selfish reasons? Are you being selfish and
don't know it? We first have to look at our own personal background.

**If you're a sister or brother raised in a single-parent household,
you have to ask, what do I really know about relationships? Have
I personally seen one? What do I want, and what do I expect out
of this? Am I try'n to fill a void? If all you know are the "pass'n
through" men your mother brought around, are you basing your
understanding of relationships on that? And these young brothers
without fathers, shit, I really know they don't know. That's why
they don't respect sisters today. They don't have a good example
of their father with their mother to go on. They, like myself, have
TV. They have music videos.**

Sex was a definite weapon. I would have it when I felt like hav'n it, fuck
how you felt. I could really want it, but withhold it, just to fuck with you.
Sex was not out of any deep attachment I felt, but because I wanted to stay
in control. The person was used, and that's it. That sounds like TV, soap
operas and movie of the week to me.

Now I have to pay attention to the type of guys I've been attract'n. That's
why I say my shit goes way back, what's goes around comes around, and I
guess I can't complain. When all I wanted to do was fuck, that's all they
wanted to do and everything was equal. Now that I'm try'n to relate to
brothers differently, I still find myself deal'n with a figure of my former
self. Men that only want to fuck me. And it seems all men. I thought
having a new attitude would attract a new type of man. But, un-unh.

This second-to-last dinner date I had, it was with a titty watcher. He sat there and talked to my titties the whole evening. I was like damn, my eyes are up here.

The last date I had was with this rapper. I've been dat'n rappers lately. Now, I know you can say, if I'm try'n to attract a new breed of man and I'm dating rappers, am I defeat'n my purpose? But not all of them have been rappers, and they all have proven to be just the same. This titty watcher wasn't a rapper. So it's like whatever their occupation. A man is a man, is a rapper, is a businessman. A businessman is supposed to act like a civil person. His civility may be a front. Not having the excuse of a rapper, he can dog me in a sly and polite way, and then I'm really pissed. I'll take the rapper who's expected to be more straight up. At this point I need to know what I'm gett'n. Plus, a rapper is either gonna show you his ass, or he's work'n hard at not com'n off like the one-dimensional image they have.

So this last date was with a rapper. By night's end he was show'n his ass. The date ended with him bring'n me back to my apartment and he invit'n himself in. The little I do know about men was enough to tell him, early in the date, that this wasn't a sex date. But do niggas listen? While we were at the movie he was with the hands and I told him to stop. At dinner, again with the hands, again I had to tell him to stop.

Now, be'n that money is spent, I'm aware that he may feel entitled to at least a kiss, if not outright intercourse. Forget that stupid shit men believe about spend'n money means gett'n automatic ass. I let him know, and he was like, "Yeah, yeah, that's chill. I don't expect you to feel you owe me something." That was early in the day. So we're in the apartment. I'm try'n to carry on a conversation. I ask him how long he wanted to be a rapper. Who does he see his style similar to? All that. Boom, he starts with the hands again. What was the "Yeah, yeah, it's chill" all about? I waste no time, and I tell him he has to leave. He redoubles his efforts and then starts to really push up. So now I'm wrestl'n with the muthafucka on my bed. We're actually wrestl'n, him on top of me, not getting up, and I have to throw him off. I'm nearly hysterical, yelling and scream'n at him to get the fuck out, I don't believe him. I looked as if I were in a fight, and I'm like what the fuck is with guys? I told the bastard this wasn't a sex date.

Almost the classic example of date rape, had he gone on. Him be'n a rapper, I'm not hold'n it against him. He was just another stupid-ass, ignorant brother. I'm not hold'n it against him as a rapper cause now I'm now see'n another rapper. I don't know, right now it's something about rappers. Maybe it's my career. I come across a lot of rappers. Plus, I can't lie, I like that "I'm the man" attitude. Be the man but don't violate me the woman. I don't have a "fuck me" sign on my back.

I feel brothers should be able to see what you're about and act accordingly. Act against what you'd rather do if you can see the sister is about try'n to have respect for herself.

AND ESPECIALLY, ESPECIALLY IF THE SISTER HAS SAID SHE DOES NOT WANT TO FUCK YOU.

You can't get no clearer.

I know men can look at a woman and tell what type of person she is. Whether she'll be down for some quick, meaningless, or whether she's not. If we are, a man should know. We'll drop hints, or we'll come right out and say it. We make it very easy because we know where men are coming from. It doesn't take much.

So if you have someone who is making things very clear, clear that she doesn't want any sex, then respect that. I'll accept the come-ons, but when it gets physical, that I don't deserve. I could have been raped. What have I done to deserve to be raped? It's as if men become deaf and they see women as one big whole. They don't put any effort in to seeing the differences that exist. And when we help your lack of effort by tell'n you the difference, you ignore it. We'll tell you what not to expect, and I still find myself fight'n niggas in my house, on my bed.

I believe I'm sexy. Therefore I automatically project sexuality. You can be initially attracted to that sexuality and want to fuck me, *BUT!* once you see I'm not about that, once you listen to the quality of my conversation, you should realize that you can't push up like I'm the easy ho you want me to be.

Listen, I know about males' egos, but I think I'm all that, too. I also know, when it comes to my career, I'm work'n hard to make it happen. I'm going to be large, so brothers better recognize.

And the man I dedicate myself to can't be com'n along for a free ride. I know just as there are female gold diggers, it works both ways. There are male gold diggers. He has to be somebody to make me feel like, damn, am I worthy of him? He has to be just as ambitious as I am. I'm work'n too hard to be gett'n with a freeloader.

I'm from small town, USA. I'm in fuck'n New York City. This is a whole different world, but that's how bad I want this shit. I'm by myself. I have no family here. I don't have anybody whose door I can go knock on and say, "Damn, I just got another audition door slammed in my face." I'm in this small room in Harlem. How I'm liv'n is how bad I want this, so you know when it's all over, I don't wanna have some half stepper with me.

I'm sexy, but I'm also intelligent. I'm very smart and I'm also a human being. I'm more than a pat on the ass, or somebody's toy, and I will let you know.

If you're not a star, then dammit, have that star quality. Carry yourself as if you're a star. I've seen intelligent sisters turn into complete assholes with men. They'll take all this shit and go complain to their girlfriends about it. I don't want to hear that shit. In a sense, what my mother taught me was good because I'm not walk'n around here whin'n about some man. Fuck that. Don't come to me whin'n. Take that shit to your man. I'm not that traditional weak little punk bitch.

This is on the parent's tip and how much unintentional damage they can do. What we're taught early in life can damage our sexual relations later in life. The image and mold girls are supposed to fall into is very fucked up. When that mold and image are contrary to how you really feel, it can cause lots of confusion. And really, lots of damage.

I suffered from the good-girl syndrome. Good girls don't, bad girls do. This was until age seventeen. That's when I first had sex. And after I had finally slept with someone, I was always hiding. I was always hiding the fact that I was sexually active. I never wanted my mother to know. I never wanted anyone to know. I was like so repressed, but I had always had the desire. That hiding and repressing does something to you.

I was hav'n oral sex before I was hav'n actual intercourse. I would suck dick but that's it. I had good-girl syndrome, and good girls don't. They can do everything but the main thing. But what the fuck is that? Good girls suck dick? Even today, and my girlfriends think I'm crazy, but I'm like I'll perform oral sex way before I let them have sex with me. In my mind, my body is like a shrine. And when I give myself to you, that's say'n a lot. It's say'n I'm ready to open up and share what's inside me with you. Share what I internally feel. But if I'm gonna just suck your dick, that doesn't mean shit to me. Maybe I sound like Vanessa Del Rio, but that's how it is. That's how I worked out my good-girl syndrome. Want'n to be sexually active and being so, but not really be'n so. A lot of women are just the opposite. They can fuck a man and think noth'n of it. But suck'n dick is out of the question. I don't see it that way. To me it's the opposite. We all place our personal values on what certain things mean.

I started masturbating within the last two years. I've started so late, again, because of the good-girl syndrome. And even when I started, I kinda felt kinda like I was do'n someth'n wrong. Like someone was watch'n me and I shouldn't be do'n this. Like I'm be'n bad? But this is something we have to acknowledge.

Our bodies, our sexuality, we have to get to know them. Inside and out, we have to be able to talk about this to our partners. Masturbation is something I try to do regularly so I can make myself more familiar with my body. It's so I can be more secure with my body. Correct all the inhibitions I had toward sex and my body. Caressing and massaging your body lets you know that it's more to it than an insertion and just hav'n an orgasm. Discovering all the pleasure that can be brought to my body, discovering those pleasure spots makes the act even better. When your partner knows this, it's all the more better. But he'll know only if you know what to tell him. Then you won't complain that your man isn't good or doesn't know what he's doing.

When I masturbate it's easy for me to have an orgasm because I know what I'm do'n. I know what feels good to my body. I don't use a vibrator, but I'm gonna start.

During masturbation you discover a lot. But during sex, sometimes all you get is straight sex. You have the occasional suck here, kiss here, but it's still basically straight sex. Through masturbation you can simulate and discover all that you really like. How you'd like the penis to move inside you, where you'd like to be touched most, how you'd like to be touched. You can discover that anal stimulation is exciting. You can then translate all that to your partner. But don't make it like a mechanical teaching class. Move here. Touch here. You have to have style. You have to guide your partner into it, and guide in a way that they don't know they're be'n led. Then after, you can say I like the way you caressed me here. How'd you learn that? Then watch niggas lie.

You can also outright discuss what you like and dislike. All this is to correct what I call sexual setbacks. I didn't know my body and I didn't have a healthy attitude toward sex. I abused my body. I misused it. Sexual ignorance is what leads to a lot of bad relationships as well as unwanted pregnancies. Girls not know'n anything about sex can get caught out there. They go and do it on the sneak tip. They get caught out there, have no idea they're pregnant. Find out too late. Panic. Try to ignore it. Hide the shit, and the next thing you know, here comes baby.

We're physically able to have a child at twelve and thirteen. Our bodies are ready. Our periods have started. But that doesn't mean we're ready mentally. So why not have the proper knowledge about sex? I can't believe there's a debate whether sex education should be taught in the schools. Aren't schools supposed to be about education? Why not educate about something that's hurting a lot of young Black girls? It's common sense. Why is there debate over sex education in schools? Because then we'll do it? Like it's not being done now? Like maybe with education it'll be done the right way.

Here in America we have this belief that if you teach a little girl about sex she's gonna go out and become a slut. They throw girls in parochial schools and think that's gonna stop their natural development of sexuality. These Catholic-school girls are the ones who are experimenting like crazy. You suppress them and they're gonna come back even harder. You suppress anyone and they're gonna go hard. Or they'll have a suppressed, fucked-up life. You have now affected so much of their other personality traits. Everything else is on this suppressed level. They're shy, they don't speak up, they're weak, they can be taken advantage of. We're creating more problems. What happens when it's time for that girl to relate to the world?

Sex needs to stop be'n such a taboo and hidden issue. It's like with anything. Try to hide it, people will want to know why it's be'n hidden. How many "Let's keep it from them" sisters do you see with seven pounds in their arms?

Brothers need to understand that it's not all about women receiving an orgasm each time we have sex. It's the closeness that we crave. Part of the enjoyment of sex is the attention that I'm receiving, not the orgasm. That's what makes sex feel good. It's all about simple affection. A lot of women are look'n for affection. Look'n for that form of love we may not have had from a father. Hopefully, you're with your man to get this. Although we're look'n for affection, we get confused with how to get it.

Right now I'm involved with a guy whom I haven't slept with yet. Even though I want to sleep with him, I won't let it happen. I'm tired of meeting men and sleep'n with them right off the bat. I'm a very sexual person. I'll meet a man, be sexually attracted to him and say, fuck it, let's do this. Then I'd regret it. Especially if we don't work out. The more I'd get to know the brother, and see that he's an ass, the more I'd start to regret that I'm sexually involved with him. I'd know the regret wouldn't have to be had I waited and kept it on a non-sexual level. Had I done it that way, and then realized because of his personality we couldn't work as a couple, cutt'n him off wouldn't be so hard. It's hard to distance yourself from someone, no matter how much of an ass they are, once you've slept with them. And don't let him be a good lover. A good lover but an asshole.

You're like damn, if only I didn't have sex with him. It's hard to walk away from a good piece of dick. They're hard to come by.

I had to change because I found myself becom'n like a nigga. When I knew it was all about me, and that from start I knew I wasn't try'n to have a relationship, after I'd sleep with the guy, I'd basically kick him out of my life. I just used him. I didn't care about them and who they were as a person. After enough of this, after see'n this is what guys do and it hurts women, I said to myself, I don't want to be like that. That's all that happened. It wasn't some big, major incident that made me change. It was just realizing what I was do'n. I don't even know if the guys really liked me or was just going for the same. I didn't give them the time to explain. I didn't care. And if one did like me, I'm sure after the way I cut him off, he wouldn't want me to know that he liked me. He should have been call'n me a bitch. But that's all in the past.

So, now, if I want a relationship with you, I really have to know the brother first. No matter how bad I may want him, I have to put my desires in check. And brothers don't help. They'll get upset and say you know you want it, and they'll be right. Half the time I do want it. I'd want it just as bad as he does, but I have to say no. I need to wait. I need to know who he is. I need to know more than his body. I need to know where his mind is. What he wants for himself. What he wants from life. What he wants from me, besides the obvious. I now need to know more than just surface bullshit before I sleep with someone.

A lot of women don't feel this is right. Putting on these time limits. They'll say time really doesn't matter as long as the feelings are there. But that's the problem. Those feelings can be just lust. You may think it's something more, but it's not. How can it be so deep and you don't really know the brother?

If the feelings are stronger than lust, and you think it's near love, you still can wait. What's the rush? If he felt the same way, he won't be go'n anywhere. That's when you'll know what you really have. He won't be pressed about gett'n some. The time will come. Wait, take your time and know what you have.

I'm start'n to make brothers and myself wait and I'm gonna stick to it. I don't agree with the thought that if you make a guy wait too long he won't want it anymore and the sex won't be good. I think just the opposite is true if he's really interested in you. It's like Eddie Murphy said in *Raw*. If you've been starv'n for food and someone gives you a soda cracker, you'd be like, "Goddamn, that's a good soda cracker. That's the best soda cracker I ever had. What kind of soda cracker was that?" It would be worth the wait. I had to realize, if you want a relationship, you can't sleep with the guy on the quick fast, because he'll then think you're a ho, you do this with ten other brothers, how does he know you really like him, and he's out.

This brother I'm see'n now, we're tak'n our time. I really like him and he doesn't have a problem with wait'n and I like that. We're gett'n to know each other, our likes and dislikes, our personalities. We may discover we're not meant for each other without ever hav'n sex, and we can part company with no regrets. At least I can. If the sex happens, it'll happen because we'll know we're truly try'n to make something work. I'll trust that I'll know when the time is right.

I'm start'n to use condoms and I feel better about that. Like so many others *still* are, I was ignorant. I just didn't have a fear of catch'n the Magic dick. It's fucked up how if I wanted a relationship, sleep with him quick fast, it doesn't work out, my frustration would be, "Damn, I let this ass have a part of me." Not, "Damn, I hope I didn't catch AIDS from this muthafucka."

And brothers don't give a fuck. They'll look at a girl they wanna get with and they'll say, based entirely on how she looks, she doesn't have anything. She looks too clean, so she ain't got shit. She looks too good to have something. Shit, if she looks good, how many other brothers do you think have already pushed up? That good-look'n, clean-look'n girl can have some good-look'n, fucked up shit up there. But everyone's think'n "not me."

Everybody, not just brothers, sisters too, because it works both ways, everybody needs to come correct. I'll even lean more on sisters because we're the ones be'n chased. We should set the rules. We have what men want, so why don't we say how it should go?

Sisters aren't even in control of their own bodies. If a man wants my body, it's on my terms. First you have to care for me. You have to respect me and I have to respect you.

I didn't change because guys started chang'n their ways. If I left it up to them, I'd be fuck'n all the time, and without a condom. So, I had to make the change. And make it by myself because it was what was best for myself.

Sisters be chang'n for brothers and shit. They don't have to do that. Do'n all kinds of shit they know they'd rather not be do'n. If you're unhappy and miserable, look at why. Don't fuck him on the quick fast, get hurt and be like, the dog, well I hope the next one works out. Sleep with the next one, get hurt and be like, the dog, well I hope the next one works out. You're not even address'n why things aren't lasting. It's about say'n enough. If you don't like the way things are go'n, don't blame men, blame yourself. If you're worthy of blame, face up to it. You have to be honest enough to say yeah, OK, maybe I am fuck'n too many brothers and hoping for the best. That's not the way.

For the most part, brothers do need to change their shit anyway. They need to get serious. When you do see that someone you like, ask yourself are you ready to put in serious, committed time with the person? Not just try to bone her and then work on the relationship part.

We should be look'n for something that will last. How do we know it will last? Because both people will be honest with everything they do. So if we come with honesty, we should have something that's lasting. If not a relationship, at least let's get a working friendship outta the deal. Friendships are to cherish. Everyone has a friend they've had longer than any relationship. What does that tell you? Friendships last longer than relationships. So if brothers and sisters can start to develop friendships with each other, that's a positive beginning. It'll last beyond you two not working out as boyfriend, girlfriend. You'll have only what you started off with. The friendship. And ain't noth'n wrong with that.

These are the type things that we need to hear. All we know are negatives. Negatives that's be'n kept alive by negative people. It's like where are the people who love Black men. Love Black women. Love themselves. We're badly misrepresented. The same as the news people pick'n the worst person to interview. "Yeah, I seen the whole thing. I was drink'n my forty when it happened." We're like, couldn't they find anyone else? They couldn't ask the sane-look'n brother stand'n next to the fool? We love to keep highlighting the fools. We love seeing the fool. The idea is supposed to be that by show'n the fool, other fools will see themselves and correct their foolishness. Highlight the negative to bring out the positive. Well, we've been shown the fool for hundreds of years now. After a hundred years, someone should say that idea ain't work'n. Show the positive. The fool will see how he's supposed to be and he'll correct himself. Try that theory.

You have to understand how we're conditioned. You have a TV with two channels. Which would you rather watch? Channel A to see ten weddings, or B to see ten vicious murders? Is that nature or nurture?

I believe we've been told to like what we think we like seeing. If you keep show'n me ten beautiful weddings on channel "A," that's what I'll become used to seeing. That's what I'll pay attention to. And if you keep show'n me murders on channel "A," I'll pay attention to that. I'll grow to like only that.

The way things are, show the positive and the negative will know they don't fit. They'll adjust. Everyone wants to fit in. We're trendy and if the trend is one way, everyone will follow. People will change their shit in a minute, just to fit in.

The way the negative is shown only glorifies and continues it. I don't see how much good or correction can come from constantly show'n the negative.

Did you not run down your negative side in hope that people will listen, learn and a positive change can come about?

All my shit ain't negative. I added my positive change. I believe, since we've been shown nothing but all negative, we have to show nothing but all positive. After that we can have a balance of both. My negative wasn't pointless like so much of the negative we see. I would hope it was more constructive. If you personally have only negative to show but you feel you can work it into a constructive positive that can actually help others, then show it. I meant everything I said to have a positive effect. Everything. Even the extremes. Sex, masturbation. How many people are willing to talk outright about masturbation, and feel comfortable? We don't know shit about ourselves, and we're fuck'n ourselves over. I feel we should be open enough to talk about anything that can help us. Especially if it's something we're hurting ourselves and each other over. These are extreme times, we need extreme measures.

We need to go deep, because we're in a deep situation. We need to go deep, explore, discover and announce above all this other bullshit that we're a beautiful people, we need each other, our relationships are tight, and then can't nobody fuck with that. Let the fools be fools.

III
Waiting to grow

coffee, tea, café au lait, corn bread or croissant
Shih Tzus chas'n alley cats
To Sir with Love and *Menace II Society*
Oscar Micheaux, Lloyd Richards, Cope 2 or Lee
Nick's 24hr Bodega or Dean & Deluca
Upper West, Rahway State, MIT, GED
Museum Mile then death row?
commendation, suspect
the Nile, Seine, Coney Island, Jacuzzis, passing gas in bathwater
hematite, agates and crystals, gold teeth and hoops
PBS and Def Comedy Jam
existentialism, lock down
lock blocks to Paul R. Williams and Frank Lloyd Wright
ham & cheese on white, Epicurean tastes, or at least a nature burger
    from Zen Palate
make love or fuck'n without a word
from kings and queens, B-boy
the whole wide world and all its glory, colors
shapes, sounds, dynamics
or only 9th & X to 10th & Y, back to X & 9th

so what do you wanna do tomorrow?

angela

angela, 24

11212

student

I think we're definitely lost. Lost from self and definitely lost from each other. Women are lost because of this modern-day attitude that tells us we're independent. We walk independent, we talk independent and our attitude is independent. We're supposed to be on our own. We don't need a man, we can do without, but we come to find out that we do need men. We know that we love men and can't do without them. So, now we have this attitude, this clash, this conflict of idea and fact. We haven't realized the idea should have been how to have a man and still be your own woman. I think we've gone overboard with this independence thang. Yes, I'm independent, but I'm independent with a man. I need me a man, thank you.

I can make my own money and do for self, but I'd like to share it with a man. A Black man. Whereas other women on this independent, power kick would make their own money and feel they then don't need a man for anything, I don't. Is that money gonna hold you and keep you warm on a lonely winter night? And I'm not talk'n about buy'n a heavy-duty blanket with your independent money. I'm talk'n about another body giv'n you warmth and affection. Sharing emotions and experiences. Women need to appreciate brothers and realize that we do need them, that we need each other. We need to know this if we have any sense of unity and self-preservation.

Men are lost because they realize there are eight to thirteen women to each man, and they act like it. If they can get it from door to door they will. It's like, life's mission is to get your thirteen. They know there are gay men out there, and they know there are men who are incarcerated, so they feel the need to pick up the slack. It's like, now there are thirty-nine more available women out there, let me go get 'em.

We've lost our values. I know there was a time when women didn't have to have sex before they were married. That allowed for the relationship to take on a whole 'nother dimension outside the sex. The couple developed a relationship with each other that allowed them to fall in love and be willing to marry one another without knowing each other sexually. That says a whole lot about the quality of their relationship. It says even if you're not good in bed, I still love you. I didn't marry you for that. I married you for all of what we shared before we became sexually intimate. The sex would be just a benefit, and to have and raise a family. My parents were like that. At least the sex didn't come until well into the engagement. Can you imagine a couple today, a young couple dating, being boyfriend and girlfriend, eventually with time becoming engaged and they haven't even had sex with each other? They became engaged because of their non-sexual love for each other. The love for each other's character and personality. The friendship they have. My point is not to endorse the ending of any and all sex between relationships before marriage, but I'd wish to point out the level of respect that went into these non-sexual relationships, that's what the focus should be. Sex wasn't the focus as it is today, the person's character was. OK, today's relationships include sex as a dimension of it, but don't let that be the only dimension, please don't. Remember and include what the primary focus to relationships were all about: the person's character. The ideal person to complement you as a person so you'll have something more than what is only sexually based.

Our generation has been lucky enough to have the pill and even more, abortions, that other form of birth control. What is that? You should not have unprotected sex and figure, "If I get pregnant, I'll either have it or have an abortion," yet this is what's go'n on. If the guy has big money, he can pay for three, four, five abortions, he has no problem not us'n a condom. That's a crazy thought pattern. And sisters are like, "OK, if I get pregnant, I'll just have to get an abortion, but I shouldn't get pregnant because my period just ended." We're tak'n chances with the inefficient rhythm method. Sisters my age. I'm not talk'n about these little teenagers runn'n around. They do it too, but they're young, irresponsible, don't give a fuck and they'll most likely have it, but my age group, sisters who should know better, who are work'n or in school, they're do'n some stupid, crazy shit. Figur'n, they can just as easily have an abortion as a form of birth control.

This attitude goes across any particular class of sisters. You go to some

of these clinics, and you're like, what the hell? What are women and young women do'n?

We've really been unlucky as far as abortions, the pill and all this sexual liberation stuff, but we just don't see it as such. It's certainly come with a price: AIDS; one out of every two marriages ends in divorce. What is that? Just a normal, accepted fact. One out of every two marriages ends in divorce, the sky is blue, I bought a new pair of pants yesterday, I'm twice divorced, I'm twenty-four. Crazy shit. My parents are still married, knock wood. They have been for twenty-five years. If we compare the differences of how things were done and gone about then as to now, that should tell us something, but we don't know any better.

Today, well, we can see why so many relationships are lost. We haven't developed that quality outside the sex. In fact, the sex has become the basis as to whether or not we wish to remain with our partner. If the sex is good, "Ump! I'm gonna marry that chil'." If not, to the curb you go. I know sisters whose first question is "can he fuck?" That will be the basis of the entire relationship. You can be nice, in school, work'n, got it go'n on, but if you're not good in bed, sorry. Their attitude is, I can get a nice personality anywhere. I can get Joe College anywhere. I can get Mr. Work'n'man anywhere. I cannot get Mr. Does Fuck Me Good anywhere, so if you're bad, move it along, and that's not right. First of all, if he's not good, you take the time and show him how to be good. You open your mouth and say what you need, and what you like, so that you can get yours. Maybe you're not good and he needs to tell you!

Do we even know the quality of our lives is substantially negative and in a state of emergency? You can be talk'n and some people are like, "What is she talk'n about?" If it ain't an issue comically addressed on one of our few Black sitcoms we watch, everything is OK. Other than that we don't know squat. So, now we need to be educated that there is a problem. Black people are in a state of emergency. I'm tell'n you this and there ain't no punch line. This ain't *Martin* so we can wipe the smile off our faces wait'n for the joke. We are in a state of emergency.

I get sick and tired of every man I go out with look'n at me with, "well, how soon can I hit it?" It's like, yeah, yeah, yeah, you're a nice female and all, but how soon can I hit it? No matter where you are. No matter where you meet them. The only difference is the approach. In the corporate world they're always noticing and commenting on my clothes. The cut, how it's fitting. I think it's fitting conservatively, I'm dress'n for corporate

America, but they always see it differently. So the bottom line is these are just lines. Surely they don't care what I think of the stock market this week.

Then there are the brothers I meet out on the street and it's like, "Oh, God, I have never had a woman like you. How tall are you? Come, let me do something that only I can do for you."

Then in clubs: Well, you never know what you're getting in clubs so that's not even worth the comment. Wherever the approach may be, the aim remains the same.

W hen it comes to deal'n with men, I'd like to have control of myself, but not necessarily the situations. I believe in the traditional roles men and women have. There's a lot to be said for tradition. Again we're in this modern age and attitude, but I believe in the difference between men and women. We're made differently and so we're best suited for different roles. I would be happy being the domestic while he pays the bills. I've been made a spoiled girl.

Isn't that what this new age and attitude is rebell'n against? Being confined to a limited role?

There's a difference between being confined and restricted to a role and being viewed as if I can't do anything else. I voluntarily allow myself to be that to which I'm designed: mother and nurturer. I will voluntarily keep the home in order while being mother and nurturer while still having my life, and having it as I want it. Remember, I said I believe in being independent and in control of myself, but if you look at it, what do you have? A man works eight hours, five days a week, every week, to bring home a paycheck. Wouldn't you really want to switch places with me? It's not about just being home cooking and cleaning. That takes two hours. The rest of the time is spent like the vacation time everyone who works wishes they had. Cultivating self. Museums, galleries, shows, walks through the park. Living life. I only wish my husband or man wouldn't have to work so he can share it with me. But bills have to be paid. If I had to work, I would, but I wouldn't be as happy. Cuz like everyone else you'd rather be do'n something else. Who is happy working a regular nine to five? No one. Day in and day out. We can't wait till vacation time. We can't wait till five o'clock. And if we put in overtime we're bitch'n.

That's where women have gone overboard. They're crazy if they want to work all day, all week, just to prove to men that we can. We know we can. I think we were smart to decide to let the

man work and we'll stay home. That was a helluva smart decision. I know what I can do. I'm work'n and pay'n my way through
school, but to avoid work after graduation, I'll play the domestic
in a minute. I'll already know I'm intelligent and have an education, so let me apply this intelligence and kick back while he
works. This need to prove that we, too, can go out there and
compete in corporate America, you can have it. I know I can
compete. Women have gotten suffrage. There are anti-discrimina-
tion laws. OK, now that I'm working alongside Joe and Bob, who
still see me as a piece of ass they just want to hit, now what? The
attitude is what needs to change. Accept me as a strong Black
woman who can compete if I choose to do so. Don't view me as
something you just want to hit, and I won't view you as the
shallow piece of man who just wants to hit it. Let's give each
other more depth and credit than that.

So when I'm married, if we both have to work, fine. If not, let me be the
mother and nurturer I'm best designed to be, and let me continue to
cultivate self. We've made that agreement long ago. We've said, OK, you,
man, work, keep the world running smoothly, as it already is, that's a
simple enough job, we'll sit back and take it easy, but look what happened. Can't leave y'all on your own for a minute. Look at the state of
things. Wars, killing each other, blow'n up everything. So, I guess women
do need to come to the rescue. Then we could work and rest harmoni-
ously.

I don't want a man who's work'n just for the material things. Work'n for
the million-dollar house, the million-dollar car. Then, after we have all
these material things surrounding us, we don't have an us. Too many
couples hook up with the other just wanting showpieces, and they'll use
each other as a showpiece. I have the beautiful home, the beautiful car and
the beautiful wife. Look at this on display. Things that have no depth.
More tragically, you've been work'n like dogs to get these material showpieces and you haven't had the time to instill depth in the other. Maybe
many couples can be happy with those things and happy with each other
just be'n showpieces, but like with everything that is material, it gets worn
out. Outdated and you grow tired of it. Then, boom, divorce. People go
into marriages with divorce as an option. The same irresponsible people
who go into sex with abortion as an option. If and when they get bored
with each other, "Oh, well, I'll get a new home, a new car, a new husband

and a new hairdo." Pre-nuptial agreements tell you this isn't forever. It says up front, when we separate, what's mine is mine, and your little shit remains your little shit.

Brothers need to respect sisters—as if we haven't heard that before—but it will continue to be said until it sticks. Until it sticks and sinks in and doesn't need to be said anymore. If you're not respecting a sister, you're not fighting the power. We are both Black and in this country and that is strike one, two and three against us. We're out. Now we're fight'n to get back in. Now we need to work as a partnership. I need to respect you and you need to respect me. You need to respect yourself and I need to respect myself. It shouldn't be about gett'n over on each other.

Honesty is important. Though honesty can dig your grave sometimes. I mean you don't want to tell someone you're see'n someone else, but if you've met someone else that makes you happier, be honest about it. You wouldn't be hated for it. How can I hate you if I'm not what fulfills you as a person and someone else is? I'd be hurt, but I'll get over it and in the long run I'll be happy for you. I'll meet someone who fulfills me and whom I fulfill. It would have worked out for the best. The thing is, while brothers already have someone, they're getting with someone else only for some ass, and who wants to be honest with that? But you should. Say you wanted only the ass. We may let you in on a little secret. Then we both can laugh and resume things. But will it really go like that? No. So leave the extra ass alone or make sure the person you're with is special enough so that you would not want to hurt her if she found out you're stray'n. We always, always find out. We always know. Y'all are so sloppy at it, it seems you don't care if we find out. Well, we do care. So do us a favor. Don't have us think'n we're a special someone to you. But then you might not get the ass, so then you'll have to lie, boy this is thick. And I don't mean be a better cheater.

Let's just start with the basics. We need to be honest with what we're looking for and what we have to give each other. Forget the pussy, forget the dick, for now that's not the issue. I find there are too many of us pretending that we can offer so much, have all this and that go'n on, and we don't. Brothers do this all the time. Tell you they have this and that, then when you hook up they expect you to have forgotten all of what was said. I'm like, didn't this brother say he was a manager of some group? That's the latest line. Everybody has something go'n on in Hip-Hop. "Yeah, I'm lay'n down tracks for my nigga." "I'll be in the studio next week, so I'll page you the week after." Then after we've gotten together and I ask about things I'm told the group broke up, niggas ain't really down, you haven't heard from them in weeks, and so you had to go back to work'n at KFC. You can front for only so long before you're busted and we have yet another failed relationship. Another something built on a foundation of lies, which when revealed can't help but crumble. Tell me up front you're managing the deep fryer at KFC, but you have aspirations of work'n your way up to the register. Tell me that and I have a friend for you. No, just bugg'n. I may go for you myself if you're good in bed. No, I'm bugg'n, but the bottom line is be up front and be honest. If you're work'n at KFC, you're positive, you respect me, I'm attracted to you and you're earn'n an honest living, then you can be the one for me. Beyond that at least say, you'd like to manage a group or you'd like to one day be in the studio. Don't say you're in negotiations with Shai to be their open'n act. The lies are so elaborate you figure he can't be ly'n, he has to be tell'n the truth because who would stand here and make all this up and expect a lasting relationship? Or is that it? Say anything to get in the drawers and that's it. Worry about the lies later. But by then you're out. No need to explain 'cause you're gone.

Brothers will even front in terms of education. When I meet men who are not in college or who haven't gone to college, and they find out I'm in school, they put on this false ambition. "Yeah, I'm gonna go to school, I'm gonna get a degree." I listen and wonder if even a high school diploma was obtained. You can look at some brothers and you can tell, they're never going to school because you can't let go that 40. You're hold'n on to it so tight, waving it around in my face, while try'n to talk to me about "What's your name?" and "Yeah, I'm gonna go to school." More dishonesty. More front'n. Tell me you're just a Black man try'n to survive. I can relate to that.

We're always gonna have that support for Black men, because there's always that ounce of hope. The Black man has a lot to offer. I'm a strong believer that all men are not dogs. A lot of what women get from men is what they provoke. Sometimes women bring out the worst in men. If every Black woman the Black man comes in contact with is constantly speak'n down to him, condemning him for not be'n what she thinks he should be, how can a harmonious union take place? His job choice may not even be what he thinks he deserves, but he knows this is America. This is America. He needs your understand'n and support. The Black man is frustrated enough without a Black woman having to talk down or look down upon his position in life. We need to speak support. Or just be a support. It isn't worth say'n what the brother already knows about his situation if he's the one deal'n day in and day out with the oppression. It's like when you're driving and you're lost and someone says, "You're lost." You know it, so shut the hell up. What you should say is "Maybe you should turn left, I think I know that area." Say'n, "You're lost, stupid" in that tone you know Black women can give is only go'n to make matters worse.

I know it's hard be'n a Black man. It's a job I wouldn't want. Unfortunately I have something between my legs that I can toss around if I wanted to. I can use feminine persuasion, but you're not gonna persuade a white man with what you have. Unless you're both gay. So as a brother, it's really hard.

So the next time I hear about sexual harassment, I can ask how much was harassment and how much was a woman throw'n around feminine persuasion?

It's all wrong, but the game is survival. Until men stop oppressing, as we constantly tell you, then what are we left with?

If all women stopped using sex to get their way in any capacity, do you think men would then give up the due respect?

I would like to think so. So that's to say it's up to women. I hear you. One half can't demand respect while the other half uses feminine persuasion. But a lot of times the harassment is in response to innocent flirtatious signals women give. Just innocent I-recognize-you-as-a-man flirts. That's our nature as relating to the opposite sex, but men don't know how to discern. Men have tunnel vision, they cross the line and want you in bed after work. Men know nothing of subtlety or romance. If you did, you'd flirt back, see how far it could go, you'd see if this stuff is real. If it's not and you can see it's only flirting, and not to be confused with "She really wants me," then you can chill. Most times we're not aware of our behavior because we're be'n natural. Are you moment to moment aware of how you walk, how you behave, how you exude male sexuality, especially when play'n sports, like basketball in the park, brothers with their shirts off. You're not aware of what you're giv'n off, you're just be'n brothers. But sisters will see you and keep the excitement on low. We'll talk to you days later to see if stuff can be real. We know you were just be'n you, and if you don't really like us we're not say'n, "Well, you shouldn't have been out there play'n basketball, giv'n off natural male sexuality." But when a woman acts natural and lets you know we don't like you that way, men will start sexually harassing and then be in shock when the suit hits you. You're then like, "Well, you shouldn't have worn that dress that agreed with you."

So, getting back to be'n a Black man, cuz this is important. I can remember in elementary school, the teacher would treat the little Black

boys differently than the little Black girls. The girls are given more attention as if naturally expected to be better students. The boys aren't expected
to do well. If that's the attitude, it's gonna be picked up by the boys. At
that young age Black boys are be'n shaped into the irresponsible Black
men they're expected to be. Children know neglect. They know this lack
of attention and focus they receive from teachers. That's why they become
disruptive and apart from the rest, because teachers are distancing them
from the rest of the class. As children they're full of sensibilities.

**The boys will go ahead and re-channel their energies into being
class clowns and troublemakers. They're rebelling but you don't
know this. They really don't know the basis behind their actions.
All they know is "I receive less attention so let me entertain
myself." Then if you have one that is studious, the teacher believes he's gifted. He's a miracle child. No, maybe his parents
didn't buy into because he's a boy, less is expected of him. Parents are just as guilty as the teachers. They'll give the girl a
coloring book, and the boy a toy gun. Look at the two skills
developed from that.**

If you notice children in school that are brother and sister and they're
both smart, their gender had nothing to do with it. They both come from a
home where the parents equally instilled in them a sense of learning. The
boy's potential wasn't compromised in any way. If that's not the case, if the
parents' expectations from the boy are just as low as the teacher's, then
he'll get to school and you can forget it. The girls are the focus and the
boys are ignored, except for erasing the blackboards, straightening the
desks, opening and closing the windows. You end up with the brother
with the 40 say'n, "Yeah, I'm gonna go to school."

As a brother, as a Black man within this system, you gotta work hard.
Hard work never killed anyone, except slaves, but that's another issue.

I look down on brothers who turn to white women. Five to six years ago,
within that time, I've dated two white guys. They were both curiosity
things. I was ignorant at the time. The second one, which occurred in
college, I became just another notch on his belt. Something for him to go
and say, "I did a Black girl." His parents were from Georgia and they
weren't hav'n it. I should have seen through his game. Not that a white
man wouldn't pick a Black woman over his family, but I should have seen
things as they were.

So, the same with brothers, I know it's mostly curiosity. It's for all the
wrong reasons. And if they marry them, well then I know they have a

deeper problem. They have no sense of unity for the Black family. And I know for the average Black man looks are everything. A female *muss* be fine, if noth'n else. A fine ass, hips, breast, all that. So when I see a brother married to the dowdiest-look'n white woman, even white men don't want her, you have to stop and think, what the hell? The brother is usually dark skin and obviously has a color complex. A self-hatred of his color and he wants to have little light-skin children to redeem himself.

I'm light skin and I have the worst time when men actually tell me, "Oh my God, I've always wanted a light-skin woman." I can't believe anyone would actually come out their face and say something that ignorant. You're practically say'n, "I've been brainwashed by the white man and I have no self-love." Say'n, "I've always wanted a light-skin sister," how is that supposed to make me feel? Now I have to question every brother's motive when he talks to me. Is he brainwashed, or is he attracted to my personality?

This color thing. Brothers need to realize we're all women and it's really all the same once you get in it. Let me put you in a dark room with a sister, and afterward tell me if she was light or dark skin. If she's a sister, all you know is that it was good. All you can say is "Well, I definitely know it was a sister." So that realization should force you to ask what is the reason behind your preference for lighter skin.

This color thing is all psychological. Unless you know your reasons outside of be'n shaped by white America, which I can't see, because as long as white America is in control and you live in America, then you think as white America thinks. Until you show me otherwise and regain your natural love for color, you are lost. I believe color just naturally looks better than non-color. A baby will respond to a toy with color over a pale-shaded toy any day. Even white people know this, despite what they say. Look at what they do in the summer. They've created their tanning salons to go to when the sun isn't out. So color is better than non-color. That's a universal agreement. The Black man just needs to wake up and join the universe.

Black Black men are beautiful and why they would want to purposely lighten their offspring is beyond me. Black men are just beautiful. The darkness. The mystery. The power. When you look at them, my God, I can talk about them forever. For a while, as a light sister, I questioned my own taste for dark men. When I was younger, between eleven and twelve, there was this boy in my class who liked me. He said the only reason I didn't like him was because he wasn't light like me. I didn't like him because he was fat, but that was something that stuck with me when I started to date. I would intentionally not look at the light-skin guys and would gravitate to the darker-skin boys. Then later I discovered, in comparison, a dark brother does look better.

The darker the skin, the better they look. There are no bad features in a dark brother. The color doesn't allow for flaws. The attention that the color commands. How the eyes surrounded by black skin stand out and grab you. Then the nose, the mouth, the neck, the chest and below, it just gets better and better, everything just says, "Black Man." A chocolate, chocolate man is like the sexiest thing you'd ever want to lay on. Lay your eyes on. But lay on, too, for that matter. They really are. You're the sexiest. You're just edible.

We need to become more comfortable with our natural beauty. All this fake hair, fake eyes, fake nails, fake breasts. What's with all this losing touch with who we are? I remember when if you had stubs for fingernails you just had stubs for fingernails and you painted them and you went on your way. You took care of them and they grew naturally. I don't believe in all this unnaturalness.

The more Afro-centric people would give me a hard time about my perm, but I like versatility. I wear makeup, but I can go without it. I don't feel I can't compete without it. My fingernails are just there. And if they never grow again, they just don't. I'm comfortable with who I am.

We need to realize all the products and models on TV are ideal for the white man. That's what he likes. That's the way he wants his white woman to look. We pick up on that and think that's how we should look. No hips, no ass, thin lips, thin nose. Well, our men like us full. Ass, hips and lips. If we controlled the media and commercials we'd see this. We should know this anyway. Let a sister walk down the street in a pair of tight jeans and put a mainstream, commercial media girl next to her. Who's gonna become invisible? A brother will let it be known what he appreciates, so why complain about hav'n a full ass? Sisters know they wouldn't have a man if you didn't have an ass.

We really need to be work'n together toward our unity. Those who jump all on the people with weaves, fake eyes and nails are only adding to that which keeps us separated. Again, it's in the way it's approached. You can't help but get defensive if someone is com'n at you all hostile with

"Why don't you take those fake wannabe white, store bought, sick-look'n hazel contacts out your head." Now, who's gonna say, "Yeah, you're right." You're gonna get defensive, call her a jealous bitch and now you're curs'n each other out. If the approach was "Black and brown eyes are superior to all other colors because of melanin which is special and unique to Blacks," that can open up an enlightening dialogue. This may allow the person to see the beauty within their own eye color and make them think, independently, as to why they would want to change a superior eye color to an inferior color. Then, on their own, they can say, "Yeah, why did I spend my money on these fake, wannabe white, sick-look'n things. I know I'm beautiful without them."

We have to be more diplomatic and concentrate on unity as the goal. And politics aside, those fake eyes really look sick. It looks unnatural. I mean it looks as if a piece of plastic with some color is hanging on your eye. I understand we like versatility and we have the right to beautify ourselves the way we like, but if it looks tacky, it looks tacky. If they looked natural and I was fooled into think'n you had hazel eyes, I'd have to give dap. Sisters with natural hazel eyes look natural. The real and the fake look worlds apart. It's like the weaves where you can see the stitching. Now, some weaves look good, like Robin Givens's, but she has that kind of money. I have yet to see some good-look'n colored contacts. Oprah looks unnatural, and she has money, so that should tell you they haven't made the colored contact that looks natural. Sisters look like their eyes hurt. But, anyway, that style is on its way out, thank God. But I still see the sisters from the islands wear'n them. But I know it's a late thing with them. They get our style and fashions two years later. I'll just have to wait two years till it goes out of style with them.

I can appreciate style and change, but our change always seems to be slanted toward whiteness. But I understand this is white media-controlled America. That's our ignorant excuse we have to overcome.

It should be a shame when Bo Derek and white people have to tell us braids are beautiful. Now we've embraced them and it's the style. We didn't see the beauty until white people OK'd it for us. Now everyone and their mother has braids. And it took us ten years after Bo Derek to feel safe and comfortable wear'n them. When you tell a Jew to remove his yarmulka and he does it, when he feels ashamed to wear his culture in public, I'll feel the same.

We need to be more exposed. There are a lot of things we rebel against in ignorance because we think it's white. We don't like tennis or something like that because that's a white thing, when nine out of ten times the games that they're play'n came from us and we just don't know it. There are guys who have done lots of things with me that they would never have tried on their own and they enjoyed it. I had to go see a live orchestra for class and I thought of Carnegie Hall. I asked this brother if he would go with me. He said no, that it wasn't his style. He was the gangsta type, but I pressed him and he said OK. So we get there and he falls asleep. It was boring, but in the end he liked the idea of check'n out Carnegie Hall. It no longer remained some big mystery place, someplace Blacks don't go. He was surprised to see the number of Blacks that were there. From that one experience, his scope of things starts to open more. More than Flatbush Avenue, Brooklyn.

Something new doesn't always have to be the latest CD or the latest movie. There's a world beyond the street-corner brothers are used to hang'n out on. And I mention the need for exposure because this is something that I as a Black woman like to do, and if the Black man feels alienated from a lot of cultural things, he need not be. A lot of this stuff is us. It's Black. It has African roots and foundations, and it's something we as brothers and sisters need to share in learn'n and experiencing. A little secret to brothers: Instead of clubs, you can meet a nice sister at an art gallery or museum. She's usually by herself and other brothers won't be there cock-block'n.

In the same respect, I've been known to tap a 40. But I have to have a cup. I thrive on be'n one of the guys, but a level of respect has to be maintained. And hopefully that isn't the total extent of what you're about, a 40-ounce. I love socializ'n with Black men because I love Black men. I'll venture into your world just as I want you to venture into mine, but I'll do so with all the respect I maintain for myself. Too many sisters socialize with brothers and they do it with no respect for themselves. They let brothers have their way, then they're cry'n about not be'n respected. You have to set the standard. Brothers will do what you let them. Me ask'n for a cup when drink'n a 40 tells a brother something. He automatically knows he can't go but so far with how he can treat me. Sisters who are like let me tap that and they're guzzl'n from the bottle like Shenahnah, a brother is like damn, what else will she do? What else will she put to her lips, just like that?

Another thing brothers should know: Females will always give you a number far less than the actual number of men she's slept with. We will always say about five. Six the most. We can be as active as the next guy, I know our number doesn't compare to yours, because we still involve feelings with those we choose to sleep with, but that number is most likely more than what you're told. I know every man wants a virgin, but sorry, sisters are not hav'n it. You need to know we're just as sexually active, but on another level. So don't think you can play us and we'll still be there, hang'n on and think'n you're the only man for us just because we gave it up. We gave it up because we felt for you, but once we notice it's one-sided, we'll quietly move on. No more drama. New day, OK.

Be up front if all you want is the sex. I would much rather you tell me you just wanted to hit it. Then I could see where you're com'n from. I could check you out, see how big your hands and feet are, and see if it might work. Maybe I'll say yes. It's all about be'n honest. Don't try to wine and dine me and go through all this "I'm interested in you as a person" when you're not. I may be think'n I'm gain'n a new friend. If I say I'm not interested in a sexual relationship at this time, and you still want to see me, I'll be all gassed up. I'll think, finally a male friend who's cool with just be'n friends. But when you're schem'n just to get some, and then I never hear from you; when all that "Let's go out, let's go here, there and every-where" was just so you could get me in bed, then I'm like, you nigga. What a waste of my time. If you don't get the ass, it would only be a waste of your time. I would be enjoying myself. I'd enjoy the trip to the theater, the shows, the galleries. I'll take it just for what it was: a trip to the theater and enjoy it. I'd enjoy your company too, but after the truth comes out, I'd still enjoy the memory of the places we'd gone. I'd only be upset that you couldn't be honest with your intent. You're sitting in the theater wishing the movie would hurry up and be over so you can get me back to the crib and screw my brains out. Then at the end of the night when I say thank you and good night, you're all frustrated because you really expected something. You thought somehow, some way we were gonna end up in bed. You spent all this money, so now I'll automatically want to screw you. When it doesn't happen, I'm now a dick tease, you believe you wasted your time and money and you never wanna call me again. So be up front from the beginning. Then, the next time, you do call, and I love this, you'll be more direct. "Uh, whatcha do'n? Can you come over and spend the night?" But now you played yourself. No, I'm not com'n over to spend the night. You should have asked that from jump instead of tak'n me all over the city, hav'n me think you were interested in me as a person.

Be up front from the start. Tell me if you think I'm sexy, you want to take me out do whatever else. Tell me if you think I'm sexy and all you want is a one-night stand. Tell me what you want and I'll do the same.

Why is it so hard for men to come right out and speak to you? What's with this, "Pssssssst. Pssssssssssssssssssst!" Who taught you that? I'd like to hear your voice. And then you're offended when I don't respond. I'm now a stuck-up bitch who can't speak. Next time try "hello."

Love is a very special kind of feeling. I don't think that men feel the same kind of love women do, and if you really can't, then you need to at least understand our kind of love. This brother that I was in love with expressed his love by say'n, "Well, I'm around you, right?" He said, "I wouldn't be around you if I didn't care." But it's more than be'n around me. It's certainly more than say'n that simple shit. It's say'n *you love* be'n around me. Telling me how happy I make you feel. I don't know for sure unless you tell me. I can only guess or assume. It's better if you tell me. It's better if you tell me what I'm do'n that you don't like. That way, if you just break out, I'm not wonder'n what happened. Is it something I did? Are you just crazy? Is it another female, what?

It's special little gifts that show you care, that you remembered our favorite color or flower. When we're in love the brother is in our thoughts wherever we go. We think about you. We smell you. We feel you when you're not there. We like do'n any silly little thing with you. Love is when you're totally comfortable with the person and you want to know every little thing about this man. From the hair on his chin to the hair on his toes. Love is total feelings. Now, is it like that for men?

I've had men tell me after a couple of weeks that they're in love with me. Now, I'm like, get out of here, what is this, you don't even know me. How can men claim love after two weekends and you don't even know me from Adam. I mean really know me. I'd suspect love for men is "She made me come real hard." Or you're tell'n us what you think we want to hear, and you really don't feel a thing. You don't feel anything, which makes it easy for you to play us. If you don't feel it, don't say it.

That scares me, when people use the term "love" so loosely. Love isn't something that comes around every time someone opens their legs. I used to think, "Yeah, I love him cuz we did it." Then I grew up. I think too many people are still using that as a criterion. If a woman says that after a short while, it's because she's been investing some serious time into pouring her love into you. If she's slept with you, she's investing even deeper feelings into you. She sees the future with you. Everything is now taking on a deeper dimension. Men don't need to feel anything, and certainly not love, in order to sleep with you. All they need is a body.

Women need to not be so gullible. Men need to understand our view on sex and love. It's not the same as yours. You have to think for two the next time you have an erection. Don't be so selfish. Know that it means more to her than just the act of sex. Know that we think with our heart, so you need to think with your head and not your other head.

At the risk of sounding vulgar, I must say that Black men, brothers, really do tear the pussy up! I mean, really tear it up. Those with the biggest, they're the ones that wanna show you, have to show you just how much damage they can do. They're the ones who need to be the most gentle. I don't like all that pumping as if your ass is on fire.

It's all in how you do it. Motion and detail, not maniac sex. I don't like walk'n as if I've been sitt'n on an elephant. I mean it really becomes painful. And one good night with a couple of good sessions is enough for me. I don't need it every night, every minute, every moment we're alone. Every time we come in from being out, the night doesn't have to end with us banging walls. Falling asleep in each other's arms is better. Brothers, find that romantic bone in you. I know it's in there.

For those that are not as well endowed as others, remember foreplay is a big help. For those that are well endowed, remember foreplay is still important. Take it easy with those thrusts. Don't act as if you're try'n to draw blood. Everyone. Large, medium and small, do not rush foreplay. If you do, that tells me you're considering only your own needs and that leaves me disappointed, you may as well use your own hand.

Don't waste so much time on the breast. There are lots of other parts that feel just as good. Be adventurous. The hand and fingers are erogenous zones, give it a try.

There are those who think that go'n down on a woman is nasty and dirty and they won't do it. Shame on ya. Then there are those who love go'n down, they think that's all a woman wants and they drown themselves. They go into overkill. We have to find a happy medium. The sounds that are produced sound better than it actually is. That is what keeps a man down there, but you need to come up for air. Really though.

Men need to realize what orgasms do to women. And once that occurs from oral sex you need to stop.

Our bodies get tight, but feel light. It's a warm, continuous

ocean flowing from head to toe. We're highly sensitive and charged, but relaxed. We're on the verge of tears. You need to read our bodies at that point and stop because it's difficult to speak, and I don't want to have to kick somebody in the face. It's an overwhelming, out-of-control experience.

I'm gett'n warm think'n about it. Is it like that for men?

We savor the feeling, and go on the memory, so we don't need it every day, every minute. We'll cherish that special moment. We're happy and satisfied with that special time. It's like we're still involved with that moment and don't need to so quickly re-create it. We're still going through the afterplay. What men do is try to quickly re-create that moment. You're out of the afterplay and ready to nut again the next day. Most men don't even know what afterplay is.

And, also, if we don't hit that orgasm, and you're still go'n at it, we'll fake it. I know women fake it a lot. Brothers, don't be fooled by all that hollering. Women fake it more than you think. If what you're do'n is not work'n, instead of hurt'n your feelings by say'n, "Stop, get off," we'll just fake it. That's also why we don't need it every minute, because y'all don't make us come each time. So we say to ourselves, do we feel like hav'n this man hump on me for two minutes? Let's cuddle instead. Or if we do give in, because you're so damn persistent, we'll fake it so it can be over.

What's up with the honesty. Shouldn't you say we're being inefficient? Don't be fak'n that shit. Have us think'n we're do'n work if we're not.

You're absolutely right. It works both ways. I guess that's something women should start do'n, because we do fake it, a lot. More than you know.

I think the way you feel about the person plays a large part in how good the sex is and whether or not an orgasm occurs. In fact, I know it is. Remember, for a girl, her feelings are involved with sex. So if she really doesn't feel for you, her feelings are not involved and an orgasm most likely won't occur. But we can still like you and enjoy the sex. Maybe fake the orgasm. But when the feelings get deeper and we're more relaxed and ready to totally give ourselves to you, and you're moving right, and everything else being equal, madd orgasms are occurring. We're flow'n like a river.

Understand that our gett'n off is not totally dependent upon what you're do'n. It's not based on what you're do'n, because you're most likely try'n to get yourself off. So it could never solely be based on you. If that was the case, it would be over in a matter of seconds. We need more than seconds. If men reversed their selfish thought, if men went from "I'm mov'n in it to get myself off" to "I'm mov'n in it to get her off," the session will most definitely be better and most definitely last longer. You can come with us because when we orgasm, most times you can't help but come with us because our walls contract, become tighter, and that's just too much for you to handle. Which reminds me, through vaginal exercises we're also able to contract on our own, and that's part of how we fake it, hav'n you think'n we've reached orgasm. I may be giv'n away too much, but I guess I have to be honest. But when you focus on pleasing us as well as yourselves, it works out good for all involved.

The point is, ask us if we're satisfied once you've ejaculated. If not, we'll wait. We'll let you recover, like we know you have to, and then it's our turn to be satisfied. Don't be so selfish. I know y'all would throw a fit if we came in five seconds, pushed you off, rolled over and went to sleep. Y'all would be back on us so fast. So you gotta look out for the sister. And sisters gotta tell you even if you don't ask. We need to say, "Wait a minute, baby, I need to get mine."

Sisters, the things you think you can't do with your man because he's your boyfriend, you gotta do it. You can't be think'n he'll think I'm a freak. If he thinks you're a freak, he's more liable to stick around. If your feelings are right, go for it. Take hold of that thang and do what you want.

Brothers, don't hold our heads and bang the back of our throats. Let us know exactly what it is we need to do. Let us know if you're enjoying it. We may not know what we're do'n. So when we use teeth, don't yell at us and punch us in the head. It hurts.

Someone punched you in the head?

It wasn't exactly a punch, but imagine if someone sunk their teeth into you, you'd react.

I know men have feelings. You need to let them show. Let a woman know about them. We won't think any less of you. Tell me you're jealous when I go out with my male friends. Don't accuse me of cheat'n when you know that's not the case. Tell me you want me all to yourself and you don't want to share me. We know it can't really go like that, but it's nice to hear. I'll tell you I get jealous, but I know I have to give you your space.

Show sensitivity, but don't get out of hand and start whining. Some men try to prove they're sensitive and they whine and they sound like a little bitch. Check yourselves on that. Express you're hurt when you're hurt, and leave that whining alone. Admit your fears. Let us share in your feelings.

Brothers! Brothers, please stay up to take us home after sex if we say we wanna be home at a certain time. I now hate those late night, psychic hotline, three-hour-long Soloflex commercials. And those get-rich, no-money-down commercials. I should be a millionaire by now. I'm also gonna order that Edgar Morris crap, I'm now so convinced. Brothers, just try and stay up.

Lastly, I'd like to say when it's over it's over. We love deeply. We commit deeply. We hurt deeply and when we cut off, it's final.

The same depth, time and sureness we put into deciding to sleep with you and become a part of you, we put equal time and depth into deciding it's over. So after you've messed up for the last time, accept it. No more begg'n forgiveness. No more chances to hurt us again. If the sex with that other sister was meaningless, you should have thought of that first. We don't want you anymore. Go ahead and try to make it work with that sister. It's over. Don't call. Don't leave messages. Don't send cards. Don't ask our girlfriends about us. Nothing. It's over. If you're hurt'n, you need to suffer and learn this lesson so you'll appreciate and treat better the next sister. You won't take her for granted and you'll learn about commitment. In the end we may be able to still be friends, but understand that the relationship is over.

If it's a case where your feelings have changed and you want out, let us know. Women will badger themselves over a failed relationship as being their fault. What did I do, what did I say? What didn't I do? Did I not go down enough? We'll make up all sorts of stupid things. If you don't tell us that your feelings have changed, and it's nothing to do with us personally, you gotta say it. I know it's hard. I know it's easier to just stop call'n and start paying less and less attention until the person gets the message, but that's the punk way out. The sooner, the more direct and honest, the better. Be a man about it. For the sake of us all operating in peace and unity, be a strong Black man. Stop be'n a little pussy about things.

donyale

donyale, 22

native californian

freelancer

I don't expect much out of a relationship in its early stage. I only let it grow from the beginning into what it becomes. By not expecting what has not been established keeps everything on an honest level. Women too quickly invest feelings and expectations in men without knowing their stance on relationships. We have to understand what people basically want if we're to devote time and energies in them. We shouldn't expect anything more from them until they show an interest in wanting more. If a man wanted to commit himself to you, he'd let you know. He would not want another brother interfering with what he wishes to establish.

Women need to stop forcing the issue. We very quickly invest these feelings unsure of what this prospective mate wants, and it causes nothing but disharmony. But that's also part of being a woman. That's what being a woman is. We very quickly feel. We're in touch and operate on our feelings and emotions. I think we just have to balance it out more with common sense.

Besides us having to use more common sense, it would help if men got more in touch with their feelings and allowed their emotions to lead them a little bit more. That would make for a happy compromise, and kinda even things out for us relating to each other. A little bit of heart, a little bit of common sense and a little bit of compromise.

Once in a relationship, I'm fully committed. This is also what it means to be a woman. I also believe this is what it means to be a man, so I expect my partner to be fully committed. And commitment is something we both have to decide on. I know women who've become intimate with a man, and assume they have a new boyfriend. I don't expect commitment just because we're dating or because we've become intimate. Once intimacy has occurred, that's the time to examine whether you actually want to commit. How does this person make you feel? How's his personality, his responsibility, his sensitivity. How is his family? How does he treat his mother? And how does his mother treat him? However that is is how he's been used to women treating him. How is he in bed? There are different yardsticks for different people. For some, it may be wise not to become intimate until the two of you have a commitment. It's too often, we want the commitment just because we've slept with the man, and we don't fully know his character and background. Once you know who this person is, or have a substantial idea, you then know whether you want to go the full distance.

My belief is to be open and honest at all times. I can't stand deceit. I'm real cool, just tell me how it is, I can go with the flow. I don't mind dating more than one man, and having a man dating more than one woman, if that's the way it's decided it's gonna be. Once we decide we're gonna date other people, let it be that way. If we decide we want to date only each other, then let it be that way. This decision should be based on us having grown so close that we don't feel the need to see other people. Maybe while we were dating and seeing other people, we realized and appreciated just how much more we had.

I don't open up very easily and so when I commit and do open up it's a big deal for me. Partly because of who I am as Donyale, and partly because of past experience.

I like to talk, as most women do, but I also like to listen, as most women do. Listening, I found, helps in getting the man to open up. Women complain that men aren't open enough, but do we listen? We may find that they're more open than we thought, if we'd only listen. Men don't communicate like women, so we need to find out how they communicate and listen. I've found a man's way includes a large number of non-verbals. It is there we have to be aware, be patient and pay attention. At the same time, men, Black men, should make the effort to include actual spoken communication. Everything is compromise. We're different as man and woman, so we have to meet each other halfway.

I don't judge. I think the worst thing a woman can do is to judge a man. The worst thing to do is listen and then judge. That says you really haven't been listening, because men don't tell us things to be judged. Without exactly saying so, they tell us things for our support, or understanding, or just to get something off their chest, not so we can judge and make negative comments. This is part of why they don't open up, as we complain about it. A man might say something and a woman would jump all over him. Now he's like, forget it. Then we will nag, nag, nag him to express the next thought. Express something, anything, but we're the one who shut down the communication. We can forget it. If someone feels they're not being understood, and is receiving the wrong feedback, why should they go on?

We also sometimes act as if we wanna hear some good gossip, not something serious our man may be trying to tell us. We definitely need more patience and understanding with each other. I would recommend a couple read together. Read and listen. It helps you get a feel of how the person expresses different issues and things of importance. Then when you need to talk, you'll be familiar with hearing and listening to the tone of what that person is communicating. Picking up the tone is important because the person may not be as direct with what they want to say. That's where the saying "that tone in your voice" comes in handy.

We can also read it separately and just know that when we're together, a genuine effort of communication and relationship is going on.

It seems we almost have a ready defense and opposition toward one another just because we're male and female. Yes, we are different, but that doesn't mean we can't ever equally relate on many things. I feel because we are male and female, we work best as a unit. If we see it that way, we'll go from being defensive to forming a perfect union.

I know women want closeness. Women want understanding. Women want honesty. Women want men to be sympathetic.

Women want men to remember the little things about them. Men need to know that the little things mean so much more than the big things: a phone call saying I love you; a flower; any little thing that says thoughtful gesture.

Men definitely need to focus on the little things. Be in tune with what the woman is feeling. Be aware of moods and feelings. You'll be surprised how much the little things really mean. You can blow a woman away if you give her a three-week-anniversary gift.

Why is men's first instinct to lie? Most men will lie about any situation in which they feel threatened. That's always something that bewildered me. You can tell men, "Look, you can be honest with me, that's all I ask." And if they do something dishonest, and they're caught, they'll make it even worse by trying to lie their way out of it. You're caught in your dishonesty, so why not at least be honest about your dishonesty.

My girlfriend is in a relationship and her boyfriend is cheating on her. I know he's cheating on her. She knows he's cheating on her. He knows he's cheating on her. She'll call him on it, and he'll just continue to lie and build lie upon lie trying to maintain his innocence. She'll have proof and he's still building lies. Like Eddie Murphy in *Raw*. The girlfriend catches her man in the physical act of cheating, and he says to her, "It wasn't me." As if the girlfriend is going to say, "Maybe that wasn't you in our bed with some other woman. It looked like you, but it wasn't. A couple broke into our house and used the bed, I'm sorry, baby, I thought it was you."

I guess men are just natural-born gamblers. They'll defy the billion-to-one odds that a woman will agree it wasn't him, and take that chance and lie. That is a born gambler. Whatever the impractical, impossible odds, they'll take it.

Why she's still with him? Now we get into self-esteem, and feeling you can't do any better. Love, and the time invested.

But we wanna know why you're cheating. Is it something we did or didn't do? I'll leave you anyway, but I'd like to know why you did what you did. I don't understand, "It's a dick thing." Can you give me more to go on?

And what's tripped out is, once you cheat, and we find out and leave, you then go through this please forgive me, please forgive me, I was wrong. You show all of this pain and agony. You act hurt, you look and feel so sorry and pitiful. Now you're the most sensitive thing in the world. Why aren't you like that, why haven't you discovered all these feelings and emotions before you cheated? We now see the depth of your love and emotions, but it's too late. This is not the time to display them. That should have been done during the relationship. It's too late, because we're also hurting. This goes back to men needing to open up, meet us halfway and let us see this love side of you.

I've come to know that when a man hurts, when a man cries, he really, really hurts. It seems since men don't allow their emotions to show, and they're always denying emotions, and when you do finally emote, it's all-out. It's for whatever the immediate reason is, plus all the other past denied emotions.

I think of my ex-boyfriend in all his machismo, and the time I saw him cry, I think his pain at that moment was much deeper than anything I ever felt. I couldn't take it. But, yet, that drew me closer to him. Him opening up, letting me feel what was in his heart, recognizing his pain, letting me share in that, made a much, much better relationship.

When I have my son, I will definitely expose him to all different types of people and cultures. Travel with him so he'll have a wider understanding of this world. I want him to have a wider scope, outside of the United States, where he may only learn to be an American. I don't want that. America has mis-shaped and mis-educated our Black men's minds about themselves and about women, and I don't want that. If he sees other cultures, his mind is not narrowed. He can be aware of how different men of the world view and interact with their women. He can conclude that there is no one set way of behavior. Everything is cultural. Or called cultural when it's really political, because it's to the man's advantage. He will understand this. He can learn, with my help, the proper way is to respect and treat others the way you would like to be respected and treated.

I find that the men I know, who, through their parents, were exposed to diverse travel, literature and education, seem to have a greater understanding of themselves and of women.

I don't want to raise a stereotypical son. A son who stereotypes race, sex, homosexuality and religion. I will make an effort to raise a son who accepts people as people. Accept what they choose to believe, how they choose to live their life, and not let prejudice dictate his decision to befriend them. I want him to have an understanding and concern for all people. I think all you can do is expose. That's something that's severely lacking in how Black men are being raised.

And if you can't afford to travel, the libraries are free. PBS is a station other than NBC, ABC, CBS and Fox.

Many of us were raised on *Sesame Street,* then we discovered the other networks, and haven't been back to PBS since. Do parents today even sit their children in front of *Mister Rogers' Neighborhood,* or are they in front of a violent game of Sega and Nintendo, learning that winning and aggression is everything in life. You destroy whatever's in your way and you're the winner. That is very much an American game.

When raising a Black child in this society, you have to pay close attention to negative influences and negative role models. Society doesn't. We have to. Society's only concern is does it make a buck? If it does, go with it. We have to be the watchdogs. Black parents especially, because many things are produced with age-old stereotypes, either conscious or unconscious, but in any event, they are oftentimes stereotypes at our expense. Or at a woman's expense. The bad guys still have darker complexions, if not dark clothes, which is subliminal, but effective. The heroes are white and the woman is still only a sex object.

I personally view relationships as positive. Not all men are dogs. That has been my experience. I believe if you feel all men are dogs, then it is dogs you're choosing to deal with. It's the men you're allowing into your life. I know there are situations and brothers who are no good, but that's why you take your time getting to know someone. You know the quality of man you're getting with. Of course it would be wrong of me to stereotype, but we do allow ourselves to fall into types. And if you're from a certain place, you hang out at certain places, that says something to me, and I'll be cautious about dating you. That's not to say I won't. I'll let you prove my suspicions wrong, or you'll confirm them. No matter where you're from or what you do, I try to listen to how you come off. That basically decides it.

There's such a thing as women's intuition, and it helps to use it. You'll end up not having to say, "He's a dog." Your intuition or common sense would have told you. Or you should know something when after the movie, his entire critique is "That bitch was crazy." I know we won't be dating again. You may think that's a minute example, but it's only a matter of time before I'm crazy, or something else. I won't let it get to that point. I am not that pressed to overlook the minute, which really is a small part of the whole. I don't have to wait to see the whole. I've had only positive relationships, and it's been for a reason. Luck doesn't get all the credit.

Along with knowing the right person for you, relationships are tough today. People are scared. There are diseases out there and you have to be careful. Young people can't rush into anything nowadays, at all. You and your partner both have to know what you're getting into.

People need to keep their eyes open and care about self. As well as your partner, you must be concerned with you. Women allowing men to have sex with them without a condom just because he says he doesn't like the feel, or that he's had sex only with clean, good girls is no reason. Or as long as they're on the pill everything is OK.

Unless you know one hundred percent that you're both HIV negative, a condom should be used every single time. I know plenty of people who haven't tested for HIV. They know that they've had unprotected sex many times and yet they refuse to go get tested. They think, "well, the people I've slept with haven't died or contacted me, so for now, I'm not worried." Or there's plenty of, "well, if I have it, I don't want to know. Just let me die."

Within a relationship I don't expect a man to spend a certain amount of money on me to show his affections. I don't own a calculator. I will say I like to do interesting things in life. I like theater. I like nice restaurants. I love good food. I treat myself to these things. They don't necessarily have to be expensive, just interesting. So the type of people I go out with, I'd prefer if they shared my interest. That's part of what makes relationships work. Knowing what you like and knowing you'd like your mate to share some of those likes makes for a workable relationship. But how many people know what they like and then look for those similarities in a prospective mate? How many people come together because they like how they were grinding each other out on the dance floor?

I've dated someone who was 6'5" down to someone who was 5'9". I've dated someone who was jet, ebony black to someone who was very fair skin. I've dated a millionaire; I've dated students. I've dated someone who was the vice president of his father's company; I've dated a starving artist. They've all shared my interests. I don't have a particular type, it's the person.

Women who feel there's a shortage of men may be creating the shortage by limiting their choices. Some will say they will never date a garbage man, or a blue collar worker. Or he has to be 6'4", dark, broad shoulders, and have a six-figure income. If that's how you think, yes, there will be a shortage of men. For me all he has to do is capture my interest, and share my interests.

W omen crave closeness and stability. Like I said, we attach very quickly. And most women who attach very quickly have probably come out of a relationship that didn't end well. Generally, we rebound like that. We'll get out of one relationship, feel hurt, and to get rid of the hurt, we'll fly into another relationship. Because of the bad relationship we'll feel the need to prove ourselves worthy of love and affection and closeness and commitment from another person. We'll attach to someone else to experience those feelings again.

Women love being in love; feeling loved. Women like one-on-one relationships. Women like to say, "I have a boyfriend." We generally don't like the dating game. If you ask any woman what would she rather do, date five men or be in one monogamous, close relationship? The woman would choose the monogamous, close relationship. We like to be in the dating game, get someone compatible, and get out.

Black men and women need to realize and accept the differences. According to this country's traditions, there are differences. As long as neither is willing to change, then let us recognize that and stop acting as if things will change. Without the recognition and willingness to work within that recognition, there's going to be very little progress. We need to recognize our states of mind before any compromising relationship can work.

If you feel the need to have more than just me, let me know. I'll either choose to share you, or I'll choose not to. I'll most likely choose not to, but some women will choose to accept it. Everyone is different. Don't assume I won't accept your lifestyle and lie to me.

Some women may work harder at trying to make the relationship monogamous. Trying to make him forget about sleeping around. They try to make him desire only them. I feel you can't make a man do anything. All you can do is be yourself. You shouldn't have to put in any extra effort to make him stay. He has to feel what he has inspires him to stay and be monogamous. This "I'll accept him running around" while you're working your ass off to make it monogamous, doesn't work. If he's dating other people, our arrangement will be that I am also, and there will certainly be no deep feelings of involvement. If I started to feel deeply, yet he still felt otherwise and wanted to maintain an open dating policy, then I'll have to bow out. If I'm comfortable with it, then I won't be trying to make it monogamous. Once I want that, it won't work. But I've also noticed when the situation is you can date whomever you want, as soon as he sees you with someone else, he starts to second-guess the arrangement. He could have been dating the world, but let him see you with another man, it's a different story. Men can't really handle the thought of another man being with someone with whom he's intimate. It'll either be ego or true feelings, but he's responding. In an open relationship, if there's a response, I guess it should be ego. If it's feelings, the relationship shouldn't have been open. Someone wasn't being honest. If I agree to an open relationship, I'll know I won't trip once I see you with someone else. I would have taken inventory of my feelings for you. An agreement says I care for you but don't care if you see someone else. I'll care if she's treating you bad, but I don't care about you enjoying someone else's company. My agreement says we're on until I feel monogamous about someone.

No one person should feel that they have to be dominant at all times. No one should feel that they have to be passive at all times. If so, there's a problem. If both are dominant personalities, there has to be a conscious give and take. If we're planning a trip, I'd like to handle the arrangements. He can dominate the rest of the way. Or he can plan the next trip. It's give and take. It's knowing what roles men and women like to assume and going with it. Although I may want to drive on a short trip, I know men and cars. It's their toy, and they'll throw a temper tantrum if they can't play with their toys. Men would also want to drive because the man drives. It's a man's thing, translation, control thang. It'll help if you can try and get over the control complex.

Women can stand back a little within relationships. They can wait and let the relationship grow and not force closeness. That's the main thing. We know how we are. Now we have to know how men are. Don't force and try to manipulate anything. People know what they want, and they usually make it known.

Any breakups should come because the two of you have outgrown each other, grown apart or for a mature reason. There should still at least exist a friendship. I'm still friends with my former lovers.

As for men, you can open up. You can give a little bit more. Be a little more sensitive. All the usuals.

Understand that little things mean a lot. That may be something new. The littlest thing will affect us. A card when there's no occasion or holiday. Just your appreciation for us being together. An unexpected show of appreciation goes a long way.

There has to be compromise and changes for what can be changed, and an understanding for what cannot be changed.

IV
it's your thang

Cheeks

cheeks, 20

connecticut

painter

On the issue of sex, brothers need to learn the act, OK. It's not just stick it in, stick it out. Brothers need to understand that you can't just stick it in, get yours and leave us hang'n. Come on, what is that, and I'm gonna let you know. The men have the nerve to walk away say'n "oh, I fucked her," when in actuality he's the one that got fucked. There is a big difference. I mean, I FUCK MEN. They don't fuck me. I hope I'm not gett'n too graphic, but this hidden shit has to go.

So, yeah, I do work. Brothers think they're do'n something. They get all hot and sweaty, and meanwhile I'm yawn'n. Guys may think they're do'n a very good job, but in actuality, he may not be do'n a damn thing. I mean, I know I can hop on that shit and bam, what's my name backward, OK. I mean, I've had guys walk away like, damn, what did I just go through?

I fuck, I am not fucked. Even if I'm on the bottom or whatever. It's more than pump'n. It's more than just stick'n it in. Sex is a full-body, full-contact activity. Men have to learn this. It's OK to get worked over, break that male ego down. Like I've had men say during sex, "Whose pussy is this?" I'm like, I don't think you know. Not yours. Brothers just gotta stop fool'n themselves on that dick trip. They think since they have this male organ, they're do'n you the favor, but in actuality I can go get a vacuum cleaner or something, turn it on and call it a day.

You can only trip when you know how to use your whole body and mind. Until then shut the hell up. Your shit is weak.

What mainly upsets me right now is this double-standard psychology. If men sleep with many women, he's the man and all that, but when a woman does it, she's a slut and a whore. That pisses me off royally, because I'm not a slut, and I'm not a whore. Women love sex just as much as men, and even more so, I think. I know when Auntie Flo-Flo starts coming around, and those hormones are kicking up, sex is like a must. For women it's more of a strong hormonal thing. Our psychology has just been reprogrammed. Men seem to have a constant state of "Yeah, I wanna do her, and her, and her," and it doesn't end, it's constant and the intensity stays the same. The attitude, the motivation, all on the same level. Once you get it, your intensity falls like a brick. With women, when mainly at that certain time of month. It's not a constant twenty-four–seven like with men. But when it hits, it's like a crack fiend need'n his pipe. It's that much of a physical craving. Our bodies are going through changes. Our hormones are talk'n to us.

When a guy wants sex, he sweats any girl, he gets it and then he's fiend'n for the next girl. It's not the sex per se, it's the conquest of the girl. With men it's more psychological. It's a chance to say to his boy that he got with so-and-so. It could have been the worst sex in the world, but a year later he's still talking about the time he got with so-and-so. It's like prestige. Guys like say'n to their boys, they just got some from a girl more than the act itself. The sex could have been bad and all of two minutes, but he's bragging to someone that he fucked her.

For women it's the sex we need. We don't need the psychological part of it, which is to brag to our girls. The physical is all we require. That's why you'll see a certain guy and say, "How did that duck get with that?" That duck just happened to be at the right place at the right time.

I carry condoms because . . . just because I do. It doesn't make me a slut. It doesn't make me a whore. It doesn't make me a ho. It makes me socially conscious. It's just in case. Carry a condom, save a life. I need to do a condom check now, I might be low. Hormones don't only kick in at that certain time of month. There are spontaneous kicks.

Better lines need to be found, badly. This too-tired line business has gots to go. I've heard things like, "What's your sign?" I'm like, STOP. I mean, this is the 90's and I'm hear'n "What's your sign?" as a pickup line. Stuff my mother heard. The guy could have used it on my mother, but not me.

Some brothers do know how to approach you. They know how to open with a nice greeting and make light conversation without harass'n you for crucial information. Guys with the "What's your name, you got a boy-friend?" are only show'n their ass. If you say yes I have a man, they're ghost. Forget try'n to make intelligent conversation just for the sake of exercising their brain, they're out. But it's that "yo, baby" shit that has to go. That's really played. That's 80's, straight 80's. And that doesn't mean come up with some new off-the-wall stuff I haven't heard, it means come up with some sane, honest truth. Come with what you mean, which is I'd like to get with you, or I'd like to know you.

Usually, I get a lot of older men who approach me very cordially because they've been through the routine and they know how to approach you with respect. That's always a welcome relief.

If you see a younger sister with a much older man and you're wonder'n why? how? It's because he treats her like a woman. He treats her like a woman wants to be treated. With care and respect. We don't want to be pressured into sex. Can we have intelligent conversation? Can we learn a few things about each other? Brothers need emergency maturing in the area of conversational approach. Don't wait until you're in your thirties and forties to start acting like a man.

I've had guys come up and grab my breast as part of their introduction. They're think'n that's cute. But if I kick you in the balls, I'm the one in the wrong.

I find that the school setting doesn't allow for serious relationships to develop. School at any level. High school, college or graduate. Any time you have many members of the opposite sex grouped together in a small setting, you're gonna have pseudo-committed relationships. Too many people are catching too many eyes. Nothing of depth comes about because everyone is runn'n around try'n to get theirs. Even those who *know* or seriously believe they've found their perfect mate can't resist the temptation of hook'n. They'll sneak around and hope he or she doesn't find out.

It's a new day. Hell, I'm over eighteen, I can do whatever the hell I want and I don't give a cuss. I hate this old-fashioned perception of women that these image police are try'n to keep out there, when that image is out of touch. Do they not understand, I'm not the girl I used to be? I'm not what you read about in textbooks, and even some of these so-called modern women's magazines. Even with *Essence,* I'm sometimes like, "What, who are they talk'n to, because this is not what I'm see'n and hear'n every day." We're either lying to ourselves or lying to these interviewers and it sounds like both. Who's gonna tell a complete stranger, I'm a freak. I cheat on my man. I experiment with bisexuality when the climate is against it. They'll say, "I've experimented, once." I think not. The shit is ongoing. I know so many straight sisters, with boyfriends, who'll be at a little all-female gathering, get tipsy, only tipsy, not drunk, and then start going for it. We've created this atmosphere where it's unsafe to confess, yet everyone is involved. Sisters will tell *Essence* "No, no, once, no, never, maybe, my friend does, I thought about it, but no, no and no not me," and shit gets reported as up-to-the-minute reality. Yet shit is running rampant. Why is AIDS, of all things, on the increase? A life-threatening disease, and it's on the rise. You'd think there would be a downward trend in sexual activity. If we're not open and honest with what we do, I can see us being irresponsible when we're do'n it. "No, no, I don't." Meanwhile, we're sweat'n the test results. If we're in denial of what we're do'n, we'll do it in an irresponsible, undercover way. We're like, "This is the last time because I shouldn't be do'n this." Well, since it's the last time, I'll take a spontaneous chance and not use a condom. Next week, "No, this is the last time." Why not accept the fact of whatever it is you're do'n, bring it to the forefront of your brain and go about it in a responsible manner? Condoms and background checks is all it takes. Then you can do whatever you want and as often as you want. If you accept what you like to do, you'll be more professional about it. You won't be undercover, rushed, rash and just plain stupid. You won't feel like you deserve whatever bad happens to you because you shouldn't have been do'n it in the first place. Accept what you're do'n and be careful. Be conscious and be smart. Clinton and every president on down have been accused of gett'n some on the side, so let's face it and stop be'n hypocrites.

I believe monogamy is conditioned. I know it's not in my nature. If you can find one man who'll satisfy all your beats, then go for it. I haven't. Until I do, I gotta have it, from him, him and him. I can be with you and let the next guy know I'm attracted to him, let you know I'm attracted to him, and let him know I'm with you.

Where does it end? When we get into an agreement between two that they feel they can be monogamous with each other, and even still, it's not a promise, it's just a feeling. So if you find yourself want'n some from someone else, at least you didn't promise anything. Promises are made to be broken. We prove that every day. I don't make them. I won't ask you to. You can honestly state how you feel, but that's not a promise. I'll accept, "I feel so close to you that you're all I need." I know that that's at that moment. That's how you're feeling at that time. Sexually monogamous feelings change. Maybe after years of being together, just once you find yourself wanting that brother that moves you sexually. You don't want to leave your man for him. You love your man. You have so much more than what only equals sex with your man. Hav'n discreet, only sex with this guy that moves you is nothing to feel guilty, ashamed or end what you have with your man. And the same for men. It's really not that deep. Whoever said it was wrong and whoever accepted it as wrong were wrong.

How come everything that related to how Black people look and behave naturally is wrong? It's really stupid. Running around, try'n not to get caught, being ashamed of responding to natural desires.

This thing of ownership needs to be put in check. I don't say I have a boyfriend. I say I have a significant other, or others, depending. We have too much of a slave-master mentality. This is mine. I own this. What is this? I'm like, you didn't pay for me. You didn't give birth to me. You didn't plant the seed. You didn't water me and help me to grow. None of that. You didn't breathe air into my body and give me life. Therefore, you do not own me. I am not yours. If I owned you and you owned me, then we'd never have breakups. Just as a slave couldn't walk off and claim independence. We couldn't ever leave one another. But that's not the case. I can leave you mid-stroke. What you may be claim'n as yours may be out with another, then what you got to say, "She took my man." No, he was never yours. People are not ours to claim or own. I thought we settled that.

You can say you have something special with a person, and you share each other, but you do not belong to each other. You and that person have every right to leave and go your separate ways. You may personally not want to get with anyone else, but you can't demand that of the other person.

A question I have is why is there such a big urge to ejaculate with men? Women like the whole process. The orgasm is not the sole pleasure factor. The whole thing feels like, damn this is good. It feels like a big, beautiful oooze. Like, oh, yeah, I just smoked twenty blunts without choking. It's very mellow. When it's slow and good and with someone I love, I'm cry'n like a baby. That's what it feels like to me. The feeling is the total joy of the body. It just feels . . . indescribable.

My legs start quivering and, I'm like, how, why, how, why, ohh, ahh, damn, shit? It moves to a higher plane, more than just the physical. My mind becomes clear.

I think men miss all of this because they're so concentrated on the ejaculation. The person also has something to do with the intensity of the orgasm. Sex is of the mind. If guys worked more on develop'n their feelings for that one person they know they feel special about, they would feel the difference in orgasms. For many men there is no difference between sex and love. I fuck, I have sex and I make love. Before you think you need that vacation, cultivate those feelings, explore them, take time to feel them out, don't take them for granted and so quickly be on to the next person, then back to your mate. Experience the difference so you'll know when you need a change just for the human sake of change, and when you're with the one you love, you'll know that it's paradise. That's how it is for me. Sometimes I just need a break, but I know I have the real bomb at home. Guys need to get over the psychological trash and start experiencing what their bodies can really do for them. As it is now, they're just runn'n around stick'n it in everywhere and are not experiencing what their bodies can do for them with that one special person. Take the time to get to know the best of both worlds. Love and sex, there is a difference. We need to acknowledge this truth about ourselves.

I think men and women have to learn to be civil toward one another first. We need to create an atmosphere that says, although I don't know you as we walk toward each other down the street, we should feel safe enough to say hello and feel this can be a friend of mine. We should feel the person doesn't particularly want anything, be it physical or material, but I'm acknowledging this brother, or this sister, because they're a part of me and I'm a part of them. We're Black people with a common background, culture and heritage. "Hello, brother." "Hello, sister." That's all. You can try to kick it, but let that be civil and let the response be civil. "Thank you, but you know, it's like another brother beat you to it, but you got it go'n on." Now there's room for friendly dialogue. You may even become friends, and from there, who knows? Or the two of you can just go on your way. Nobody feels dissed or feels as if someone's a bitch. I'm talking about an atmosphere that says respect first.

We need to learn the meaning of the word friend, and then see if we've found that in the person we're try'n to call friend. I have a lot of male friends—that guy I was just talking to is a friend of mine—and it's a friendship not based on anything he may selfishly want from me or I from him. It's a non-sexual friendship and yet we're friends. Generally, the thought is if I can't sex you, then we can't be friends. Or, if I can't sex you, then I don't even want to know you as a person. That means, I'll be your friend once we have sex. That's how we generally translate he or she is my friend. We fucked, so now we're friends. Other than that I'll have nothing to do with the person. I can have a friend. I may have sex with him, I may not, but we can still be friends. We can still hang out together, enjoy each other's company and end the night without any sex whatsoever. And this can go on for years, because we're friends. How many others translate their so-called friendship in those terms?

When you're special friends, the person makes you feel especially different from your other friends, there has to be a trust and honesty between the two of you. For example, I have a significant other; I hang out with a lot of his friends, and it's no trip. It's madd cool. He knows what we have and there's no need to trip over who we know and who we hang out with. We trust each other's responsibility and we don't need to question each other about shit that's really meaningless between us. That's the ultimate meaning for the word trust and respect for the other person as an individual. No one owns no one.

When I hang out with my girlfriends, we'll go to a strip club and I'm going, "Hey, baby, come here. Let me put this dollar between your string." Now, if that bothers you and you're gonna stress over it, then I'm not the one for you. As humans we're so complex we need complexity to keep us going. Who eats the same dinner every night? We need to say we're young, we're attracted to many people on this surface sex level, and then work from there. I have a significant other whom I feel special about, yet I may see other people on a surface sex level and I may not, but, at least that's my prerogative. We're free, no one binds no one. I'm growing, I'm learning, I'm maturing, and maybe one day my significant other and I will have grown closer and closer together, while at times apart, and now we feel we're ready to settle into each other, and everything will be justice.

Our problem is we have a problem say'n we may feel attracted to someone else. If that happens, at least acknowledge that to yourself. Start from there. Don't try to fool yourself. You can love your man and still feel sexually attracted to someone else. You sex them and that's all you want. Don't try to make it anything more than it is or could ever be. Some women fool themselves that they're now in love with two men, but really, other than the sex, the person is nothing, means nothing. But because of the sex they're fool'n themselves. Separate the two when it calls for it. I know people who are attractive, they appeal to my sexuality and that's it. We can't really be social because we may be two totally different sociable people. But that doesn't mean I can't fuck your fine self. We can then realize why we're in love with our partner, and now love them all the more. You got a different release out, you don't feel guilty about it and your head is clear. Sometimes you just need a vacation. Stop believing all this bullshit about sex. We're already do'n it, so let's see the sense and normalcy in it. Don't be preacher, teacher, president and preach sexual morality as monogamy, when you have a *friend* named Gennifer Flowers. That would make me crazy. Say'n I should be do'n this, yet feel'n and actually do'n differently. Either say, yeah, I have sex and I make love with different people, what does that have to do with the price of tea in China, or just say no comment and shut the hell up. Since the atmosphere is still hypocritical, just shut the hell up and know at least you're true to yourself. You're free and responsible. If my man is responsible and not endangering my health, I don't need to know who he slept with last month for ten minutes. I don't need to know who sucked his dick last year while I was at work. There are bigger issues. People are hungry, dying, unemployed, countries at war, shit, we need more lovemaking, and we're try'n to suppress it, so don't bother me with "Did you know your man was hav'n dinner with what's-her-name and probably slept with her afterward?" Yeah, well after what he probably did or didn't do, he and I were out protest'n for change. What were you do'n besides be'n in me and my man's business?

We're so caught up in the trivial, we're kept ignorant from all real issues. I mean, we're here mak'n an issue out of how we have sex, something that's so natural that we don't need a discussion and people are steady dying and being exploited. That's how we're kept ignorant of the real issues. Give 'em some bullshit to debate, meanwhile the power elite are the ones really fuck'n us in the most forbidden, dirty, perverse, immoral and indecent way. Let's be real, settle this shit and move on.

freda

freda, 27

noneayabizness

Brothers need to know, or maybe they don't need to know, that women are out there do'n the same thing that they are. And it's been in effect. We're be'n just as doggish as men have been. No, it's not help'n the problem any, but we didn't create the problem. We didn't invent the game, we're only now play'n it with you. It's about time. It's only so much a sister will take until she comes to her senses and starts dish'n out the dirt that she's been dealt for so long. The same way men will claim to have that one special person in their life, but yet have something on the side, women are do'n the exact same thing. Two wrongs don't make a right, but it damn sure makes it even, as they say. It's not like we really want to do this, but my attitude is if you've been burnt once, twice, three times with relationships, you either start mak'n some changes and learn how to play the game, or you get burnt a fourth, fifth and sixth time. So the next relationship you don't dedicate that one-hundred-percent effort. You hold back in anticipation that this nigga is not for real and he's gonna F-up. That's when you're learning.

You get you something on the side for as soon as he messes up. Or get you something on the side when he does F-up. Most of the time he will. We'll know that he's out there mess'n around. Mess'n with one of your girlfriends, and instead of pull'n him up on it, mak'n a big stink over it, we'll just go out and get us someone to do the same thing.

And you feel that's justified?

Hell yeah. I do.

And you'd do it?

I've done it. I'm do'n it. I believe all men are dogs. There's no ifs, ands or buts. I've accepted it. I've learned to work with it. I know that if what you have is no better than the next man, and with the exception of him mess'n around he treats you good, why change one dog for the next? There's no hope. I can have some fun, too. Brothers think we don't know when they're cheat'n. We know, but we don't say anything anymore. As men say, we know it's your nature. It can't be helped. You still love us and all, you're so full of love, you just have to love the next sister. Well, I'm full of love, too. I'll quietly do the same and everything remains peaceful.

Now guys can stop think'n they're so slick. You've been do'n it too long, women have been gett'n burnt for too long not to know. If we suspect, we confirm it with sister, mother or girlfriend. They'll ask what are the signs? Why do you suspect? We say why, and they'll confirm it. "Yep, that's what your daddy did, your uncle did and your other uncle did." We notice the changes every step of the way. At first, there's a behavior for when you want to hook up with us. There's a change in behavior for after you get it. And a change in behavior for when you're think'n, plann'n and act'n out your dogg'n. But now we no longer say anything. We keep quiet and you get more and more sloppy. The only thing I'll say is from now on we'll be us'n a condom. If you ask why, I'll say because I just wanna use a condom from now on. Fuck my pills.

Stay with the dog that you know. If both of you are friends, you get along well, and he's good to you, leave it alone. Some men can be real sweethearts. They're nice, kind and very respectful. They just have to go and get them some from another woman. And they can be nice and a sweetheart to her. I understand. I just want you to be as understand'n when I do it. Don't say a word. Let's just keep the peace. I won't bring your dirt to your face, you don't bring my dirt to mine. Let's not even look at it as dirt. Let's just keep everything clean and pleasant. Most times you're so busy with your side thing, worrying and making sure your ass is covered, you don't dare think we got something going on. When you call and say you can't make it because you have to take your grandmother to her checkup, and I know your mother went with her yesterday, I'll say, "OK, baby, talk to you later." I'll call up my side thing and do what I wanna do.

My girlfriend's man is cheat'n on her and her attitude is "so what." She's do'n the same. We're gonna get something on the side for either two or three reasons. We're hurt and we wanna pay you back. You needed not do anything and we just want the extra dick. Or maybe we love you, but the sex is bad and we just have to get some that's good. It depends on who you talk to. It's strange, you never hear a guy say he needed to get some extra ass because his girl is bad in bed. She can be do'n everything to the brother, hook'n him up, and he'll still find himself in another bed. But for women, we'll have more of the "bad in bed" excuse because men are so selfish. But, yet, many of us will hang in there. At least, many of us used to, some still do, but I know plenty who are like, fuck that. I gotta get mine. We may be using the extra brother to get off, but it's all good, because he really doesn't care. He's gett'n his with no strings attached. Another reason may be because we met and like a new guy and we're plann'n to break up with you. In this case we can use your infidelity as the perfect excuse, or we can come with it and say there's someone else. I like the honesty.

I personally don't go into relationships plann'n to cheat, but if he messes up, I'm not gonna act like my heart is broken. If he's not cheat'n, then neither am I. Even if he's a bad lover, maybe I'm not gonna cheat. If he cheats, I've now found that desire within to get someone else, too. One situation was like that and he denied he was cheat'n. Without video what can I do? So now I wouldn't say anything.

Another situation wasn't even because he was cheat'n. He was a bad lover, but I still wasn't gonna play him like that. I tried to talk to him about it. In a nice way I tried to tell him that I wasn't being satisfied, that I wasn't being fulfilled, and he took it as a put-down. He held it against me. It made his feelings for me less. I tried to explain to him I wasn't try'n to hurt him. I wasn't try'n to put him down and make him feel any less of a man. I was try'n to help our relationship. Through my frustration and his withdrawal, I found myself in the situation to cheat on him.

For a minute I felt guilty, because the first time I got with someone, the sex wasn't even sex. He came all over himself before he even got it in. He was so excited, as soon as he pulled down his pants he jetted. I was like, damn, is it really all that for men? You just can't wait? You nut from just the anticipation? I was like, maybe this is a sign that I shouldn't be do'n this. But I got over that.

I thought I did everything right on another occasion and my man got some other girl pregnant. Now, this nigga was smooth and I never suspected. But when the girl got pregnant and started mak'n herself known, I was like, ain't this a bitch? There comes a point when you say fuck it, I'm going for mine. What else can I do? Sit around and cry? I'm out there. I'm still decent. I'm still loving. I'm cautious. I'm aware. If I'm with you, I know what to expect. I can still care for you, but the other foot is firmly placed in reality and is ready to step off in another bed.

I've given up on love. I've been out of love for two years and it hasn't killed me. I now know it's something I can live without. Women are taught we need a man, we need to be in love and have someone love us, but that's not how it is.

The whole love process is dead. It's not like our grandparents, where love was forever. It was monogamous and it was deep. Where fiftieth and seventy-fifth anniversaries were celebrated. You know, gold, silver, platinum. When was the last time you heard about one of those? My last time was when I was a little girl and it was my grandparents. Today, marriages barely pass the paper anniversary.

This generation is not the marrying kind. Love is something that's viewed as "I love you cause you're the father of my child." Or, "I love you because we're fuck'n" or "you fuck the best." I was in love with a good fuck, and he was a fuck-up, too. Thank God I ain't try hold'n on to him. Today's love is able to make you understand and accept that "It's a man thing, it's a dick thang." Well, OK.

If I'm thirty-five and still single, I'll accept it. I won't boo-hoo. I would not like to have a child without hav'n a father for it. But if there's no father, there's no father. I don't need a husband. If you can be a father to your child, that's all I ask and I'll be happy. I look at my girlfriends with their sons and daughters and invisible fathers and I make sure a condom is at hand.

Right now all the brothers I know have children and I really don't want to be somebody's stepmother. Not now. Maybe later, when I'm stable, but I don't want a ready-made, instant family. Even though he may not be a complete father to his child, not if he's all up under me, but the mother keeps him involved as much as she can and now that involves me. So, I'd prefer no ready-made families. I know that's a lot to ask but I'll ask it. I don't wanna have to deal with an immature mother and the father of her children. They're still most likely try'n to keep the man for themselves, so now you're catch'n all this 'tude. Fuck it.

I don't care if I stay single or not. Brothers come with too much baggage that I have a hard time deal'n with. Two and three children with two and three different mothers. Niggas beat'n on women. I don't want to deal with any deep shit right now. I don't feel like be'n embraced now. Everyone who tries to embrace you has one hand in your pocket and the other behind their back.

Pleasure is chocolate chip cookies and vanilla ice cream. That's how I get my pleasure. Occasional sex, but more often, cookies with ice cream. My view isn't pessimistic, I think it's realistic. All the advice in the world isn't going to change a man. This is a man's world. He's in control. He's arrogant. He thinks he's always right. He set the rules. All I can do is learn how to play by them. Women can't really tell men anything. You're just too hardheaded. We can only tell ourselves something. The same way I told myself something.

This interview can come out, men can read it and go "yeah, un-huh" and roll right over on their bitch. Get up and stop by their woman's house. We'll still be look'n at messed-up relationships.

Your view of us hasn't changed in thousands of years: from the European caveman dragg'n his bitch by the hair, to how you now see us in music videos, movies, commercials, sitcoms, you name it. Even if Black people came to power, as we're supposed to, because we're the lost and chosen idiots, things still won't change. I've noticed we've already followed this established order so well, we'll continue the same shit. Only the skin color will have changed.

I don't have any advice for anybody. Everybody is already advising themselves. Who am I?

It would be fucked up if, now that women are starting to play your game, you'll say, "OK, no, let it be me for you and you for me." Fuck that. Too late. You do your thing and I'll do mine.

j o d y

j o d y ,   2 6

s t u d e n t / b a r t e n d e r

a l l   o v e r

*B*e'n a woman lov'n a woman, in comparison to a man, do you think you can better love a woman?

I would say no. To me love is love, so I would say no. I believe I could more understand a woman, but that doesn't mean I could love a woman more than a man. I think I may have an advantage on understanding what a woman goes through, her sensibilities, emotions, how a woman feels and what affects her. This allows me to better relate and deal with a woman as a lover, but through communication a man, too, can come to understand, know and learn how a woman feels. This would allow for a better relationship. The same betterness I would have because I understand and know women, I just don't have to ask the things a man *should* ask. As a woman, I know.

Women think on the same level of logic and this is an advantage. Men and women think totally differently. Like, if we had a problem, we'd go in two separate directions to solve the problem. We may solve it, and we may arrive at the same conclusion, but we'll take two totally different routes to get there and we'll endure a lot of headaches along the way. Two women with the same problem will take the same route, get to the solution quicker and avoid the headaches. Women have the same thoughts, especially me and my lover, our zodiac is the same. We're born only two days apart and in the same year, so we have the same mentality. We're both stubborn, both open-hearted, we have the same type qualities and being women makes us even more connected. A man and a woman under the same zodiac are still different. Two women are in there. I can start a sentence and she'll finish it.

Also, I feel women are more loyal to each other. We'll stay in a relationship longer than a man and woman would. More than two men would, I found that out too. Men are just as disloyal with each other as they are with women. That makes sense. Men are men. Gay or heterosexual, only their preference is different, their wandering nature isn't. Two women could stay together for years. A long, long time. Maybe too long. The relationship will seem like forever. But it's all loving. If you understand how loyal heterosexual women are, they're dedicated to one lover, it goes to follow, women are women, heterosexual or gay, we're loyal to each other.

Men can be loyal, too, but when you get down to nature, women have this innate affinity of bonding. Men don't bond as much as women bond, you know, because of society and all, but women are allowed to go with their nature while men aren't. It may have been man's nature to bond, but you let something happen. And today you make no serious inroads toward recapturing it. It's like, what's done is done. You accept it and bathe in ignorance.

Women will eat together, we go shopping together, we're more free and open with each other. Women undress in front of each other, we don't have to be gay or exhibitionists, this is just what we naturally do. We do things together so much more than men do together. We talk more. We talk about family, work, our trifling lovers, aspirations and frustrations, we just talk more and we bond. Men play basketball and watch football together and that's your bonding. Things to further your macho, destructive, male sexist attitude. When you talk, after you're done with watching sports, it's about sports. After that it's about women. How many you had, who you'd like to get with, what's the word on this sister? What kind of communication is that? No wonder you can't talk to women. You can't talk.

Many heterosexual women are finding solitude in other women. But I think that we're always homosexual or bisexual, we're just closeted, or certain women will always go back to men because that's what they're more strongly attracted to, and you have society shaping decisions. But bisexual activity among women is a high percentage. If they're straight heterosexual and they're just out experimenting, they'll most often go back. They may dabble every now and then, but they know where a lot of satisfaction can be found.

If a woman's experience is that bad with men to make her turn to women and stay with women, well then that's deep. That really says something about the relationships between men and women. I don't know of any cases like that, I've only heard, but they're rare. For the most part, you're either straight, bisexual or gay. From my point of view a lot of women are bisexual, but from your point of view they're heterosexual.

How many women have told you they sleep with women? Many have told me they have a man, but here they are in my world.

From the women I know who have crossed for experimental and out of curiosity reasons, they really like the experience of receiving, non-sexually, what they've always wanted from their man. And that's romance. Women want romance and women are romantic, so when they go out with a gay woman, that's what they get. They get what we naturally give as women. Romantic dinners, candles, roses, flowers, love notes, the whole nine. Men don't be think'n on that level the majority of times. I mean, just simple stuff. Women love to be listened to while talk'n. We love to communicate. Men give us a hard time with just talking, and when they do, we're not really listened to. Now, a woman will give another woman good conversation, we'll listen. That's what makes the conversation good: listening and giving feedback. Men tend to half listen and have a habit of interrupting while a woman speaks. Men tend to lecture and not communicate. They'll dominate the conversation and that's still not communication. Men just need to learn how to talk *with* women. Not to women, but *with* women.

Women can sit and cry while watching a movie together. The sharing of emotions is special. If a woman watches a movie that touches her, and the man is like, OK, what do you feel like eating, that's frustrating. We want to talk about how we've just been affected. We want the person who watched the movie with us to be affected. To see what we saw, feel what we felt. Two women can share this experience.

Men can either take this information and use it or they can sit on it. But they'll probably sit on it, because you can't tell a man anything, especially coming from a woman. But you better listen because a lot of women, heterosexual women, may take this information, open their minds and go get what they crave from another woman and never return.

Threats are always good. But it's a reality threat.

Men are romantic, but they're not so much to the point where they can just sit and hug and just lay up and watch a movie. Create that closeness outside sex, and women will do that. We'll watch something like *Beaches* and sit there and cry with each other, knowing that we're connecting and sharing in something that we know just affected us. We love to know that we're not alone in what we're experiencing. You're not gonna be left with a cold and indifferent feeling. Just hugging don't have to lead to sex all the time. Straight women will tell you they don't get this type of bonding with men. They'll try to hug and cuddle, and the man takes this as sex time. A woman going out with a woman is a woman going out with someone who knows her, understands her, has cramps every twenty-eight days the same as she does, and it's nice to know you're with someone who understands you, who knows you. The same as when you're in an all-white atmosphere and it's a relief to find a Black person you can relate to. That's how a woman with a woman feels.

If you can understand how close women are already, we do so many things together from the time we're young, going through adolescence, sharing in emotions, crying in each other's arms, it's no stretch of the imagination to see a woman turn to another woman sexually. At first it may be for the non-sexual support and understanding she knows she'll get from a woman for whatever problem. She'll receive affection, attention, love, sensitivity, all the things we love, and before you know it, you give it the right circumstances, timing, situation, that close contact will grow and grow. *The Color Purple* wasn't a stretch of the imagination. Shug and Celie. It was a page straight from reality.

For the public, many sisters will keep up the straight front, but let the need for understanding, attention and close affection come, that their man is not providing, it's back to the other side of the tracks. It's frustrating in two ways. One, because you're playing second fiddle. You almost feel like you're being used. What if you develop committed feeling for her and she's still running back to her man? Two, it's sad to see Black men not able to love a Black woman that loves him correctly. If a sister runs to me and we're just friends, I'm frustrated over point two. If I've developed deep, deep feelings for her, I'm frustrated over points one and two. But this helps a lot of women deal better with men. Now, you have to think, every time she says she's going out with her girlfriend, what's really going on? Men are so worried about is she seeing another man, you relax when you see it's just her girlfriends she's spending a lot of time with, but guess again. Now you can have a new worry. But don't really worry, because as I said, it's not like women are leaving men for other women, they're just having a positive, on-the-side, fulfilling, you-don't-have-to-know sexual rendezvous.

A friend of mine is bisexual, but to the world, heterosexual. She's involved with a woman now. She lives with her. They're just two female roommates to the world, you'd think nothing of it. Women share apartments, they do that. What woman is gonna move in with a male stranger if she needs a roommate? And these are sisters you as a man would talk to in a second. We no longer fit a stereotypic look. Now everyone has a short natural haircut. It's cultural and we're shedding the Euro-centric influence. Now you have no physical characteristic way of knowing who's gay and who isn't.

My lover, slim, light skin, all legs, very attractive, she's hit on by men constantly. Light skin, OK? That's another problem we have, but that's for another time. But she's attractive anyway, in spite of, not because of her light skin. She's also gay and you'd have no way of knowing other than her telling you. So now, every time you throw your best rap and a sister still gives you no play, you can wonder. There's a good chance she might be gay. And if she tells you she's gay, you still treat her with respect. She now doesn't become a dyke bitch instead of the usual "bitch" you'd usually say. It's not her fault or your fault she's not attracted to you.

Homosexual or otherwise, women are just more comfortable with each other. Women will get together, sit down and have these women's talks. Not to male-bash, although women do that too. I've sat in on a few sessions and listened to "He did this to me, he did that to me," and I'd tease and instigate and say, "Yeah, he's a dog ain't he, girl?" It's all loving. But we'd get together and bond no matter what the occasion. We'll go somewhere and eat and talk. The talks are always planned around eating, that's intricate to the bonding. Like a mother teaching her daughter to cook, two women bonding revolves around food. It's an extension of that mother-daughter, womanly bonding ceremony. The son may want to help, but he's told to set up the table and go play. Now I see maybe he should be included so he's used to talking and bonding with women from an early age. That means it's mostly our fault men can't relate or communicate to us. Yes, this would help correct today's problem, big-time. Everything is not without reason. How can we say it's your nature if we as mothers are not including our sons in the bonding process along with our daughters. We have to find some way of including the son because he's being ignored. Women, it's your fault men can't relate. Now let's pay attention to how we raise our sons. Because of this neglect, men don't cry in front of each other. They may want to cry in certain situations, but they're worried about being called a punk. They think, No, I gotta be strong. Who's teaching them this? I think you're a punk for not crying, you're human too. Do you not have the ability to cry? Are male tear ducts different from female tear ducts? Are they all dried up? Then what's the problem? If you're hurt, if you're affected, let it show. As long as you know you're a man and are secure in your manhood, be human about what affects you. Then men have the nerve to talk about someone who's gay.

Someone who acts by their nature when you don't. Yes, let's rethink how sons are raised.

Like this male friend of mine had his male friend come over to his house. They were just hang'n and kick'n it. It got late and the guy spent the night. My friend has a full-size bed and his friend is sleep'n in the bathtub. Why is he sleep'n in the tub? Get in the bed. They didn't want to get in the bed with each other. What's wrong with gett'n in the bed if you know you're not attracted to each other and you're only going to sleep? That was so stupid. He told me, they weren't getting in the bed with each other because they weren't like that. If they knew that then just get in the bed and go to sleep. What's the problem? The bed is also used for sleep. Do that head-to-feet action you do when you're six years old. Despite how you're raised, I think you should be intelligent enough to get over some things. There is such a thing as self-thought. If that's how men logic things out, going only by what they've been told, without even analyzing the stupidity of it, I can see why the world is full of racial intolerance and homophobics.

Women have sleepovers all the time. We're all in our nighties, sitt'n there talk'n and hav'n fun. When guys were younger they had campouts and thought nothing of it. As you get older you move from the tent to head-to-foot to the tub to just going home. Tired as hell, but you can't sleep in the same house with another man because you're not like that. You'll just head home instead. Four, five A.M. in the morning and get in a car accident because you fell asleep behind the wheel. You'll tell the cop you had to leave your boy's house because you weren't like that, and because the cop is a man, he'll understand. Justifiable accident. You're not charged with reckless endangerment.

Women, we'll talk ourselves to sleep. Talking about everything under the sun and then fall asleep. We'll leave in the morning, because that makes sense.

This one guy who was a friend of a friend kept try'n to talk to me, and I'm tell'n him I'm gay, and he's going, "No, get out," and I'm, "Yes, it's true." We became friends and one day he threw me for a loop. He said let's talk about sex. I said OK. He said he's never performed oral sex on a woman and wanted to know how to do it. I said what do you mean you've never, what's wrong with you, go ahead. He said he was afraid to do it because he wouldn't know if he was do'n it right. Also, he was worried about catching something in the mouth. I had to let the brother know.

First of all, oral sex is no more hazardous than mouth-to-mouth

kissing. In fact it's safer. The mouth has way more bacteria. The mouth is a literal breeding ground for bacteria, all the food residue, why do you think there's bad breath? Most people don't brush but once a day, in the morning and that's it. Eat three meals and then want to kiss you good night. A well-kept vagina is safer than a mouth any day. Most people don't know this and they continue with all these stereotypes. Men, take you butt down south. You love it when it's done to you, so what's the problem, we love it too.

So, I told him, if you're hav'n all these doubts, why don't you make it romantic. Get in the shower with her and the two of you bathe each other. That way you can see for yourself it's been cleaned. I mean, it's gonna have a taste to it, but it's gonna be a taste that you like, you're gonna be attracted to it. It's not an acquired taste.

He was like, give me details on what to do, how to do it? I said, well first of all, what are you doing? He's like, well, when I go to bed with her, I touch her this way and that way, and she doesn't like it. She says it hurts. I said you must be touching her too hard. Sounds more like you're grabbing than touching. If it was a soft touch it wouldn't hurt. No matter where you touch a woman, if it's soft, it's gonna feel good or it's gonna tickle. If it hurts, you're too rough. Men are strong and if you're especially talking about the pearl area, you have to develop a gentle touch. You're not giv'n your boy dap, you're taking a woman in your hands. Just like you don't want a woman rough-handling your jewels, be gentle with the pearl. You don't want someone biting down on you and chewing, and we don't either.

Breasts are another tender area. You can't be grabb'n them, unless she instructs you to grab them a certain way. Some breasts are more durable than others. Unless you're instructed to suck harder, suck gently but firmly. You'll get a sense of when to apply more pressure. Her body language and the intensity of the passion will instruct you. After a while the body craves more stimulation, the tolerance level for a little more roughness is higher and so you may then act accordingly. But don't come out like gangbusters. You can also go softer, too, because of how sensitive the body is. A soft, steady, concentrated application can be ecstasy. It's very important to listen to body language. Listen to what your partner is moaning. It's not words, but you should be able to understand.

I told him to just take his time. Be sensual about it and let her body signals be his guide. He was asking time limits, and what's too long or too short. There are no set time limits. Like the song says, you do it till you're satisfied. Think of it as kissing. You kiss around it, teasing it a little, preparing it for what's to come. You can blow on it. Breathe a hot and heavy breath on it. You kiss and suck on her thighs. You caress the mons. Play in the little afro. By this time they're going crazy in anticipation. You don't let them suffer anymore and you go for it. You French-kiss it. Softly. Gently. And all the while paying close attention to her body language.

Then he asked, well where exactly is the clitoris? It's funny, but a lot of men don't know. So I drew him a little picture and showed him where it was. I saw him sometime later and he says, he did it. He says he was in the right spot, he took his time, he was soft and gentle and he knew what he was doing. So I say, well, what happened? He had the nerve to say he got tired and stopped. After all that time of finding out where it is and what to do, finally getting it right, and he gets tired. Then I gave him some tricks on how to have her orgasm sooner so he won't have to get tired. The next time he came back he was like, it worked. I said see, you didn't have to be down there for half an hour.

He said, since he's done that, their sex life is now totally different. I assume she had never had an orgasm and now her floodgates have been opened. Now they're more free and open to try other things and experiment. Now that she knows he can please her, she wants to get constantly busy. He said before she used to not initiate things. Please a woman sexually, have her orgasm several times a session, you now have a new woman.

A lot of women expect the man to already know what to do, and if they never reach an orgasm they'll never know. Some women think a certain plateau is an orgasm, but when they finally have one, they're like, oh, shit. It's like a kid with a new toy. Some women won't discuss what a man isn't doing right because they feel he'll get offended. Or the woman herself don't know. But she'll ask her girl. I feel, if we're so quick to talk about it with our girlfriends, we should be as quick to talk about it to our male lovers. If you want the problem solved including your man, I can't help you. I can help you only excluding your man. Gay women don't have that problem. One, since we're so used to talking things over with our girlfriends, we'll just as easily talk about any sex problem with our lovers. Two, sex is rarely a problem because we already know the female body. We know its sensitivity, its anatomy, its response to touch, the time involved in intensifying passion, us being multiorgasmic and tending to that fact, and we more or less know how to make that perfect love.

Sex should be fun and exciting. Different places in the house. The bathroom, the kitchen can be cute, lots of appliances. If you have a car, drive to a make-out point and make out. Don't tell her. Surprise her. Women like that kind of stuff. Spontaneous stuff. Different positions are cute. We don't like that same sex, straight missionary position all the time. Women fantasize a lot. Especially when we start reading these books that feed our nature. Waterfalls and mountaintops, that's us. The love and intimacy between two women is just so beautiful because we're both in there with the romantic scenery and atmosphere, music and wine. People make the mistake of going with the stereotype that one woman must be the man in the relationship. One has the masculine, dominating character, the other submissive and passive. One's the Butch, the other, the bitch. Wrong. I'm very feminine. My lover is very feminine. We're two women. The only difference between us and other women is our attraction to whom we sleep with.

Sexism is one thing gay women don't have to deal with in relationships, thank goodness. In heterosexual relationships, sexism is gonna be a problem. Regardless of how open this brother is, it's gonna be one time when he says something or does something or refers to something that's wrongly based on gender and the woman is gonna be like, what did you say? Some women think they know their man and are in shock when he finally says that from-the-heart sexist statement. Before then you may be like, unh-unh, not my man. He don't feel that way. He'll agree with me about this. Then he'll say something real stupid to prove you wrong.

It's always some issue that'll come up to show how sexist a man is. We'll call our girlfriends and say let's go out to eat. The next day, let me tell you what that Negro said to me. He had the nerve to tell me that daaa, daaaaa, daaaaa, daaaaa, women shouldn't daaaaa, daaaaaaa, daaaaa. Now it's my turn to be sarcastic. "Unh-unh, not your man. I thought he was different." Then when she gets with him later, she's fired up from talking with her girls, and now it's another argument.

Women won't let stuff die either. Men will forget about it day one, and it stays forgotten. Not a woman. Let her discuss it with her girlfriends and it'll go on and on and on. We'll bring something up thirty-one days later. Remember that day you said daaa, daaaa, daaa. He'll be like, what are you talking about? We'll go into detail, you were sitting right there, you had on such and such and you said, and I quote, daa daa, daaaaa, daa daa.

That's the down side of being in a relationship with another woman. Women don't forget. One will go, remember that time, last year July, you said daa daa. The other will go, yeah, but the day before you said daa daa. We'll go further back and further back. We can't deny remembering, because we will. A man will go whatever, I don't remember, but whatever you say, you're right, OK, case closed. He'll have no idea, no recollection of what you're talking about, but for the sake of peace, he'll admit to being dumb, stupid, an idiot, wrong and once again, you're right. Two women will keep pulling stuff from way back, try'n and top the other and win their case. That's why when my lover and I have an argument, I say look, we have to squash this today. We have to sit and talk it out today. Because I know if I don't and if we go to bed angry and with it unsquashed, we'll be hav'n this for the entire week, so I try to squash it then and now. Even though I'll have to admit to being wrong, although I'd know I was right, I'd give in just to have it squashed. That's the advice I give men. End before you go to bed. If you don't you probably won't get any sleep. You're supposed to be up worried about the problem the same as she is. If you want to watch the game Sunday, squash it Saturday, because a woman will carry it over. I know. I know how I am. I know how my girlfriends are.

Men will always have a sexist view. It's a man's world, for now, that is. When I had a boyfriend in high school, he said something and I was like, what? What do you mean women can't be fighter pilots? Why, how come? He couldn't give a non-sexist answer. I'm like, see, that's the problem, you don't know what you're talking about. He said, she'll have to go to war. So what? If a woman wants to fly a plane in a war, that's her business. It's her country too. We wouldn't have to fight for our chance to fight in a war if it weren't for men in the first place. Women don't need men to do us and the world any more favors. Just let us get a few more judges, senators, mayors, governors, presidents and vice presidents, and you'll start to see the improvement. Women come from a spiritual, all-inclusive level. We're not selfish. We look out for all.

Your sexual orientation is decided at birth. I know mine was. Some people say your father wasn't there and you had only your mother to identify with, that's why you're attracted to women. Then if your father was there, you were molested. If that's not it, somebody did something to you somewhere at some point, if not physically, psychologically. A whole lot of Freudian penis-envy bullcrap. You hate your father so much you hate all men and you turn to women. You love your father so much you want to be like him. You love your mother, you hate your mother. Enough is enough. It's decided at birth, case closed. We come up with every reason except the biological reason.

I've dated men. I've had boyfriends. And I've never had a bad relationship. I tried to fit into the so-called *normal* way of life of socializing with men. I had boyfriends and I had sex with them. I was do'n that while all the while thinking I'd rather be with a woman because that's what I was really sexually and emotionally attracted to. To be touched by a woman, to be held by a woman, to be in the company of a woman, and find identity is what I wanted. No one introduced me to this. No one coerced me. I was never raped or molested by a man or woman. I had an equal balance of male and female influence in my life. I wasn't a teenager rebelling. In fact it was as a teenager that I was trying to conform. If anything, I was rebelling against my true self. I stayed in the closet and denied who I was.

I did not choose to be homosexual, like choosing to wear a pair of pants or a dress. The same as you didn't choose to be heterosexual. I hope you didn't choose to be heterosexual. I would think you went from infancy to what you are. You naturally went with what you found yourself attracted to. You didn't say, well let me see. Right now I'm sexually neutral, so should I be heterosexual, homosexual or bisexual? Eeny, meeny, miny, mo. Maybe I'll be hetero this year and homo next year and bi the year after. Then I'll abstain for three years, then cross-dress, then get a sex-change operation and sleep only with women. Then I'll change back and still sleep only with women. Then men, then both, then this, then that, you know what I'm say'n? It's crazy.

You do not choose to be gay. Like in 1956 in Georgia you would choose to be born Black. No, you were born that way. You had to accept it and you suffered for it. If you did have a choice, you would have chosen to be white because you wouldn't want to be hanging from a tree the next day. You would choose not to have to go to inferior colored schools, ride the back of the bus, live in ghettos, be discriminated against and be called nigger day in and day out.

If it was a choice, why would I choose to suffer at the hands of homophobics? Why would men *choose* to be gay? They're gay-bashed every day. Killed every other day. Who would want to choose to place themselves in constant danger? There's masoch-ism and there's masochism. Who would choose to be called a faggot, sissy, queer, pussy, dyke, Butch? The same as nigger, spook, coon, darkie, spade, jungle bunny, you name it. You accept it and like being Black, you be proud of it. I'm Black and a gay woman. Why would I want to burden myself twice? Though being either is not a burden. It shouldn't have to be. It's others who have the problem.

Homosexuality is not a sickness and not a disease. We can

raise children without raising them to be gay. I was raised by heterosexuals, why am I not a heterosexual? Therefore I can raise a child and they'll be whatever they were born to be, OK, thank you, case closed.

Gay people being told that homosexuality is wrong and not normal or natural are forced into a position to say bullshit and what else have I been told is wrong and not? What have I been told about Jews, Asians, Indians and everybody else that's not a male WASP? What have I been taught about religion, sex and women? Once you realize you've been lied to once by liars, you'll start to see all the other lies.

To be attracted to more than one person is innate human nature. Our cultural history is not monogamy. Large families were needed to help cultivate the land, tend the home and maintain the posterity of the family. The men had their roles and everything was communal. It was for the whole, not the individual. There was no place for selfish possessiveness. Selfishness wasn't *taught* or *learned* the way we're taught it because that was not in the best interest for the whole. You go to an African home, you'd be welcomed like you wouldn't believe. Like the brother or sister you are. Fed, sheltered, you'd have a place to stay and sleep like you were a long-lost son or daughter. Love wasn't singular, it was plural. All wives were still highly respected and had stature.

This marriage business doesn't have its history founded in I love you, you love me, let's get married and it'll be me and you forever. For us, our people, it was about adapting this human nature of polygamy to work for our cultural benefit. We ain't know nothing about you took my man, selfishness, greed or none of that. And still love was involved. It was communal love. I don't mind being loved by two and three people. And I can love two and three people.

Monogamy within the European world came about for the same reasons slavery came about. To take ownership of a person. To take control of women. It sure wasn't for the cultural reasons. Marriage wasn't because I love you. It was because I now own you. You take on my name. Forget your identity, have my children and they'll have my name also. It was economics of a different sense. If you marry a woman who was left land and property by her father, and that only being because he didn't have any sons, you then acquired all that property and land. You ain't give jack about the woman. That's selfish and exploitive and it carries through to today. Then you bring the Church in to ordain and justify and sanctify marriage and it's complete. The woman is put in her place, according to the male, patriarchal rulers.

Today, if you think the person you're with is the only person you're gonna find attractive, that's ridiculous. It's not our nature, it was never our nature. We've confused the activity of sex with the feelings of love. You can have sex with someone you love, but you can also have sex with someone you don't love. Sex is only physical. It's a physical act. When you love someone, it's mental, spiritual and you can express it physically, through sex, if you so choose; through a hug if you choose. If you love someone, how does that restrict you from engaging in mature, responsible physical sex with someone else you're attracted to? Let's get over the ownership of others. Telling them what they can and cannot do with their own bodies, just because you love them. That's another turn-around. If you love somebody, you let them do what makes them happy. You don't place restrictions on them. We are first and foremost free individuals, then you can love me, but I'm still free. Your love doesn't straitjacket me. No one's love should. I shouldn't become your property. But we buy each other every day. Dinners and gifts and marriage contracts, now you're mine and I better be the only one you're screwing. What is that?

If I love you, I love your freedom. What you do with your body is your business. You could even include me. If I'm with my lover at a club and I see someone I like, I'll say she's cute, let's have her. It's like that. Somebody will get her number and we'll be in touch.

Men do it. They have their woman and they'd run around with another. Be open about it. Does the love diminish every time he so calls "cheats," every time he does this physical act that his love for you has nothing to do with? Then understand he loves you mentally and spiritually and his physical activities have nothing to do with how he feels about you mentally or spiritually. That doesn't change by him having sex with someone other than yourself. We don't think, he screwed that girl, he must love her. We think, he screwed her and he should be screwing only me. We think selfishly.

Sex is just humans having fun and enjoying the fact that we're able to enjoy more than one person's being. Let's unbrainwash ourselves, because that's what we've been. We've been told how to have sex and with whom to have it.

Gay people are more open to their nature. We've accepted our gay sexuality and in the process, we've accepted our sexuality which is polygamous. Therefore, we can accept sex for what it is, just sex, not what society says it is. Something done only between husband and wife who are in love. Yeah, right, and how many people adhere to that? Now it's time for polygamy to come out of the closet, because everybody is practicing it.

Sex is just sex. It's not love. Why all the added fanfare? It doesn't mean this, that and the other. It means just sex. When it's with someone you love, it's different because you love the person. Special feelings are involved with the act, but special feelings will go along with anything you do because you love the person. That doesn't mean you or they shouldn't do several physical things but with each other because you love each other. That's stupid.

Do you have to first love everything you do in order to do it, or is it done because you just feel like doing it? You have the feelings to do it, it's safe, harmless, enjoyable and you don't feel guilty. If you love macaroni and cheese, do you have it every single night for the rest of your life, or can you have something else, enjoy it and still be able to love macaroni and cheese?

Until men can really know or at least understand, because you'll never know, how it is to be a woman, there will always be sexism, abuse and harassment toward women. As long as that exists, things are gonna stay the same. The little progress will continue to be negated by what's still be'n taught and believed. We'll continue making progress in quicksand.

When you go to the corner store, you just go. Women can't do that. When we go, we have to worry about being harassed. If I go to the store, before I hit the corner three guys have already said yo, baby. Sometimes we say forget it and don't even go. If it's something we can do without for the time being, we just wanted a soda or something, we'll say forget it, I'll drink water. Some days more than others, we just don't feel like being harassed. Some days we say, I'm in such a good mood can't no guy jump'n in my face mess it up. We'll go get the soda. Isn't that deep? Going out to get a trivial item like a can of soda has us going through all this pro and con. How much do I want the soda? Is it worth three or four guys asking me my name? Is the weather nice out? If it is, that means more guys will be hang'n out. Damn, it's a nice day. We have to go through all this. If *you* want a soda, you just get up and go. Come back with your soda and enjoy it. I have to drink water. But water's good for you, so now I have to look at it like that.

My roommate just went to the Laundromat up the street. I guarantee you at least three guys have tried to stop her. She just wanna do laundry. She ain't even thinking about men. She's gay, but she still has to go through this.

Imagine you're in a world of gay men. Imagine you're hit on every day, three to five times a day. No matter where you go, no matter where you're at. To the Laundromat, to the corner store for a soda, men are constantly hitting on you. You're thinking about the soda or whatever it is you're try'n to do, but you're constantly interrupted by men going hey, brother, can I talk to you a minute? Frustrating, isn't it? It's frustrating for a woman. It's doubly frustrating for a gay woman. We ain't thinking about men, but yet you're constantly in any woman's face.

If it's too late out, forget it. You can go to the library and don't have to worry about leaving by a certain time. We have to make sure we leave before it gets dark. We have to worry about sitting in a well-lit part of the library. We have to worry about where we sit in a well-lit section. Does this table with three empty chairs invite some guy over to interrupt my studies? You just go and do what you have to do without a second thought. You don't have to worry about your space being invaded. You can stand on the train, mind your business and go on to your destination. Women? I can have my head in a book, my Walkman on and some guy wants to know what I'm listening to and what book am I reading?

I have no problems responding to a nice greeting. I will respond. But when it's rude and disrespectful, as is most times, then I have a problem and I'll let you know. This is what continues sexism. A little kid sees this and goes, oh, that's how you talk to a girl.

I'd like to have children, but only by adoption because I sure ain't gonna have one naturally. I have the maternal instincts to want and raise a child because I'm a woman, but I don't want to give birth. Another stereotype is that gay women must don't have maternal instinct and they don't like or want children. I love children, I just don't want to give birth. I'm also not gonna have sex with a man, and I'm not gonna do artificial insemination. I don't wanna go through the weight gain, swelling, mood swings and delivery. I can't handle monthly cramps, I know I couldn't handle being pregnant. I know gay women who want to have a full pregnancy and delivery, but that's not for me. Several heterosexual women don't want to give birth, so it has nothing to do with being gay.

And my main reason is we need to adopt more. Thousands of Black babies need Black homes. Thousands of Black babies are already here, can we care for them first? Then we get in an uproar when white families adopt Black children.

Once we find our own identity, we'll be all right. Forget what you heard and educate yourself about everything. If you begin with and understand that this country, this system, was established for the benefit of the few, and that automatically means that the non-few suffer, ask yourself are you the few or the non-few. Ask yourself who's suffering? Who's dying? Who's out of a job? Who's called derogatory terms and why? What have you been told is unnatural, not normal, immoral? Ask yourself, is it so the few can maintain control and power? Ask yourself are the few still in control and in power? Once you realize you're the goat, you're the back being stepped on, then you finally would want to straighten up. And in order to straighten up you would reject all the lies, educate yourself and take control of yourself. You'll control your sexuality, your personal form of religious worship, and everything that doesn't make intelligent sense, you'd reject. If you'd only think about it.

And don't educate yourself at Harvard, Yale, Brown or any of the elitist few. That's where you're really brainwashed. We need to take that Malcolm X route. You decide which book you want to pick up. Learn this world's history of exploitation and oppression at the expense of the colored masses. Travel and educate yourself. What sane person in power and control is gonna tell you the truth? Is Harvard really gonna tell me? Tell me that mental and *physical* slaves are necessary for this country's survival and that the masses are the guinea pig? I intelligently think not. You think physical slavery doesn't exist? Get a degree and go apply for a job on Wall Street, then apply for janitor and see which one you fill quicker.

So, find yourself, no matter what state you're in or what age. If you ain't dead yet, you can still learn the truth and teach it to someone. Teach your grandchildren. Tell them the conclusion you've come to in your seventieth year in life.

If you're middle or upper-class and think you can rest easy, learn the truth. Adopt some Black children and pass it on. I can't stand some ignorant upper-class "I've-got-mine" Black folks. They make my flesh crawl. If we take back our identity, we'll be all right.

Because I don't have much intimate contact, literally or metaphorically speaking, with Black men in terms of relationships, I really can't say much. I can say only as Black men and Black women, I wish we all could better relate just on a human level. Non-sexually, humanly speaking, I wish we all could come together, communicate and live in peace and harmony. The gay community has unity, for obvious reasons. There's a lot of love and understanding. We have our people who'll trip, too, but for the most part, there's a tremendous amount of patience and kindness. Should everyone turn gay? Well, things may be better, but, no, don't do as I do, do as I say. Don't judge. Don't hurt. Don't ridicule. Be patient. Kind. Understanding. Loving. Apply that to whatever lifestyle you're living. If it's the Black man and Black woman that especially needs the most help, then apply it twice as much.

CooPeratiVe loVe

Chris

chris, 22

marylander

self-identified

I try to follow and remain true to whatever force it is that's guiding me and telling me what to do for my own good. Whether it's relationships, school or anything I may have to deal with in everyday life, I try to follow that guiding voice, that guiding force. It's difficult because, like any child, I was raised and taught the societal rules that people try to play and live by. It's difficult because it conflicts with how we may really think and feel. It came to a point where I had to start making decisions. Decisions about my life and taking control of it. Whether I was gonna continue following what I was told, or was I going to live by what I truly felt and believed to be in my best personal interest? I chose to go with what I truly believed and felt. Not to disrespect anybody who follows what they're told, but I just can't live like that. Personally, it makes no sense if you don't look at what you've been taught with your own personal discretion. Accepting what you've been taught without giving any personal thought to it is stupid. This is what allows people to be raised by Skinhead, Ku Klux Klan parents, and not, in their twenty-first or thirtieth year of life, as mature, free-thinking adults say, no, wait, this general line of racist thinking is wrong. It's about making decisions with your life, no matter what you may have been taught. Be it morals, values, what you eat—I'm now a vegetarian—everything that you think has an important impact on how you may best, happily live your life, you have to question and decide for yourself whether to accept it or reject it. If what I was told didn't conflict with how I naturally feel as a person, I'd follow that truth. The truth is indisputable.

What I was told was that it's one man one woman. You get married, have children, grow old together and die. This scenario sounds very familiar. It's like what you see on TV all the time. A happy-faced depiction of what someone says is the way things are, and it's not. We're not that simple. We're not all the same. We're not all the time happy-faced and watered-down. We are all not mother, father, child, dog, cat, happy and harmonious.

There are various natural dynamics that interfere with this desire for a clean-cut and simple lifestyle. All of how we think and believe is contrary to a clean-cut and simple life. Because of our state of denial, many lives are lived in conflict and turmoil. If only we followed the very truth and dynamics we rebel against, the clean-cut and simple life we seek can be obtained. We try to make the unnatural work. You can never go against nature.

I've concluded that the way I was raised to live isn't exactly, in my opinion, what's best for me. So, when it comes to relationships, the traditional idea of man and woman falling in love, being everything for each other, committed with no other needs of fulfillment from anyone else isn't working for me. That doesn't mean that I can't be in love with someone, because I have been in love, it just means that I can love more than one person at one time. That's what works for me and that's how I choose to live. This is what feels natural and what I'm comfortable with. If I am in a relationship, it's an open relationship that allows me to relate with other people to whom I'm attracted, interest me and can help further my growth. I get what I need from my companions and they get what they need from me. No one has any constraints, no one is held back from doing what may complete them as a person. It makes more sense to me that way.

The first thing people think of is, oh you just want to have sex with whomever and do it, and to tell the man he can do it is just letting him have his cake and eat it too, but it's not that shallow. Sex is not the issue. It's not the biggest factor in being allowed to have your freedom, and I don't even look at it as something that big to even get caught up in debate over. It's about personal growth, positive growth. Positive contacts and relationships with people. Out of the billions that are here, all with different insight, knowledge, experiences, can I relate to just one? Who was it that said find that one mate and then shut yourself off from everyone else, and we agreed? Who said limit yourself and we said, OK?

It's been a four-year process that's brought me to where I now am. It's been a process that has opened my mind as to how I now choose to have relationships with people. What happened was I was truly in love with this one person. He was such an influence on me in so many ways, intellectually and spiritually, I was truly attracted to this person. I was a freshman, eighteen, he was older. He was an extremely powerful person. I was in love with him, and I felt he was attracted to me. Although not confirmed, I felt that our relationship was a very personal one. Now, the whole time that I've known him, he's been somewhat involved with this other woman. From spending so much time with him, I got to meet and know this other woman. It was funny. Before meeting her, I knew who she was, although not formally. I knew that she was the one he was once in love with. When I met him, they were still very good friends. When I was introduced to her, she automatically didn't like me. I didn't even notice it. I had to be told that she was giving me all this shade. She felt very insecure whenever I was around. She was jealous and felt that I was moving in on her territory. I didn't look at it like that. I felt that she and I could be friendly, and we could be cool with each other even if they were still emotionally involved. I, realistically, was only his friend.

Over a few years my relationship with him progressed and I remember one time I had called him, and he was talking about this other woman. The gist of the conversation was that even though we fall in and out of our relationships, you can still very much love the person even when you part company. He had formally broken up with this other girl, they weren't intimately involved but they were very much spiritually intimate. To hear this had hurt my feelings so much and so deeply. I felt at that point that he and I could never really be in a relationship. I felt that if he's in love with another woman, then it's no point in me trying to take him away from her. I felt, obviously his need for her was very deep. But at the same time I was like, he's a beautiful person and there are things I can learn from him. Why can't we still be friends?

We stayed friends, I was under the impression that we would go on being friends, but *my* relationship with him continued to progress into something that seemed deeper than just friendship. I felt connected to him because of the many things we shared, but not in possession of him. He had his personal needs to take care of outside what I could do for him, but that didn't lessen what we shared and enjoyed. I stopped feeling the need to wish he was all mine, because that just didn't seem logical to ask of any one person.

So, like, now, my whole thing was, isn't this against what I've been taught? Isn't this weird, what's going on? And why am I not feeling jealous, or upset, or just forget about him. But to forget about him seemed so stupid and childish. I was comfortable with having him only as a friend. He was still close to this girl, and I didn't trip. I felt if she made him happy, then he should be with her. They should be together in whatever relationship they had. But that's not to say that we couldn't be together in our relationship. I felt, if he can make me happy and give respect and I can do the same for him, then we could continue sharing what we had and without the perception of ownership.

Ever since that experience, I started to look at this dominant concept of relationships. I started to see you can have feelings that are totally different from what we've been taught. I felt, yes, I can love him and he can love me. But at the same time I saw that he or I can love another and no one is trying to take anything away from anyone. If that's my or his happiness, if that's what my or his truth is, then that's what we should have.

I still can accept that two people can be everything to each other. I can see that. If that's what they're sure they've found in each other. I'm just saying that for me, what I've come to understand about myself, the path I'm on, and the type person I am, if one person has only his knowledge and experience, and I'm on a path to acquire several different bits of knowledge, then that one person is limiting. Not to say that I couldn't find myself with one person, but it might not be a one-on-one commitment. I would still have to allow myself to be open to different people if I found myself attracted to them. Right now this one person being your everything is just not making sense. Maybe in twenty years it'll make sense to me, but right now it doesn't make any sense, so I'm just gonna live on what I understand to be true and what makes sense to me. More so, what makes me feel comfortable.

Don't you think the same way you've been taught one man one woman, you've now, because of this brother, this experience, been taught to accept open relationships?

I've thought of that, and I believe I wasn't made to feel this way because of my deep feelings for this man. You have to go with your heart and feelings. My heart didn't say you're so jealous and possessive you should have all or nothing. My heart didn't feel torn to see him with another woman. I felt it was right. He's happy and he should be. I was also happy with what I had. I wasn't fantasizing that we'd one day be together. I believe that this situation only showed me what my true feelings are. It would have come sooner or later.

You could have developed this logic and remained happy instead of heart-broken.

But I didn't think, "Well, what am I gonna do?" It struck me as doesn't it make sense to have several people in your life? Who are we to be so selfish of another person's freedom? Who is anyone to hold back another from personal growth and happiness?

It's about touching people's lives. There are several and so many things in this world. We as humans have the capacity to appreciate and love various things. Including amongst these different things are, most importantly, people.

I wasn't accommodating myself to a situation just to have a man. I could have said forget him and gotten another man to call my own, but that's not where my spirit is. I would be selling myself short to cut this man off, and thus cut off my own personal growth and development. I'm not that selfish with myself as well as others.

And I know that he's not the only one. I can see myself with another man, love him, and *because* of that love, encourage him to see anyone else he took a personal and spiritual interest in. His growth is beyond me. The same as my growth is beyond him. But we're still very much an intimate and integral part of each other.

We're so indulgent in the wrong things in life. I feel people indulge in their egos, overindulge. My ego doesn't keep me from enjoying a relationship with the man that I love, knowing that he gives and receives love from another individual. I don't have a big ego problem. I don't feel less of a woman just because he's not "my man."

It seems to me that the average person is so insecure. I mean, the fact that Black people have had everything stolen from them, and we have so little power in society, it seems to rule over someone, to own someone, seems to be the first thing we think of doing, simply because we own nothing. With nothing, the quickest, most tangible thing we can obtain is another person.

A girl will talk about "her man," and a guy will talk about "his woman," and there's all this talk of possession. My answer to that is I don't want to feel like I'm owned or I own someone. If they need to experience the intellectual, emotional, physical or spiritual influence and stimulation of someone other than myself, who am I to keep them from growing and obtaining what they need?

If anything, I would want them to have everything they need. I can't expect to be everything for one person, nor can I expect anyone to be everything to me, and you're free, so you're free to expand. There are so many different facets to me as a person, how can I expect one person to answer all of my needs? I really don't see it happening. And I really don't see myself as being the person who can do that for any one body. We can be together in the long run, but that's only after a lot of fulfilling, maturing and growth has taken place.

If I really love someone, then I want them to get everything they require to make them a whole person. To help them find happiness, to help them to progress in accordance to whatever it is they were brought here to learn, experience and accomplish. To me, that's what true love is. I want to be free to experience all the things I need to experience to become whatever it is I am to become. If that means that I need to deal with one or two brothers at the same time to do it, there is nothing wrong with it. If I can have really beautiful love and respect for someone, and we can celebrate the beautiful things of life without having to indulge in insecurities and ego tripping, indulging in ownership and possession, then that's wonderful. There should be no room or time for all the other nonsense.

If I can feel love for more than one person, then I should have the right to live and act upon those feelings without someone trying to make me feel guilty. That's what this society does. It tries to make you feel ashamed for what you naturally feel. Society tells you, you're cheating. You then have to sneak around to do what you naturally feel. If you free yourself and accept who you are, you can do things without guilt. It's so stupid to feel guilty about what you naturally are. Don't fall into that fallacy, it's stupid, it's dumb, it makes no sense. For Black people especially. We've been told so much of what to think, how to speak, how to dress, what to call ourselves, it's time to question all this and find and take back self-identity.

Say I was involved with one person, and I met someone else whom I found attractive. I find that I'm totally intrigued by his mind, body and soul, should I then go, well I'm already in this exclusive relationship with someone else, so forget him? I may feel there is something really beautiful about this person, and I could learn from this person. But I can't cheat on my man. What is that? How 'bout, I'm cheating myself. I'm denying myself. I'm cheating myself of pleasure and further knowledge, experience and evolution that I could gain from this other brother. I feel I don't have the luxury to be pass'n up things that could help me deepen myself. It's too many people who have a lot to offer. There are special people who have been designated to come into our lives to help us with what we're here to do. Our thing is we don't accept the gift. We always turn from it and continue walking around lost, angry, confused, mad at the world, mad at those we love and mad at ourselves.

I can truly respect and accept people who are married and find happiness in their marriage, are faithful to each other and all that. That's a good thing and I'm happy for people who find happiness in that, especially if they're as faithful as they choose to be. I hear and see a lot of contradiction among people who choose monogamy. It would seem they would question what they have been told by whomever if their spirit leads them to do differently.

In my opinion, on one level marriages are legal and financial arrangements. On another, they're just an expected tradition. Without thinking, people go into these traditions. They don't think about what they truly need and mean.

We too often and too soon place the completion of ourselves in one person. We don't enough look for self and the completion and fulfillment of self through the many and various experiences life offers. People too soon give up and marry someone they'll soon be unhappy with. We have to fulfill ourselves first, before we can be satisfied with another.

I don't understand why we too soon give up. Enjoying life is not hard. We make it hard, but what life itself offers us is not hard to experience. Why we don't see that it's meant for us to grow and become as varied and complex, yet as simple as the human being is, I don't know. Why we don't strive to use more than the only ten percent brain power we do is beyond me. But it seems, our lack and our denial contribute to our miserable state because we cut ourselves short and too quickly limit ourselves. We do this on the various levels of which we have limitless potential. Why we choose to be sub par and miserable is confusing.

Why do we torture ourselves, being unhappy and unsatisfied with the one person who *isn't* our everything? One person, who has *cheated,* when what they're really doing is unconsciously fulfilling our natural desire to make contact with various people.

We feel we can't even befriend another, or we'll be suspect of infidelity and immoral activity. We're not even taught in school about other cultures. This is what keeps us in wars. Has it occurred to us, maybe we're going about it all wrong? There are so many people and cultures on this wide earth, why do I so quickly want to grab my next-door neighbor? Hold on for dear life, and go through this slave tradition of legal arrangement? I'm trying to find myself, my own identity, not lose it to someone else. Why do I have to take on the man's name, absorb his identity? Who am I?

I see marriage, as we know it, as a tradition that may be unnecessary for me. To me marriage should be personal. Solely between two individuals and not commercialized. When it's time, my lover and I would go somewhere and commit ourselves to each other in our own private ceremony.

Just because you may be sexually active with more than one person doesn't mean you're fuck'n anybody that passes you on the street. If I'm to say I have more than one lover doesn't mean I'm fucking two or three people. It isn't just a sexual act, it's a lot more than that.

This is the thing. Sex is good,
I mean, sex is really good, but you know what's even better than sex? It's making love.
Sex and love are two different things. We prove this all the time. I personally don't have sex with anybody I don't love. If I can love more than one person, then I can make love to more than one person. Loving two people doesn't mean I make love to him and not you. Although I *can* have sex with people, I don't. I make love with people I love. Physical sex acts can be enjoyed, but two spirits in love and making love is even better. I strive for the next best essence.

I believe we've been taught jealousy, hate and this big need to compete with each other for other people. From the days of "I challenge you to a duel for her hand" to people killing each other because "you tried to talk to my girl," it's the same. We've been pounded with this thirst for competition over people. Makeup, clothes, hairstyles, it's all equipment for the competition. We're so competitive trained it's funny. A friend of mine has three sisters and he noticed whenever he would go out with any of them they would appear as a couple. It was only then, with another woman, that he received so much attention. All these stares from other sisters walking down the street, who otherwise, if he were alone, would have their eyes glued to the ground. His sisters told him whenever a woman sees a man with another woman, they'll check out the man to see what's so good about him that this sister has him. And what's so good about this sister that this brother wants her? Other women will flirt and not care about the woman he's with. If he was by himself, he wouldn't get any play. Our competitive training tells us to take this man from her. Who is she, she ain't shit, I should be with him. The same man walking down the street, the same woman and she's looking everywhere but at him. He'll say, "Hello," and she's now deaf. She'll turn the corner, see a brother with a woman and she's all in his face.

I'm not trying to say that I'm better or worse, smarter or whatever than other people, but for most people to hear what I'm saying, the way I think, they may feel it's strange or stupid or different, but I understand many have been made to feel that way. I then have to find people who feel and see things the same way I do. They have to be of the same character to know that no one belongs to anyone and that we're free to do what we want. I feel, if it's all positive and not hurting anyone, we're on the right track.

Of course I want us to have beautiful relationships, but I would really like for us to have liberation. I would like for us to find our self-identity above all else, and when that happens, I believe we'll naturally have nothing but beautiful relationships.

We may already know our identity, but we're being told it's wrong and to go against it. Many of us do go against what we've been taught, but we do it with guilt. For example with monogamy. Who's really monogamous? But we feel we're wrong. We feel we're immoral and we never fully get to know our true selves. How can we if we're feeling guilt and shame for what we're doing? It's weird, because if this is us, we should have a different attitude. One that harmonizes with us. One that doesn't leave us feeling hurt, jealous, disappointed or angry. Many of us are practicing our nature, but we're doing it with guilt. Now we have to free ourselves from the guilt, the selfishness and possessiveness, and we need to understand why this is our nature. We need to know how we can develop and grow in our nature, all in a positive direction. How we can finally live in a harmonious, unified way? The harmony society likes to sell to us, but as of now isn't there.

lalanya

lalanya, 22

west coast

actor

I don't think relationships are in a state of emergency. I just think they're not in a very good state. Relationships are obviously different here in the 90's than they were in the 70's, and 60's, and so forth. That's the first point I'd like to make. Also, in a bad way they're the same because a large number of brothers go about relationships in the negative way that they've seen their fathers, uncles, older brothers and older male influences go about relationships. It's time to play catch-up. The whole, "Yo, baby, can I talk to you a minute," is 1970's *Superfly* and *The Mack*.

And now that the 70's look is coming back, I guess I'll hear, "Hey, sexy mama, can I holla at you" coming out the mouth of a twenty-four-year-old.

In the 90's there are several contributing factors why we haven't perfected relationships. The 90's is the decade of the woman. Bottom line. This is her decade. She has her independence. Her sexual independence. Her social independence. Her economic independence. Her political independence, as we have seen with Senator-elect Carol Moseley-Braun. We have President Clinton and her First Man, Bill. The 90's woman has got it go'n on.

There is no turn'n back. She will only further herself. The year 2000 will show you an even more independent and powerful woman. Men can't handle this. It intimidates them and makes them insecure. So they immediately go into a relationship with the mind set to attack. To defend their manhood. To discredit the woman and make her feel less than she should. Not as independent as she should be.

Today's woman can say, "Fuck it. I'm out." Today's woman is no longer look'n for security from the man. She is provid'n her own security. She may be support'n the man. Hopefully, if that's the case, let him be try'n to do something with his life, but at this point certain factors are work'n against him. For example, this fucked-up economy.

In the most ideal situation, I would like for him to have his own money. I want him to have his own security. Note, I said, "his own security." I plan to have my own, and I would like for him to have his own. That eliminates any future problems with what's mine and what's yours. You buy your things with your money, I'll do the same with my money. Gifts I buy you with my money are yours. No one wants or anticipates divorce or breakups, but in the event of one, we can leave the same way we came in.

Women and men make the mistake of think'n it's materialistic or shallow to want someone with madd income. For certain motives, this may be the case. My motives are not shallow.

A large income speaks to the level of your aspirations. Everyone aspires the best for themselves. If you want the best and are will'n to work for it, not bullshit or half stepp'n, then you're say'n something about what you feel you deserve. You are making a definite statement about yourself. Whether or not you obtain madd wealth is beside the point. I'm talk'n about the aspiration, the quality of the person and what they feel they're worth. Why should I want someone who doesn't share my aspirations? Where does it benefit me if you don't wish to travel to the places I wish to visit? See the cultures I want to see. Lavish myself in the way that I want to be lavished. If you are satisfied with every weekend at the neighborhood corner bar, then I'm not the person for you. The world I live in is bigger than that.

It's not that I would date only a rich man as opposed to a poor man. It's not as blanket as, "he is rich, I will date him. He is poor, I will not date him." I would have to examine why the poor man is poor. Are you poor because you're sitt'n on your ass, drink'n beer and watch'n the games? Or are you poor because you are a victim of a racist, prejudiced society that is hindering your dreams and aspirations?

Are you a struggl'n artist and your art is not a big financial payoff, but you know about the world and liv'n life? You're well read, worldly and can introduce me to new ideas and creations. I can be with that man.

But most of the time when a man is poor it's because he's like fuck it. He doesn't want shit for himself and doesn't want you to have shit. He'll sooner hold you back than try to advance you. If he's like, "Where you go'n every weekend? Why you wanna go here, why you wanna go there? Why you wanna do this, why you wanna do that?" Forget that. I'm gone. I'll write. I'll send you a postcard. So, it's not that I wanna be with a rich man because he's rich. It's because he's do'n something with his life, and he's most likely using his money to discover life.

If I meet a man at the Kennedy Center, or Lincoln Center, I'm think'n this person might have the same interests I do. Let me see what else he's into. He can have bank, or he can be liv'n check to check. Though, in either case, both are in fact rich. Rich in culture. Both can have my time of day.

I'm definitely attracted to status, prominence and the ambitious. I know those are the things in life I want to achieve. I can learn from you. I want to learn how I can take my little artist self payoff for me so I can do the things I'd like to do.

Being goal oriented and ambitious, wanting to do for yourself and experiencing all that you can in this world is why we should all be living. People should not be waking up in parts of the world wondering where their next meal is coming from.

All the men and relationships that I've been involved with have really been of substance. My last one was a three-year relationship and we're still friends. Some of my girlfriends have said no way would they have let him go, and they say it because he had money. Yes, he had money, but "money can't buy you love." Now I know how much truth is behind that saying. It can allow you to do the things you like to do, but if you're doing those things with someone you've lost emotional involvement with, you won't really enjoy it. You have to find that person who you enjoy so you can truly enjoy any new experience. And maybe that person doesn't have a dime in his pocket.

Like my mother says, "It's just as easy to fall in love with a poor man as it is a rich man. It's the man. Except with the rich man, you cry all the way to the bank. With the poor man, you just cry." If I was in love and my heart was broken, I'd cry over both equally.

What separates me from most other sisters is that I'm motivated to get my own. Others are motivated to get their own through some man. If some women worked as hard for their own security as hard as they work toward gett'n a man with his own security, they wouldn't have any problems. That's one of our biggest faults, problems and setbacks. And I know it comes from the parent. It comes from the mothers.

I look at my mother and I see qualities that not many other mothers have. When I look at my girlfriends' mothers, I don't see my mother. I don't see that independent spark and drive. My mother projects that something which says she has her shit together, and it wasn't due to the reliance of anyone, male or female. She's self-assured and self-reliant. And you still have total femininity with my mother. She's a lady, she's a woman. She's independent and she didn't have to sacrifice having a man. We confuse the self-sufficient independence of a woman with meaning she doesn't need a man. Well, you can have both. And don't confuse me in that category, I need a man.

Look at it the way men do it. They're motivated to make it to the top. Businessman, entrepreneur, athlete, they all have that self-sufficient quality that says, "I strive for the best and to better myself." Do they achieve what they want at the sacrifice of having a woman? Do they become selfish and use their money for their own purpose? Do they say fuck women, I don't need them? Hell no. The first thing they do is look for someone to share it with. I'm the same way.

Sisters today are still relying too much on the man to do for them. We're still caught up in being Cinderella. One day my Prince Charming will come and take me away from all of this. Some of us are gonna go to our graves wait'n on that. Some of us are mak'n it happen for ourselves. We can be the Queen Charming that rescues the brother, or we can be the Queen Charming to ourselves. When you look to others, you can run into some unpleasant characters.

My girlfriend likes to go to clubs, and she's the one who is always up on the blocks just shak'n it. She meets a lot of people that way. They'll come up to her and pay a compliment. Guys will talk to her and depend'n on how they present themselves, she'll respond positive, or she'll play you off. Of those who approach and have money, she always, always has to play them off. Their character just isn't nice. They think they can come through, scoop somebody up, say jump on my bandwagon and later jump on my bed. But it doesn't work like that.

It's about where your values are. Other girlfriends of mine, who would have jumped on the bandwagon, jumped on the bed, kicked out the bed, and be back at the club, up on the block the very next weekend, shak'n it and waiting for the next Prince Charming, because the last one didn't work out.

I'm attracted to men who are smart. The guy that I'm seeing now stimulates me mentally to no end. I have always been attracted and turned on by intelligence. I can't go with J-Bone da Mack on Sixth Street because we can't talk about anything. Other than how he's duck'n people that are after him, we have no conversation.

In high school I may have gone for J-Bone da Mack. I mean I loved hoodlums. It's still something that fascinates me about them. That moment-to-moment defiance about them. But now I have to think self-preservation and go on my way.

I dated a hustler in high school. He wasn't your average everyday

hustler, and he was smart. He was smart as shit, and he was also such a
nigga. Nigga in the street mentality sense, and I loved that about him. I
love that rawness. The sheer honesty, no matter how crude. Women love
honesty no matter what form it comes in, so long as it's honest. I don't like
anyone who's gone through Ivy League and then coats everything with
rhetoric and bullshit. You would know what this hustler's thoughts and
feelings were at any asked moment. He would say, "I want you like this,
and don't sweat it." Or "I'm gonna do her, cause she's on my dick, don't
sweat it." You knew what was up, and you had a choice to leave or accept
it.

I love and I hate hustlers. They're smart and they're stupid. Hustlers are
ambitious, but it's short-term, and it stays within the ghetto. That's the
smart and stupid of it. A phat car with a phat boom'n system, a phat
spoiler kit, and they're happy. I can't go for that. A phat herringbone,
some match'n Fila outfits and they're happy. They're on the short-term life
plan. I'm on the long one.

Another reason relationships are lacking is because there is no spiritual
guidance. This is a new revelation I've been exploring about myself for the
past two years. I think by nature women are very, very spiritual. Women
are very much in touch with that sixth sense. It's spiritual to come on your
period. It's spiritual when we lose our virginity. It's spiritual to have sex.
Women are very spiritual. We show our emotions. We laugh. We cry. We
forgive. We're vulnerable. We pray. We're very open. That's all spiritual.

Therefore, when we're look'n for a man, we're look'n for the same
spiritual, Godlike characteristics. We're look'n for someone to help illumi-
nate our spirituality. That's all we're do'n.

**We're look'n for God in every man that we're with. We're look'n
for Him. The man who can help us with all the answers to our
questions. When you find that man, he's God. You worship him.
You adorn him. You adore him. Just as you would God. Just like
you do when you go to church and pray. You cater to him. You
need him. Your man is your temple. He is your God. And the
converse is true. You become his Goddess. Someone he can look
to for answers, comfort and love. He adorns and worships you,
and the two of you become as one.**

We're not putt'n anything on the man that he can't handle. It's natural
for us to feel and act this way. It would take more energy try'n to control
and not do this. It takes more energy and concentration to not treat your
Black man like a God.

If you can't handle it, all the affection, attention and love women pour on, then you are totally lost. You're detached from knowing yourself as a member of the African race. You don't know who you are and you don't know who I am.

Men have been conditioned to be these hard, fenced-up people. But I'm tell'n you, it is not of your nature not to be sensitive, not to be compassionate, not to be caring, not to love me as an African daughter. You have to return. Return to gett'n in touch with those Godlike characteristics in you. God is in you, and you have to understand the qualities of God so you can know what the qualities of yourself should be. God loves and embraces everyone. God loves unconditionally. Man should love and embrace. These are qualities we both contain. One of us has forgotten that.

Women love unconditionally all the time. We don't deny our God qualities. God forgives. Women forgive all the time.

If women can love and embrace the same as God, then men can love and embrace the same as God. What, are you better than God? Are you too good to love me the same? If I'm worthy of the love from God, I know I'm worthy of the love from a Black man. Man was made in the image of God. You were made from the love and compassion of God. He's loving and compassionate, then you should know that you are loving and compassionate. Stop denying it.

Men need to stop go'n against their nature. It seems that you're consciously work'n against feel'n the natural love that's in you. It's like you know it's there but you can't let it show through. Cut the bullshit. It's destroy'n you. It's destroy'n us. It's destroy'n the Black family. IF I HAVE TO BEG YOU, I WILL. BLACK MAN, PLEASE STOP DENYING TO YOURSELF WHO YOU ARE!

Get off that extra hard shit. You're already hard. You already have charisma, rhythm, soul, you don't need to exploit and double it into the farce you do. Find yourself. Return to yourself. Return to being God.

You'll notice women are most attracted to ministers. We're attracted to preachers, artists, athletes, all those who are perceived as be'n this type of supernatural God-figure. Take singers. Nat "King" Cole, Stevie Wonder, Frankie Beverly. Women love these men. When you sit and listen to their music, your emotions are be'n affected, we'll say, "Damn, he could really love me. He could really, really love me. I know I have a lot of love to give to him. He understands love and he understands me as a woman." When we feel that way, that the artist understands and can reciprocate our love, we're the ones you see run'n behind every one of their concerts. Women love Prince because he's illuminating this energy that women are drawn to.

Women love musicians. Monk. Charlie Parker. Coltrane. They were Gods.
These are the men we're look'n to love like God because we see that
they've noticed the God within them. This is what your everyday brother
has to do.

When we're both in touch with our spirituality, we become so much
deeper. To ourselves and each other. Everything becomes plain and less
trivial. When we reach that level of calm, when you, as a man, can say,
"baby, I was wrong." Or, "baby, I'm so sorry." Or, "baby, we don't need to
be act'n like this." And really mean it. Not say'n it just to avoid a confron-
tation, but because he knows we're way above trivial, and our shit runs
deep, when that happens, we are in there.

Or you can up and say, "Baby, I need you." THAT IS THE BEST THING
A WOMAN CAN HEAR! When my boyfriend called me one day from
across the country and said, "Lalanya, I need you, there is a ticket at the
airport," I dropped everything. My baby needs me. I'm gonna go get
needed. And it was beautiful. He was at the airport. He was probably there
wait'n after he hung up the phone. That flight was one of the best times in
our lives. We were meditating. We went to church together. We were a
team. If the relationship could have stayed there it would have been
something, but distance and circumstances had us say a mutual friendship
would be best. In fact we're now better friends. Some people you're only
meant to be certain things. But what we had, and still share as friends is
beautiful. Just to have a true friendship with a brother is special. We need
to examine and get over the "If we can't be lovers, we can't be friends." Ask
yourself, how many true "friends" of the opposite sex do I have? If none, if
they all have to be sex partners, then you should feel sorry for yourself.
You should feel a loss.

A woman's strength is natural. The pain we have to endure as women is
what makes us women. When I first started my period and I experienced
cramps like you would never understand, I had to acquire a strength I
thought I never had. A kick in the nuts doesn't compare. Men who say
differently don't know what you're talk'n about. Your insides are being
ground and ripped for hours. When my cramps hit, my aunt would tell
me not to take any Tylenol. Stick it out and feel the reward of hav'n the
strength to endure those two or three days of cramps, and when you do,
you'll know what it is to be a woman. And when I did, when it was over, I
was like ahh, shucks, now, didn't need no Tylenol, didn't need no Advil, I
am woman. I can endure anything.

This is train'n toward all the pain yet to come. Because of you men, we have to know about endur'n pain. We've come to know real well. From hav'n your children, to you break'n our hearts. To watch'n you do the wrong thing and end up behind bars or dead. To wait'n for you to find yourselves, from hav'n you taken from us and sold, to helplessly watch'n you being beaten. To ourselves being raped. Oh, we're familiar with pain, and the sooner we prepare ourselves through enduring cramps, the better.

When I lost my virginity it was painful. Emotionally as well as physically. I didn't speak to my boyfriend for two days. When we broke up I was in more pain. Then when I reflect on it, I loved it. I was soon ready to give my love and pain up to the next guy.

Now, why do women want to go through all this pain again and again?

It's because at the end of the pain is so much joy. It's because before the pain there's so much joy. The joy of loving a Black man is worth the pain.

Sex, the act of mak'n love, the intimacy, is beyond. We are experiencing something that is extraordinary. It lets us know we are something special, beyond all of what we think we are as only humans. We're soul. We're spirit. The perfect union between Black man and woman is the essence of love. Because we are by nature two very spiritual beings, and love is spiritual, together, we can only best represent the essence of it.

You have entered my body. You are a part of me, and I you. Men can feel this way if they allow themselves. I know you can. You have only to reteach yourselves. Unlearn what you've learned. Wake the hell up.

Why do women have more than one child? Because at the end of that pain is beauty. Why do I constantly go through relationship after relationship when the man has the potential to put his foot in my ass, again and again? Because I know once I finally cry it all out, exorcise the pain, I'll be a bigger, beautiful, stronger me. I'm gonna be wiser, smarter and I'm gonna have something totally different to offer the next man. And women love being in love. We'll chance the pain for the love. And not every brother is gonna bring you pain. You'll more likely get some positive knowledge. Then again, no matter how we break up, we're gonna mourn.

If I'm in a relationship for three years and we break up, I'm gonna wallow. I will throw on a slow song so I can sit there and cry. But I'm lov'n every minute of it. In a sick way, I'm lov'n every minute of it. I wanna talk about it with my friends. My friends will cry with me. I wanna go off and think about all the good things that happened. All the bad things. I wanna cry because tears cleanse. Women wallow because it brings about some type of strength, some type of enlightenment. You see things differently afterward. You're renewed and you're a better person. It's like you're born again. And being a better person comes from the relationship being healthy. The union overall was positive. It wasn't some ol' nigga kick'n my ass, got two other girls pregnant type shit. But the two of you knew you just had to part. It may have been for personal differences or personal growth, but every move was positive. It just also hurt. You're still friends, and you may even get back together down the line, but as it stands the two of you are no longer the couple. I wanna cry now. You're no longer runn'n to your girls 'bout "my man." Oh, we love to be able to say that. "My man." To have someone. To love and be loved. It's just a good feeling. We treasure relationships. That's why we wish brothers would pay attention and listen up. We don't want to wash our hands of you.

What finalized it. What really brings home the hurt is when you see him with another sister. Ohh, we're in pain. That's when we really wallow. You know he's moved on. Is she really what he needs? Is she better for him than I am? We don't even know the sister, and she's every kind of bitch, and whatnot. She could be the coolest, most rightist sister for him, but that was our man. *And* we're like, why isn't he mourn'n the breakup? Why is he with another girl so fast? Then you can't help but laugh. Men are a trip. You can still love us, remember us, but you can move on like it's nothing. That's a difference we just have to accept, and I love you for it. In the end, I'm happy for your progress. Usually, after we've found another love. And we'll still always love you too.

Men and women are different. Once you strip all the things we have in common, books, movies, music, and just sit there, you can see we're different. That's where the beauty of sex comes in. It becomes exploration. It's a reunion.

I feel before you have sex, the two of you should sit down, meditate, breathe together, bathe together, eat together. Court each other.

THE COURTING PROCESS NO LONGER EXISTS. THAT IS SO SAD.

We need to bring back the courting process. My father was married to my mother for over twenty years. They had a long courtship and a long and beautiful marriage. It was here in the heart before it was here in the genitals. This lasts only thirty minutes. This, right here, the heart, love, is ongoing. It's always happening. So when we have sex, it's because of love, and when we don't, when I just want to hold you, it's because of love. And the sex and the holding are equal. I get complete satisfaction out of both. This love right here is always happen'n. So once you capture the heart, the lovemaking is just the enhancement.

Our problem is we think the sex will enhance the love. No, the

love enhances the sex. People think once we do it, all the other shit is gonna come. Sex should be the last thing that happens. It's the topper. It's the climax to a beautiful relationship. It's the dénouement.

Let me make one thing perfectly clear. Let me direct this to sisters because we like to disillusion ourselves with a passion.

Either the nigga is gonna call you back or he's not. Either he's gonna fall in love with you or he's not. Ain't no third way about it. Don't sweat him, don't hound him, don't make yourself look like a fool.

A brother will say fuck this shit and he's moved on. Find out what he wants and what you want. If you want something more than what he wants, you gotta push it along.

If you know, at this moment, guys are shallow, at this moment before they find their true selves, their true heart, if we know that right now men are satisfied with sex and only sex, you have to withhold the flesh and work on the non-sex. At this point he'll gladly take it and step.

But also, as shallow as guys are, they know the difference between you giv'n them some ass on the first night and you taking them on a spiritual journey. Taking them on that journey that will begin to open their sleep'n world. We have to introduce them to themselves. If we do that right, they will never be the same.

If you take him on this spiritual journey with sex, he will not approach intimacy the same for the rest of his life. Or if he does, he'll know that there is a deeper level to sex. He'll know there's a difference between sex, mak'n love and fuck'n. If you two run your course and at the end go your separate ways, the next sister he hooks up with, if she's not on the deep women's level she should be, he'll be remember'n you. He'll be like, "It was so much more with my last love. It was deep, it was spiritual, it was like seeing God. We made love. We made magic. Now, this stuff here, what we're do'n, I don't wanna do anymore. My last lady, hey, I really love her. I see that now. Let me go back." It does happen. It hasn't happened to me, but it happens. It's like, you set up this standard and people will not settle for anything less. He'll do what I just said, he'll soon leave her, or he'll try to introduce the sister to this whole time, essence, love process.

So let him see that you're a God–knowing, self woman. A spiritual woman who requires a spiritual process toward the act of intimacy. Toward this act that is only an enhancement of the spiritual intimacy you have developed.

Whether the brother is bad in bed is not gonna make a difference. The brother I'm see'n right now, he's not the best, but I like him. Up to now I've had a best, but it's not like this brother can't get better. With sex you can definitely get better. Especially when it's an expression of love. I'll even say if he never got better I can still be with him, because the more I'm around him the more I like him. I already got to the point of liking him because we went through the process of courtship, getting to thoroughly know each other, and I like this much so far. There's enough of that to override the lack in sex. We became emotionally intimate first. I can't see me not be'n with this brother because he's not good in bed. And I'm not even say'n he's not good, because he's good, but I've had great. And I think we can be great. It all takes time. But then, you can't compare. That's another place we go wrong. We can't compare. We can only communicate what we like and work from there. How do we know our current man is not good in bed? Is it because you're compar'n him to a man who just happened to be a freak and he just turned you out? Did he have a big, big dick, and that's your definition of what's better? What are our standards? You have to accept each person for themselves.

Maybe he lacks romance, and you like romance. That's what I mean by not good in bed. So all I have to do is add some romance with whom I'm seeing. It's not about the number of orgasms you have. "Oh, my man ain't good because I don't have six orgasms like I did with my last boyfriend." That's weak. Maybe it ain't him, it's you. Maybe you just lie there while he brings you to six orgasms. If your man is deeper than that, and you're inactive, he's becoming bored. Of course he'll get his nut and stop. Maybe your last boyfriend didn't care if he was humping a corpse. If you demand eight inches and your man is four, what are you gonna do? If you're that shallow, I guess you'll have to leave.

Brothers need to understand a woman makes herself come. The man just helps move it along. The woman positions herself into an orgasm. You know when a woman says, "Don't move. Right . . . right there." She's help'n you a helluva lot. So, to say, "not a good lover," I could be talk'n about foreplay. Passion. Afterplay. Romance. It's much more to the act than in and out.

There are three types of men. There's the man who has this enormous penis. He has to let you know he has an enormous penis, as if sight alone couldn't tell you. This type bangs the shit out of you. You're in excruciating pain and can't wait for the shit to be over, and you'll never see him again. At least not sexually. At least not if you're me.

Then there's the nigga who's in it for the nut alone. He's selfish, not at all thoughtful, don't care if you come or not, he doesn't care. He leaves right after and don't even say bye. I also won't be seeing him again.

Then there's the brother who is the true lovemaker. He knows sex is an art. This is the man who will take the time to caress your body, suck her breast the right way. Put the oil on you. Tickle your toes. Break out the whipped cream and strawberries. He's do'n it for you. He knows he can't beat the response he's about to get from his woman. For her, he's gonna take his time. He's gonna take thirty minutes to explore you. To feel you out. Then it's on. You can't feel me out if you take off my clothes and slam it right in.

The process of foreplay needs to be gotten back to, just like courting, and just like romance. You have to take the time. With relationships, you have to take the time. With sex you have to take the time.

If you're not a passionate person but are mak'n the effort, I will really appreciate that. To know you're not totally in it for self, you're also in it for me, makes me happy. The same as I'm in it for you. That's what it's about. Different positions, oral sex, allowing the other to rest. You're do'n things for each other because of how you make each other feel. It's no big thing. You want to do it. You don't feel complete with this person unless everything is done. You already feel complete emotionally, you now want to feel complete physically.

You don't feel you're mak'n any special effort. You know you're do'n what you're do'n because the other likes it. It makes you feel good to make them feel good. When you feel, "This nigga don't deserve me to be do'n this for him," it's time to say good-bye.

I've been read'n a lot of Henry Miller lately, and I'll always go back to his book *Sexist*. He says that men would be much better within relationships if they realized, all the emotion and love, affection and adornment, whatever the woman is producing in you, she has the capabilities to produce it in the next man. However she is showering you with maximum love and attention, she can do with the next man. She can make him feel just as special. So, it's you, but it's not you. It's a woman's nature. We can take our nature elsewhere. In essence, stop tak'n us for granted. The same for the woman. She has to also realize, the way this man is mak'n you feel, he is quite capable of mak'n the next woman. We think it's totally us. "Oh, I got this nigga whipped." People do because they wanna do, and because they think you deserve it. Once they figure out you don't deserve it, you will no longer see that person. They will be out of your life and on to the next. I want to adore and worship your God-self because you deserve it, not only because that's what I want to do according to my nature. I want it to be as mutual as it should. Don't get big-headed with what I'm doing. That's not Godlike, and I can just as easily stop.

To those who feel they can handle open relationships, he's seeing two people, she's seeing two people, it doesn't work. That does not fall under the category of "I have a special person in my life." If you did, you wouldn't feel the need to see anyone else. That falls under "I'm gett'n all the shallow play I can." What's go'n on is you really don't feel deeply about the first person you're with. If you did, you wouldn't have this open date policy. You may like each other and all, but you're not deep. The person has touched you only on the surface. That's what's go'n on today. We're so shallow, we don't feel deeply. How can we have two, three, ten sex mates? Where does the deep development with one person come in? It doesn't. Everybody's "fucking friends." You hear, "Oh, we fuck, but we're just friends." "Friends that fuck." Give me a fuck'n break.

Of course all this is encouraged by Mr. Mister himself. We're play'n by his rules, and we know it doesn't work. Although we may claim to being friends who have sex, we still manage to become jealous, frustrated and hurt. Eventually we want exclusive love.

And when it's love, I want to spend all my time with you. I want to know all about you. I can't do that if I'm seeing you twice a week because you're with someone else. I don't want to ask this other girl about you, I want to be able to ask you. If you came to me with "Let's stay together, but see other people," I now know, OK, he doesn't love me the way I love him. You can worship only one God.

VI
SloW desCent

I ett

mangerlett, 21

born: '73

born again: '92

Most females will tell you this, and I wholeheartedly agree, rela- tionships have to first develop from a friendship. And a friendship that's just a friendship. First we have to define the original meaning because we've gotten out of hand with that. Not a friendship where the two of you are having sex and you claim you're just friends. Not a friendship where you call each other only when you're lonely, you don't have anyone else to call or when your date falls through. We can't have something where you know you really want more than your so-called friendship, because you'll be physically giving more. It's beyond friendship when you're sexually active with someone. You're carrying it to the next stage. How can you say you're just friends when you're doing things that boyfriend and girlfriend do? You start to develop deep feelings, and then you adjust your term for the relationship. You're now special friends. Intimate friends. You then want a boyfriend, it doesn't happen, and now you're not even associates. All because we're playing with the real definition of something, trying to stretch it into something it's not, and getting burnt in the process.

A friendship is platonic. There can be an attraction, but it's a mature decision that says we know we're not fully compatible to be in a sexual relationship. We don't feel that deeply, we may not be ready for a commit- ment, the intensity and attachment that comes with it. We can't ignore that there are personality differences too important to overlook, and it's best that we just be friends. Friends enjoy each other's company, conversa- tions, advice and opinions. There may be a sexual curiosity, which is natural, we have that about strangers, teachers, neighbors, bus drivers, cousins, but you don't go sleep with them.

I've had experiences where we were supposed to be friends, we thought we'd just have sex as friends, nothing deep, we wouldn't start demanding anything more from each other, but no, it didn't work. The friendship suffered because we became caught up in the sex. The sex became just an activity that dominated the friendship. There wasn't a commitment, and we didn't feel justified in feeling jealous if the other one had started seeing someone. But we did become jealous. We became resentful. We should have stopped our "just-friends sex," but we acted as if we owned each other, we felt we shouldn't be seeing or sleeping with other people if we were doing it, but still, we were saying we were just friends. Well, if we're just friends, then you can't tell me what to do. We had a fight and just like that it was over. Everything. The friendship, the "just-as-friends sex." Everything.

Now I'm upset that we've messed up the friendship. We didn't hook up as boyfriend and girlfriend because we knew we weren't really attracted to each other on that level. We were just sexually convenient for each other. We were just friends having sex and we let ego get in the way. You know, "Who is she?" "So, what's up with him?" This type of attitude. And saying this, not because we really wanted that person for ourselves, but because our ego said "*you* should want to see only *me,* not *I* want to see only *you.*" That's ego. When it's a real relationship, *you* want to see only that person. We didn't feel that way, but our egos felt a variation of that. We just totally messed up the friendship.

When I say be friends first, know that you're friends, but with the perspective of developing something more. You already know you have feelings beyond a friendship. You know you feel that extra attraction. You just have to be mature and make sure the two of you can be all that a couple in a committed relationship can be for each other. You're seeing if you're compatible. Seeing if the two of you can actually be friends and have a relationship. That's a mature approach.

Giving in to blatant sex is a lust thing. We have to use our brain. Since people will have irresponsible sex, my advice, but not endorsement, is to think and use your brain. This is why we have a brain, to balance our lust. Lust says, "Freak him because he's fine and I'd like to have him as my man." Your brain says, "Let me see if we're compatible as human beings first. Since I want more than sex from him, let me get to know him." If that checks out, then you can do the freak. You can't first freak him and then hope for the best. We'll like a guy, want the guy, sleep with the guy, then think he likes us. Think and use your brain.

When do we start to learn from others? GET TO KNOW THE PERSON FIRST. DON'T HAVE SEX UNTIL YOU'RE SURE OF

EACH OTHER'S FEELINGS AND PERSONALITY. Don't do the opposite, get hurt, feel stupid and wonder what happened.

We really need to pay attention, think, use intellect and listen when someone is trying to tell you something that is for your benefit. Whether the person is older, the same age or younger. If a person is speaking from experience, listen. You're being told something so you won't have to make the same stupid mistakes and suffer. I understand the resistance to an older person. We may feel they're outdated and out of touch, but they're coming from a lifetime of experience, and we should especially listen. If the person is the same age or younger, you can't use the outdated excuse. They're speaking from experience. After a week, I shouldn't be saying, "I told you so." As young adults we're still like little children. Tell a child don't touch the stove, it's hot, you'll get burnt. Does the child listen? Two minutes later you're running cold water over his hand.

If you can one-night a man with no regrets, feel no emotional ties, you just want to satisfy the kitten, I think you've become like a man. You've lost your sensitivity as a woman, and I wonder if it's due to some man in your past. If I'm the exception, and if this is the new-age woman, well, then I'm from the old school and this is how I feel. I have to know you first. I have to develop a human relationship with you first. I have feelings. I have a heart.

After you sleep with someone, we shouldn't be wondering if he's gonna ask us to be his woman.

Personally, I'm coming from a Born Again religious perspective, and I let it be known. I'm saved. That way I don't waste anyone's time. This is what I profess. Sex is not happening unless that person and myself have created a special bond. A bond that comes from the two of you growing together and really getting to know each other. First mentally, and then later on physically, once you decide "This is the person I want to have as my eternal soul mate," and after a legal bond is made. I say this because the Bible says respect the magistrate of your land. They are the people who ordain your marriage and legally bond you. If you are not joined by a magistrate, it's a sin. It becomes a sin because premarital sex, fornication, is against God's will. This is what it means to be immoral. If we'd like to live moral, we need to know what immoral is. Since premarital sex is immoral, abstinence before marriage is moral.

Many brothers nowadays lack morals. Listen to them talk. They'll tell you they don't have any morals. They're not say'n let's have sex. They're say'n, "Let's make love." That's even worse. They have no concept of the word, and what making love involves. How can we make love when you don't love me? How can we make love when you don't know me? That says you don't have an understanding of morality. You don't have any morals for the word love, or you wouldn't say this to a practical stranger.

Number two, you're using this statement as a line. You hear women appreciate sensitive men, and so you come up with this sensitive-sounding lie. Do you mean you wanna bone? I think that's what you mean, and that's a waste of my time. It's a waste because the sex wouldn't be built on anything. There is no foundation for me to justify hav'n sex in this manner. Sex is not the foundation for love. That's just lett'n off lust. If you're the type who will jump in the bed to let off lust, then that's fine for you and the person you're with, but you're creating sin. For me, I will wait until I'm married. I'm Born Again. I respect the Bible. I believe in the Bible. I believe I've relieved myself of all the pain, hurt, games and lies.

The fear that the sex may be bad, and you don't buy a pair of shoes without first trying them on, is an excuse. Sex is up here before it's down here. It's mental before it's physical. If I'm in love with you, there ain't gonna be too much that you can do that I'm not gonna like. Whatever you do, I'm like, beautiful. It would be just great. Ain't no way we could be just totally whack. If so, there are books, therapists and our personal communication of how we can make things better.

We make up these excuses to counter the Bible, but after you have no more excuses, you're faced with the plain truth that you're committing a sin and going against the Word of God. You cannot say you believe in God if you don't believe in His Laws. You consciously make the decision to disobey. And if you really believe in God, the Bible and His Word, then you believe you will suffer the consequence of committing a bold-faced sin in the face of God. Just as I believe in heaven, I believe in hell. Salvation and damnation.

I've heard the rational, "What if you love the person? What if you can see yourself marry'n them? You trust them, and they trust you, what's wrong with becoming intimate?" If it's all that, and you believe in God, what's wrong with waiting? What's wrong with show'n each other a committed, monogamous expression of love? I used to say those same things, but a sin is a sin.

If you truly feel this is the person, what's wrong with waiting? You marry this true, real committed love, and you remain true to God. What's wrong with giving that special gift of intimacy only to your husband? If you two are so much in love, what's wrong with giving each other that special expression on the most bonding and loving night of your lives? If this is what should be your *one and only,* why not give the *one and only* something that you haven't given to any others? Shouldn't we want to separate something so intimate and loving from many people to one person, the one we marry? That to me is the ultimate. Making love is the ultimate, so why not save it for the ultimate commitment of bonding with the ultimate person? Besides, I'll go back to saying any other way is a sin.

Even if the Bible said it was OK, the act is so special I'd still wait until that special occasion. I'm also trying to show that you don't have to have sex with just anyone. Bible or no Bible. Why not treasure something so once in a lifetime? Why not put a special price on yourself and your love, and not just give it away? Bible or not, we need to change how we approach sex because it's hurting us.

Guys today, with their behavior, turn you totally off. You're so turned off you become dulled to even think'n about want'n to do anything with them. The way they come at you makes it easy to wait. By waiting, you know you'll have someone that isn't like the rest. You'll have someone who respects the Bible.

My body is a holy temple. When I do things like drink alcohol, when I feed my flesh, when I smoke, do drugs, fornicate, I am tear'n down my flesh. I violate my temple. It's no other way to look at it. If we are not married in God's eyes, we won't be having sex. I know the flesh is a weak thing, and we carry it with us twenty-four–seven, but you just have to not put yourself in situations where you feel you'll be tempted. It's hard to say abstain if you're in love with someone. You just want to give yourself to each other to show how much you care and love each other, but you have to wait. You have to wait and show how much you love God. I can testify that I regret every time I had given myself to a man. Even though I said I was in love, I'm still not married. I could have waited to see if our love was truly that special to the point of marriage, and then present myself to him. And, as I look back on it, it really wasn't all that.

The sex really wasn't all that. I mean, I've had some, ohh-ahhs, but I'm not going to die if I don't get any. Some relationships, where it was like love, the sex wasn't all that. The relationships weren't true and neither was the intimacy. It was sex. I regret having that.

It all boils down to a fear of God. You have a testimony to uphold. As a Christian, we believe in the Resurrection. We believe in our Lord and Savior coming back. We believe in heaven and hell. We believe in building for heavenly gifts. The same way many people put a lot of faith and energy into building their material wealth here on earth, believers build on heavenly rewards. What you do down here determines your rewards. There are times when Christians waver and fall off their path, and I keep this in mind and try to stay focused.

As a Christian, I get strength from the Word of God. The Word is your strength. It's your food. The same way you have a daily diet, you get your strength and you keep going, the Word is my daily diet. Many Christians become weak because they haven't been building upon their spirit man. To make sure I build up and maintain my spirit man I read my Word, study it and keep my prayers. This allows me to gain knowledge and devotion to God. The Bible says, "My people are destroyed for their lack of knowledge." I wish to be maintained. You destroy yourself when you don't know. You don't know because you don't read what you should be reading. Not reading the Bible, you become weak and your mind becomes open to negative influences. This is what happened to me about a year ago when I met this guy. I look at what happened as a test. It was a test that I failed. Many times God tries us. He places obstacles before us that we must bear and overcome. My spirit man was weak. It was weak because I wasn't building on it. I wasn't keeping up with my readings, and I fell. I went out and said I want to find out about other religious beliefs and other religious doctrines. I discovered someone who was religious and who had a very influential way of making you see things in a different light. I became influenced by him because I had opened myself to this search. Aside from his spirit, I was into this guy as a woman attracted to a man. I gave into the flesh and became totally convicted. Conviction is a self-condemning thing. You feel bad for what you've done and you go into a state of repentance. Although I was searching, I was helped, because after it happened, I immediately knew that I was wrong, and that only the Bible is the Way of the Truth and the Light. It was as if God let me know, I don't have to search. He was there for me all the time. I just had to look to Him instead of elsewhere.

I was curious. I was in doubt of what I was doing, believing and learning, and I wanted to make sure I was doing the right thing. It was a test. The feeling of doubt and my initial desire for this person was so strong that it had to be a test to make me go through the process of enlightenment. If I could say, "Wow, that person looks good. I'd like to get to know him intimately. His belief, his character and his body, nah forget it," then that's not a test. If I could dismiss the whole thing just like that, that's not a test. I had to experience the step-by-step process. I became unsure of my faith, but now I am sure. I thought I may see the difference of another's belief, practice that belief and be satisfied. What I learned was you can't waver from God. You can't waver from the knowledge that you should be building on. I know I don't have to worry about ever straying again. It doesn't take too many times to find out fire burns.

My belief and faith suppress my feelings of the flesh. Once you go through conviction you feel so bad about yourself, about how you endangered your spirit man, you no longer succumb to the flesh. You feel you must prove your belief and faith. Your feelings of the flesh will be subdued by your rededication to God. This also betters your spirit and lifts you back up.

The guy I'm seeing now, I spend the night with him all the time. But he worships God, not the flesh, so it's no problem. It ain't easy, it is hard at times. The other day we woke up and I said to myself, "Mmm, sure wish I could, just for five minutes." But I turn to the Truth and let it go. It's not a sin to be tempted. The sin is in the action. Of course you're gonna have desires, but your knowledge will overcome your desires. It may sound frustrating, and maybe at times it is, but I think I'd be more frustrated by giving in and knowing I committed a sin.

When most females come on their cycle they get the three H's. Hungry, Hot and Horny. You're always hungry, you're always hot and you're always horny. So when I woke up that morning, I was feeling and fighting one of those H's. I just got up and went home. When that happens I just pray and exert my energies elsewhere. I can deal because I know I'm not going to surrender to temptation. Why go through the same thing over and over again? Why go through conviction over and over again? I've already surrendered to God.

God has so much in store for me. I feel that if I just wait, things will come. I'll just occupy my time doing His will, live straight and keep going, He'll take care of me. He knows that I'm a growing young woman and that I have wants. I know He'll take care of them in due time, when He knows I can handle them. It's like, I don't have to take this business into my own hands. I don't have to wail, "Oh, I need a man." I'll have one when I can handle one. Once I'm able to become fully responsible for myself, I can become responsible with having a man in my life. And to have a spouse is a full responsibility. It's not the little running around we do with each other, having a new partner every month or so. When God knows I'm ready for something serious, He'll send me something serious.

Most of the females I talk to say things like, "Damn, you're wait'n till you get married? Who's gonna want it?" Some will say, "Well, that's good because of AIDS, you should just bank it." The girl who said that then said "that reminds me, I gotta get some more condoms." At least I'm reminding someone to have safe sex. But most would say, "Yeah, that's good for you, but I got needs." But that's not my close circle of company.

My best friend is a Christian also and she practices abstinence. We look at it as not so much abstaining, but just waiting. Waiting until God gives us the man who is gonna treat us the way that we deserve to be treated. Someone who is God fearing, responsible for himself and is ready for a, in the eyes of God, relationship.

With the relationship I have now, it's a friendship with potential. He may be the one for me or he may not. I'm allowing myself the time to get to know this person, and to know myself. I still have much more to learn. I know I have so much more to learn and experience with this person if we are meant to be. I'm not going, "God, is this my husband?" And my flesh is not driving me to hurry up and see him as such. If I think about it, right now he doesn't seem to be the one, but you never know. I do have the privilege of prayer. I can put in requests. Right now I can ask to have positive relationships with people, male and female, and to just let it go from there.

I've noticed in high school, out in the street, sex is all we feel we have. We need to ask ourselves what do I have to offer besides my body? Right now too many of us feel nothing. If we don't have a job, don't have our own home, and not much of anything else, we feel all we have is the pursuit of sex. All we have to offer anyone are our bodies. This is how we feel we have something. We feel we have someone to call our own. This is how we fulfill being needed. But all of this is not centered in any Truth. We don't spend real time with each other, getting to know each other. We may hang out and go to the movies, but that's it. Going to the movies is only so sex can be had later. How many times have you gone out with someone, and at the end of the evening you're looking to go get busy somewhere. The trip to the movie is what you can call foreplay.

I think this unrestrained preoccupation with sex is because no one has told us about salvation. No one has told us that God has so much more in store for us. No one has ever witnessed to our brothers and sisters about the laws of Moses.

Too too many of us were not taught any moral values. Or what we were taught is totally wrong. Being taught to carry a condom in case you have sex is wrong. We should be taught not to carry condoms because we shouldn't be having sex because it is a sin. Dating is no problem. Date as much as you like. My mother tells me to date as many guys as I want. You don't become a whore until you start sleep'n with each and every one of them.

When you have sex with someone, you and that person actually become one flesh. And I'm not gonna become one flesh with you, and one with you, and him, and one with him. I'm not gonna become one with anyone until we're one in the eyes of God.

I want to accomplish some things before I even think of having a child or husband. First of all, I would like to graduate. Once I accomplish what I want, then I'll ask, am I ready to be a wife to someone? Then He may show me what I need. It won't be like a girlfriend of mine who has a boyfriend, yet she dates other people just to make sure what she has with her boyfriend is really what she wants. She doesn't sleep with her dates, she makes sure she sleeps only with her boyfriend, but she'll spend quality time with others. Why spend time with others if you believe what you already have is what you want? If I'm with someone, I'm with that person only. I don't need to date others to make sure I love you. I'll make sure from spending time with you. And she says she loves her man. That's not how I make sure about my love.

When my turn comes, God will introduce me to that one person, and I won't feel the need to spend time with anyone but my potential soul mate. And He can introduce me to two people, at the same time, but only one will receive all of my time. That's the only way I'll know if this person is for me.

I think sisters should treat themselves as if they were royalty. Not conceited, but as if they are royal unto themselves. As a man thinketh so is he. If you treat yourself as royal, you'd project that onto others and be treated accordingly. It's that simple. Change the perception of yourself to a positive, self-respecting individual and have others treat you the same.

Divorces shouldn't have to be. Especially for the sake of the Black family. People are coming together for the wrong reasons and are getting divorces because of it. If we came together as rightful Black King and Black Queen for the right reasons, then there would be no need for divorce. If you and I are together because we know we love and respect and need each other, divorce isn't a reality. When we know we need to build the unity and strength of the Black family, our little princes and princesses, then we will be together till death do us part. There wouldn't be any divorce and me suing you, try'n to take your money. It's as if people get married so they can divorce and get paid.

We have a responsibility to better our Black communities, and I mean us. It's obvious no one else will. No one else should. We live here. We should take on the responsibility. But there we go again not being responsible. Not to our selves, not to our parents, brothers to their babies, and all of us to our communities.

There are so many ways we can help with what little means we have. I'm not waiting for a big pile of money to drop from the sky so I can say we need to build a center here in the ghetto for the unfortunate Black kids. And when the money doesn't drop, I feel there is nothing I can do.

If you plan on having a child, I think we can do a lot by adopting. There are many unfortunate Black children who need to be adopted by fortunate Blacks. That's something that's feasible, you don't need a pile of money from the sky, and in doing your small part you'd be contributing to the whole. "Each one, teach one."

You'll be contributing to the community and maybe your adopted son will make something of himself and be able to build a center for the community. He'll remember what was done for him, where he came from, and have that sense of giving back. Your original intent would be accomplished and be even greater because you adopted a Black child to do it. You got two for the price of one. If you don't have one million dollars to build a center, but you have a thousand, adopt a child, raise him with self-love, pride and commitment to his community. Raise him to achieve high. Raise a genius. A scholar or the next Michael Jordan, but raise him to know himself, and to remember where he came from so he or she can reach back and help.

Brothers need to say to themselves they are Kings and treat themselves as such. Not like little whores running around with only a penis and no body or brain.

I feel every time a Black man respects a Black woman he much more respects himself. The same for a Black woman. If I respect you as a Black man, I'm respecting myself as a Black woman.

We are definitely caught up in a cycle, but it can be broken. It may be hard, but I think with us anything is possible. We've come through several impossibles, let's not stop now. Let's not think we're totally through. There are many more miles to go. So many, it's too far for us to see. If we could take a look at where we've stopped, look at ourselves and see the wrong, we would continue. We would break this cycle.

These Hip-Hop artists who use the term bitch, ho and everything else, and say they are only rapp'n about the bitches and hos they know are not help'n any. They're the ones putt'n out the message and they need to assume more responsibility.

How long can you keep call'n me a bitch? You're rapp'n about the bitches you know, but do you know only bitches? You don't know any self-respect'n women that you can rap about? Or is your own mother a bitch too?

It doesn't matter who you are, you're a bitch. I can be in a rush, on my way to church and don't have time to respond to "Hey, yo," and I'm automatically a bitch. Even if I had the time, why would I respond to "Hey, yo." We have so much to learn, change and overcome, I don't think I'll live to the turnaround. Either we'll have a complete revelation of people waking up, or we'll continue to move at a slow pace of awakening. I pray for the revelation. It's a part of my everyday prayers. I pray I'll live to see it, or at least my daughter. If my granddaughter's saying the same thing I'm now saying, we can forget it. Only God could intervene at that point. Wouldn't that be nice? Wouldn't it be nice to see the day when the Black man and woman can love and respect each other without anyone being a bitch, a motherfucker, a dog, a bastard or anything like that? And we really need God to help us out? God has to come down to make you stop calling me a bitch?

Rappers need to understand it only encourages guys to go ahead and treat a sister who is lost and doesn't have any respect for herself in a demeaning manner instead of correcting her. She'll continue to be a bitch because you continue to call her one. You continue to treat her like a bitch. You don't rehabilitate someone by continuing to feed them the destructive drug. This is what I mean when I say we need to be responsible. Responsible for ourselves and for each other. You would be a real man, a true African, if you came across a promiscuous sister, lost in her knowledge of self and abusing herself, and helped her instead of taking advantage of her. You're a real man if you tried to help correct her self-image and not only tried to have sex with her. Brothers tell each other who's a ho, who they got busy with, and who their boy can most likely get with. That's not only not a man, that's beneath being a human. To selfishly try to have sex with a sister rather than help turn her around is how lost we are on both sides. Just based on our condition alone, I need to be abstinent. I don't need to encourage any more brothers into thinking they can have me under any circumstances other than him receiving God and being serious about his Black sister. All Black women need to be abstinent until married.

If you treat me differently, I will act differently. And when I change myself, don't tell me I think I'm too good. Just last weekend this guy kept talking to my friend in a vulgar manner, say'n, "Nah, fool, this, and nah, fool, that." He kept call'n her a fool and call'n her stupid, and I told him he needs to learn some respect, this is a young lady. He said, "Oh, you think you're too good or something?" I tell myself I'm a young lady, I treat myself as such, why do I have to think I'm too good? If that's your attitude, yes, I am.

I met this guy and we exchanged numbers. I never called him because I just didn't have the time. Two weeks later, one evening, he calls and says, "Where you live, I wanna come over." I was like I don't think so. He says, "Oh, you think you're all that." I'm try'n to explain I don't know him, we haven't talked but once, and just like that he wants to come to my house. If I say yes and the worst happens, then I'm ridiculed about why would I let a stranger in my house. I must have wanted something to happen. The lost sister will be like, OK, come over, stranger. There are more respectable ways we can meet and get to know each other if you're gonna call me two weeks later. I would have loved to have gone out with him, but can we be reasonable? Can we meet at a mutual place? What if I'm the lost one? He gets here and I have him set up. He don't know me. How would he accept me reading my Bible to him? I would have loved to meet with him. But you have to meet me halfway. Then when I try to talk to the brother about what was wrong, I'm not paid attention to. Of all the good brothers out there, I don't get upset when I come across the ones that are lost. God sends me across their path so I can try to make a positive effect on their lives. Had he met a different sister, he would not have received the light I tried to shed. With me, I believe he had to take in something.

We need to pray. We really need to pray. I know we're much more into the secular and worldly than we are into Jesus, so I don't want to harp on something that's falling on deaf ears. But then again, maybe I should because this is what we need. We need to place God in our lives. Whatever God you want to call upon. Islam, Christianity, Jehovah's Witnesses, whatever. The love and principles are all the same. Finding Jesus is a personal experience. I pray we all find Him, especially knowing that having a relationship with God will help our state of relations as brothers and sisters. If we want any change, it has to start with prayer. Jesus lives, but remember, He did die for us. Let's return the love. Read John 10:3. It'd be too easy to say it. I'd like to encourage people to pick up the Bible.

tonya (part i)

tonya, 23

born: chaste

currently: chaste

The reasons for my still be being a virgin has changed from time to time. In high school, I didn't want the reputation of being a ho. I went to an elitist high school, Whitney M. Young, Chicago, and the clique I was with thought to be sexually active was to be a ho, even if you had a boyfriend. The big AIDS awareness and scare played a part in it too, as the thing not to do. Basically, relationships never lasted and you'd be marked. Reputation was everything at this point. If the guy bragged about gett'n with you, other guys would hound you, and I didn't want to get caught up in that. By the time that fad ended, like my junior and senior year, I still hadn't had sex. I think had I found a guy I really liked, I might have taken that chance, but that boy never came to Whitney M. Young. That would have been someone real down to earth. Everyone at Young was too good for everybody else.

Then, after a point, it became, well, who's gonna be the first? Am I going to lose my virginity to him? Is this guy worthy? The longer it went on, the bigger deal it became, and then I didn't just want to do it. I wanted it to mean something. So I'm going, "Is he good enough for me to lose it to? Am I doing this just to lose it?" It became who, when, where?

Also, my mother had instilled in me that you don't have sex with just anyone. She's a single parent. Things didn't work for her, she basically raised me by herself, and so I had that dynamic work'n for me. I was a little paranoid. I didn't want to get hurt. I didn't want guys com'n on to me, think'n they can get theirs. I was afraid of gett'n pregnant. I knew there were contraceptives, but are any of them one hundred percent? I also knew how irresponsible guys are. They would say they don't wanna use a condom, but don't worry, they'll pull out just before they come. Or, if they used a condom, midway through would take it off so they could get a better feel.

I literally have more friends who said they regret having sex when they did and if they could take back that first time, they would. They say they wish they had waited until they were older and lost it to someone they really cared about, more so loved. I'm in that position today. To not regret having had sex at a immature stage, so I take this future experience very seriously.

I also know how I am as a person. I look to fall in love when I'm with someone. If I don't fall in love, I know I'm not hav'n sex with that person. So, I guess to this day, I've never been in love. How many after they've broken up realized they weren't in love? They may have truly cared for the person, but they can't say they were in love. I want to make sure I'm in love. Like lust, caring for the person and sex are confused with love. I'm not trying to be confused. I can like and care about the person very much, I may even lust for them, but if the love isn't there, then I know I wouldn't be comfortable with the act of making love.

For some, well, really most, the liking and caring for a person is enough to justify sex. I think that's really an excuse, and hormones are the reason. I think people convince themselves of like, love, whatever, after the fact. I know how women rationalize their thoughts and feelings. They'll say they don't like some guy, they don't like anything about him, his looks, his personality, where he's from, nothing. Let that same guy show her some attention. Let him tell the girl she's all that, he really likes her. Let him call every day, take her out, make her feel special, and like she's just the one. That same guy then becomes fine. He then has her. What happened to not liking the guy? If she thought about it, the only thing she now likes is all the attention he's giving her. She still doesn't really like him, but she hasn't told herself this. She should be say'n, I love the attention, but that's it. She fools herself into think'n and believ'n she likes him. Now, we know what's gonna happen to this relationship. And it'll be his fault, right?

Women love attention. All a guy has to do is stay in their face and he'll eventually get her. Even if she has a man, she'll flirt. We don't care how many guys are giving us attention, as long as it's paid, we'll accept it. The day he stops, we'll wonder what happened? Has he found some other girl? Does he think I'm ugly now? Now she's in his face. Now she's try'n to get that attention back. And this is the same guy she once didn't like anything about.

I want to be the one sister who, while she can, avoids all that nonsense. I wanna be the one person who takes the advice from their best friends. I'm not the one to tell you all the dogged-out experiences and lies and deceit. No heart-wrenching stories. No other woman and no mystery babies popping up. I never thought I was pregnant, I never had to have an abortion, and no sweating AIDS tests. None of that. I have a tremendous capacity to empathize, and I'm kept in check. All I have to do is hear the story. I'll pick up the moral of it. I'm arrogant, but I'm not that arrogant to think I'm the one person who'll have the perfect relationship. I'm already accident prone, always have been. I can see myself getting dissed and getting pregnant the first time around. I could be using a condom, the rhythm method and be on the pill. I'd still get caught out there. I'd like to think I've avoided those mishaps by listening, using sage judgment and taking sage advice. If for every story, I constantly hear, "In retrospect, it could have all been avoided, I regret everything," then I know I'm doing the right thing.

People love to think the worst. They'd love to believe that I had some traumatic childhood experience or something. Some deep secret and this is the reason I'm not hav'n sex. People would say, "Well, what happened to her? What happened while she was a little girl? Was she molested?" But, I'm like, no. Didn't you say, if you had it to do over again, you'd wait until a more appropriate and mature time? Didn't you say you'd wait until you felt loved and felt love from the guy? Didn't you say the next time you'd have sex will be with someone you really trusted, respected, felt deeply for, and it was mutual? Well, that's what I'm do'n. We talk all this junk and then we turn around and contradict ourselves. You come across someone who's doing exactly what you say you wish you had done, and now that person has to have a sick background in their closet. I think it's the other people that are crazy. Some people are really out there, and that's why we have all these crazy, emotion-packed, traumatic and tragic-ending relationships. I think enough of us are really under a lot of life's stress and have a lot of adjusting to do with our own selves. To try to involve someone else when we're not yet stable, and at least to a considerable degree stress-free, is what's making for all these bad relationships. We have to be a little more centered and adjusted.

All we do is talk, talk, talk. We talk much shit if you ask me.

I want to be mentally ready for a fully mature relationship, that's all. I'm not sweat'n the sex. If I can't have a mature relationship with sex, I won't settle for an immature relationship just for the sake of sex.

I think I've become old-fashioned. Not that I have this romanticized notion of marriage and wait'n till the wedd'n night, but it will be with someone I genuinely trust, love, care about and

**would want to make love with. Not fuck. Not have sex with, but
make love. Is that really too much to ask?**

Does that sound like I'll be wait'n all my life? Should I settle and go,
well, he says he likes me, let's try and make love? Or be honest, and say,
let's fuck? I can't imagine, at this point, after learning from others, after
developing my convictions, just giv'n it away. After all this time, it's now
built itself up to being a big event. A special event. I sort of now expect the
heavens to part.

On a more down-to-earth level, I have a lot of respect for my body and I
don't want to share it with just anyone. I don't want just anyone or
everyone know'n me intimately. I'm that selfish. You have people walk'n
around, "Oh, I done screwed him, and him, and he has a small dick, he
has an enormous dick. I had him. He can't fuck. He knows how to bang.
He loves go'n down, so I'll be gett'n with him again." You know what I'm
say'n? It's crazy.

I think because I haven't had sex, I can really talk about the quality of
brothers. The quality of the time spent that should exist between two
people. I can tell if a brother just wants to hit it, or if he's with me because
he genuinely likes me. If he's hang'n around, putt'n up a front, hoping to
be the first, or he enjoys my company and wants to be with me just for
that reason. I'll know if he truly respects my abstinence by making no
attempts to pressure me, or if he has another agenda.

You usually find out where a brother is com'n from after two weeks.
That's about all the dedicated time they'll put in if they're just try'n to get
theirs. After that, once he knows he's not gett'n any, he's Casper. If the guy
likes being with you, and you're developing something that's quality, there
are no time restrictions. I'm closer and better friends with some guys than
they are with their own girlfriends. My relationship with them is platonic
and totally social. Our conversations are in depth. Everything is quality. By
being sexually inactive, I really get to know brothers. I get to hear what a
lot of sisters don't. What their own girlfriends don't. Not that they won't
listen, but I think the sex gets in the way when we're sexually active. It
would seem, once we're sexually committed, we're now freer to talk and
discuss things, but I'm learning that's not the case. I caught myself asking
more than once, "Have you said this to your girlfriend?" "No." "Why?" "Ya
know, we talk, but we don't talk all the time." I shouldn't know more
about your man than you. Is it an opposite effect? We become sexually
active and feel too open because of the exposing act? We then feel we have
to obtain some sense of privacy and barely talk? Someone would have to

explain that part to me. My opposite is, I'm not sexually active and so everything is open, revealed and reversed into conversation. Can the two be merged into one relationship? Or does sex occupy so much time, there isn't any room for conversation? If that's the case, people, once again, are not having full relationships. I'd make sure there are days where "we'll just lie here and talk."

I don't have a particular type. I'll date, and I've dated most anyone. The West Coast boys, the New York B-boys. The nerds at my high school, the southern boys, guys from the Midwest. I don't have any particular preference at all. Just be neat and have a nice appearance. Whatever your style, just have it together. There's a nice B-boy look, and then there's that overdone nonsense. You usually can tell when someone is try'n to be East Coast down, they're not from New York, and their look is like, "where are you from?" I can see they're try'n to be from somewhere, but where is the question. I'm like, pick up *The Source,* or something.

There's a cool Cali look, and then there's that too bright, floral, look at me, I'm a rainbow, I can't help but see you. There's the overdone Karl Kani, Cross Colors, Black College Alliance, Urban Outfitters, Gap, Benetton look. We look like walk'n billboards. I'm like how much are they pay'n you to wear all that? I can do my "list of things to buy" off one person. Moderation people. Wear one cool piece, and nothing else. When you have on Karl Kani jeans, Calvin Klein underwear show'n, Timberland sweat shirt and a Black College Alliance skull cap, you're overdo'n it just a bit.

Right now I'm see'n a thirty-year-old African brother. He's attentive, very nice, respectful, and so far I like him. And he's not pressed about the sex. I guess because of his age, he's had his share, he's now matured and it's about the quality of the relationship. Of course he's hinted at it, he's still a man, but once things were established, he was like, cool, and it's been all quality since.

An unexpected thing I've noticed. The younger guys I date, nineteen, twenty, they don't press for the sex like I thought they would. I guess because they think I'm an older woman who says she doesn't want to have sex, and they don't want to appear immature and play themselves, they don't pressure either. Now, the brothers my age, twenty-three, twenty-four, it's like teenage peer pressure. They want to know why I'm waiting,

why not now, you might die tomorrow, it's gonna get old and dry out, and
then nobody will want it. I've heard it all.

Then back over the fence, the older, thirty age range, are not pressed.
They state that they're ready for a true relationship. When I told the
brother I'm see'n I wasn't ready for sex, he seemed almost relieved. He's
even more open with me than I am with him. Everything is respectful and
on a mature level. That's what I look for. That's what I tolerate. You'll
never hear me say I'm dat'n someone who's too possessive or too demand'n, because if they're that way, I'm not dating them. Too cheap, too
egotistical, too selfish, too insensitive, too insecure, I'm not dating you. If I
see you're like that, you can never consider us to be dating. We can be
friends, and you'll know where we stand. That way, if, over time, you're no
longer too this or too that, we can then date with an eye toward maybe this
is it. It's a lot of fine brothers, who, if only they weren't too something,
they'd be good to go. By staying friends, one day they may say, "You know,
I used to be a real asshole." Then I'm like, "Let's go on a date and talk
about it."

I do like a touch of arrogance. I'm a bit arrogant, and I like that in a
man. Not an overpowering, I'm always right, I'm better than the whole
world arrogance, but a self-assured, confident arrogance. A sort of cocky
but likable arrogance. Some guys are too cocky and it's a turnoff.

I like openness and honesty. The brother I'm dating is that. He's always
frank and encourages it from me. He has a conservative look, maybe a bit
more gold than I'd wear, but he's from the motherland, what can I say.
Some of them get here and go overboard with what they think is the
American look. They get our movies late, like last year they got *Superfly*.
Hence the white pimp shoes, white socks and gold. The Latino brothers
wear those white shoes too. What's with the white shoes? Winter, spring,
summer, they don't care.

I think one gold chain is enough. My guy will have on two or three. I
think one button open on your shirt is enough, but he'll have two or three.
Don't let us go to a club, that's a definite three buttons, but I like him, he's
cool. No fireworks or anything, but we just started dat'n. So far, it's quality
and positive.

I haven't been through sexual relationships that bind you and make you
speak volumes on men and their sexual shortcomings. I can speak only on
the good, quality relationships I have with brothers. I understand what
you go through as Black men in this country, and it makes me love and
support you all the more. Now, if you're do'n bad in the bedroom, as I
know you are because I have many girlfriends, I can only side with them, I
can only say get it together.

From how I relate to brothers and how I know them to relate to the sisters they're intimate with, I wonder why does the sex have to that drastically change everything in how we relate? Is it that deep?

Is it just all that?

It sometimes makes me wanna do it just to see what's up. See how much this brother, with whom I have deep, quality conversations, will actually change. Just like that. Just because of male genital entering female genitalia. I mean, what's up?

It's me. I haven't done any near sex, dry fucking, heavy petting, or nothing in the way of that. I haven't been in love or deeply emotionally attached. I'm just ignorant. I expect the type of quality relationships I now have with men to continue on that level once we're sexually active. If I love you, and for whatever reason we break up, I don't believe I'll trip. If we're all quality, I expect any breakup to be civilized. I know I can be hurt, and I do cry, but I think if it's all quality, humane and decent, which is how I pick my friends, what will I be tripping off? I won't trip off him cheating, which seems to be the main reason people go crazy. I'll just uncommit myself and move on. If that's not the reason, anything else should be personalities not mixing well, too bad, we'll move on. Maybe we can just be friends, maybe not. If the mix is that bad that we can't even be friends, then we won't be friends. But as of now, the way I befriend people, how would I hook up and be a girlfriend to a personality I can't even be friends with? How would we ever get to that point? I don't think I can be duped that hard.

So, is this what sex does? Change people overnight? Or are we just hooking up with people we don't bother to know anything about. The men I know better than their girlfriends, that's not gonna be me. No other girl will know my man better than me.

I think all this time on the outside has allowed me to see the big picture, what needs to be done and how we should be going about having healthy relationships. What I've come up with seems so simple. Just get to know the person, and that takes time, and don't do anything unless your heart is in it. I have sexual urges, but I'm waiting for my heart to get the urge also. And my brain will give my heart the OK once I know the person and our personalities are like lock and key. If not, my brain will tell my heart this is only a friend, love him like one. A friend, to me, does not equate making love. It's a combination of these factors. When we go on only one, we see what the results are. The big picture tells me to learn from others' examples.

I feel I've stumbled across this insight. Like I kinda just fell into virginity. Had I not kept putting it off, deciding who and where, and not having sex because abstinence was the in style, I don't think I would have had the chance to develop all these male quality friendships. Friendships which along the way and in time showed me that this is what it's all about. This first, then the emotional attachment, then the intimacy. An inclusion of all three. That's what people weren't doing. It's obvious the breakups involve all three, but the initial coming together doesn't. You can't let one act itself out without the others being involved.

So, I'm just here waiting for my brain and heart to speak up. My third urge is speaking so well, it's fluent, that's how well it's speaking. We sometimes keep each other up at night holding conversations. Arguments that I always win. No, it's not that deep. When the heart isn't in it, the other urge isn't all that strong. It doesn't rule. My brain and heart rules. It speaks the truth of what's best for me. Sexual urges are without thought or logic. You can't listen to it. That's like, ooo, the fire is pretty, touch it. But someone else or your brain tells you better. I listen and my brain is very logical. It says making love is better. You don't love anyone at this moment, so everything is put in order. So, like, I'm a lady in waiting.

tonya (part ii)

tonya, 23

born: chaste

currently: virtuous

I've got news. I'm not a virgin anymore.

Excuse me?

I'm not a virgin anymore.

The African brother?

Yep. It was the right time. And this timing between now and when we last spoke is just ironic.

I'd say, like a mutha. Did you come, just kidding, don't answer that.

Actually, I did. It was nice. It was very emotional. It was deep feelings that I developed for him and it just seemed like the right time. It happened. And to be honest, it may sound strange, but, in a sense, I was kind of us'n him to get over the hump.

Wait up. Only two weeks ago, you gave me a mature person's development of morals and values, and now you're say'n just to get over a hump?

I didn't go against what I originally said. I did it knowing how deeply I felt for him, and he for me, it was natural. It was right. It felt right. I wasn't apprehensive or second-guessing myself. I may have overromanticized me losing my virginity a bit. But the feelings and respect were there. It felt natural and right. My brain OK'd it.

What about your heart?

It wasn't fireworks and violins. It was romantic, but I think I overhyped the moment of truth, you know? I don't have any regrets, which is good. I don't wish I hadn't done it. I also don't wish I had done this years ago. I believe my time was now.

So your heart wasn't in it.

It was in it, but I'm not in love. That's why I say I think I overromanticized the whole thing. It could have been "Wait until the wedding night," although I never held myself to that. I said it would be something near to it, and it, well, it exactly wasn't, but it just felt right.

And you said to get over the hump?

I admit, in the back of my mind, since turning twenty-one, I've always felt, damn, I am getting older and older. When, how and why am I going to lose my virginity? But, I maintained that it would be under my set of values. I'm admitting that since I didn't feel the deep love I said I would, I have to admit, part of me said, fuck it, enough feelings are there, I know his personality, do it.

So you fucked, you didn't make love.

I'm now seeing everything isn't so black and white. There's a lot of shade and complexions. Not having had sex, it's easy to simplify things, but I still maintained and incorporated more of what I believe than not. At least I'm not fooling myself. I'm not forcing any love into this picture.

You say that now.

I know myself. I just didn't mention my feelings about this hump thing that proved to be an important factor. Had I done that, it would seem less contradictory. I just should have added my feelings about it. I know I didn't. It's because it sounds kinda amoral. To do it cause you wanna get it over with. I was trying to convince myself that that wouldn't be a factor. So what does that say? Trying to keep it out of my mind, it built up and took over. Granted some of the brain and heart was there. But "get it out the way" was a fourth factor that came out of nowhere.

And I'm also not going to sleep around with every man I feel halfway deeply for and know very well. If getting over the hump was part of my reason, I now really can wait again, till I'm in love.

I think the floodgates have been opened. You've gotten a taste. Just wait. You're open.

I don't know. I think that's the safest and most honest thing to say right now. Though I am being honest when I say it will be a genuine situation like what I have now. I haven't really modified my thinking. Here's a man whom I care about. Attractive. Funny. Someone whom I know genuinely cares about me. Loves me, in fact. He's attentive to my needs. We really like each other. The evening was romantic and everything was natural. I just know I'm not in love with him. And no, I'm not say'n that for self-defense or self-protection. I'll admit when I'm in love. The main problem is women fool themselves, telling themselves they love the guy once they slept with him, and here I am stressing that I don't. And I'm not saying it so I won't get hurt, if I was in love and he left me. It would be unfortunate if he turned out to be a dog, but what can I do? But I do know him very well. I don't believe he's gone to all these elaborate lengths just so we can have sex. He played me as if he didn't want it, know'n he'd get it. I'd see through something like that. To be honest, I know he feels more for me than I do for him. Another reason I felt comfortable to sleep with him. I know I wasn't being used. If anything, I somewhat used him.

I know my emotions and I believe I'm being true to them. I'm not tripping. I feel a little closer to him, but in a way that's different from saying I'm now in love with him. If that comes, it won't be because of intimacy.

I still believe people should be friends first, and the love should be there, but I just needed to get this thing out of the way, and it was with someone who cares for me, and I care for him.

Let me cop out and say society did it. I'm plagued with sexual overtones every minute. TV, movies, commercials, billboards, magazines. That Camel cigarette ad. Maybe I'll fall in love, maybe I'll fall out of love. Maybe I'll get hurt, maybe I won't. Maybe we won't have sex again, maybe we will. I'm still virtuous.

Maybe I'll tell him, I'm sorry I used you, but I don't wanna do this again until I feel more deeply for him. Until I can say I love him. Look, I'm just trying to get through the day.

After it was over, he was the one tripp'n. In the car, he was staring at me, smil'n, ask'n me how did I feel? He kept want'n to talk about it. He'd make a lot of women happy. See, I wasn't lying. I have good communication with the men I'm with. So, he was very concerned, and asking questions, getting on my nerves. He told me he loved me. He also told me this before we had sex, but now he was really, "Tonya, I love you." I was like, will you just chill? It's no big deal. My attitude became the opposite of his. It forced him to ask, "Who was the virgin here, me or you?"

I gotta give it to you. Your first time out and you went and got some original, straight from the motherland, Zulu dick.

Well, I didn't plan it. I didn't even realize that. Yeah, that is special. I do feel like I've been baptized. I don't quite, fully feel so African American anymore, you know what I'm say'n.

A couple more sessions call me Nzinga. But it is like getting back. If a Black woman is gonna lose her virginity, it does make sense to lose it to Africa. No dis to my brothers, but not African American, just African. America has taken enough of its share of African virgins.

But I have to put this in check. He keeps mentioning, five to six times a day, that he sees this relationship leading toward a marriage. I ain't even think'n about marriage. I've got too much to do on my own first.

Do you blame him? He's thirty. Stable in his career. AND! you were a virgin! AIDS-free virgin. He was your first. That's every man's dream, to marry a virgin! Fuck around all your life, then when you're ready to settle down, get you a virgin! Only it never really happens like that.

Be that as it may, I won't be gett'n married.

You'll break his heart. He may be the one go'n fatal.

A Black man will always be there. And I do mean Black man. I wanna add this. I feel as a Black woman, I have a commitment to self-preservation. I know that I'm a positive person. I know that I'm going to be successful, and I plan to be a successful member of the Black community. I plan to be a role model for young Black children. I believe it's important for them to see a successful Black family to help shape their aspirations. It's important for them to see a Black family, period. A husband and a wife. We know about the single-parent phenomenon, so just to see a Black husband and wife is important. When you talk about highly visible successful Blacks, movie stars, athletes and politicians, many are interracial. What message does that send to our children? I'm an adult and that makes me wonder. Do I have to have a white husband on my arm to become successful?

The Black family is nonexistent. If we really want to be successful, it begins with the Black man and Black woman. That's success right there. I want to marry a Black man.

I don't think I can set the best example for Black children, trying to show the success and beauty of the Black family, if I walk in the room with a white man on my arm. I want to send a different message. I want to be a successful Black businesswoman, a successful Black wife, a successful Black mother, with a successful Black husband and family. I want Black children to say, "I want to have a career like she has, a house like she has, and a family like she has." And that family will be all Black, and proud. Peace.

VII
trepidation

Yaga

yaga, 18

don't mess with texas

sophomore

On the college tip, I believe relationships are positive. They're worth gett'n into. But on the flip side, I also know they're fucked up. They're positive, but in a fucked-up sort of way. Regardless of what happens, you will learn something. Every person you meet and deal with, good or bad, you will learn something. That's how it can be positive in a fucked-up sort of way. If the relationship was bad, you'll still learn something and can use it as a positive for the next time. You won't be, or shouldn't be do'n the same dumb shit again and again. Either case, you won't forget how you were treated. Good or bad. You won't forget how you were dogged or how you were worshipped. You should come out knowing what you will accept or reject. What you won't tolerate or what you'll be patient with. You will have more of a prepared outlook. Your shit will be more together. We should be learn'n from any relationship. Not just go'n through them to say we have somebody. Fuck that, it ain't about that.

On the real, it's time to stop all the bullshit and it's time to come face-to-face. Look me in the eye and be a man. Tell me what you want, what you're about and what you expect of me. I'll look you dead in the eye and do the same.

I mean, I'll allow for some dumb shit to pass on both parts. It's like when you're a freshman, you're stupid and naive. You go for the smooth shit and you get caught out there. You're eating the shit up because you're new to the atmosphere, you're new to this flavor, you want to hurry up and get your shit on and you might not be so quick to the game.

As a freshman, you may not think or believe you're naive or be'n taken advantage of, but, don't worry, you are. You may have just come off that "I was a senior, I had it go'n on in high school" kick, but now you're back to be'n the dumb, lost, new, naive freshman. I don't care how hard you try to play your shit off, you're still a freshman and you're much vulnerable to game. Unless you already live in this city, you know this place because you have people that go here and it's like you're a senior, unless you already know the atmosphere and operations, you're vulnerable. Everyone else is look'n at you as young and dumb. They're look'n at you the way you looked at your freshman in high school when you were a senior. So, it's time to wake up. When a brother kicks it, you're just a prey. You're fresh, new and temporary. But that's to say, after you wise up and gain some knowledge and know-how, you'll see things in terms of how dumb you were, how much you've grown and how positive everything was. Whether this process is right or wrong is not the point. If wrong, yeah, I'm down for change, but in the meantime, let me be a little prepared. Let me know that I'm viewed as naive, get-over-on-freshman so I won't so easily be gotten over on. Let me not be so arrogant in think'n my shit don't stink. Let me be prepared in know'n that I'm in for one learning experience. Let this be a warning to all freshman sisters. Your freshman relationship may not be all gold. Especially if he's a sophomore, a junior or senior. Anything but an equally lost freshman, but even they get here and immediately try to Mack, but whatever, keep your eyes and ears open. So if shit hits the fan, you don't have to cry as long. You'll know it's just ritual. Don't take it personal. Welcome to college. It's all a part of your education.

The first thing we need to do is speak up. Relationships shouldn't exist in silence. When there's nothing but sex, the relationship is silent. When there's nothing but movies and then sex, the relationship is silent. Relevant issues aren't discussed. This is college now. When you get into a heated discussion with your boyfriend or your girlfriend over politics, over the economy, sexism, racism, and you've exhausted yourselves to the point where you just want to fall asleep afterward, that's when you have a balanced relationship. It's not silent. You're able to discuss, talk and communicate. You're able to enjoy each other's company just for the sake of being in each other's company and when you wanna fuck, you fuck.

I don't want a boyfriend who's gonna call and say nothing but, "Damn, my team lost." Or "Yo, what you do'n? I'll be right over." Come over and the sex is on. Relationships where you're just hav'n sex, out of here. That superficial just-sex relationship should have been exhausted your sophomore year, high school. If you wanna regress and act like an excited little freshman who's never been out, you're awed by this new atmosphere, you're hyped by all these new brothers and you just have to go buck wild, well, then go for yours. Get it outta your system and then settle down to business. This is college. I keep say'n this is college, because people are gett'n buck from day one, till their last day, and I ain't too sure about that. To see juniors and seniors at the clubs every weekend, and on days during the week, I'm like, damn, either they're that smart and got their shit together, or they ain't learn'n a damn thing. I can't do it. Maybe I'm judging people by my standards and they can do shit like that. Well, more power to you. Maybe I'm overanticipating how hard these four years will be, and it's not really like that. Maybe it depends on your major. Without naming names, you do see a certain school represent'n more than any other during every club night. They know who they are. Liberal arts. Fine arts. School of business. In that order. Oh, communications ties with fine arts.

If you're mature enough emotionally, and you only want to have sex, speak up and communicate that. Make sure there's an understand'n that you're not look'n to get deep. The problem comes when people don't say what they mean. They talk this open relationship shit, and leave you think'n it has strong possibilities of turning serious. Bullshit. Open relationships don't work. If the girl is agreeing to it, she's front'n. She really wants a relationship, she really likes him, but if the guy is say'n he only wants it open, the girl will find herself agreeing to this crazy shit. It's only a matter of time before she finds herself hurt.

If the guy is talk'n open relationship, he's simply talk'n about hav'n the chance to get more ass. Get it, and have you agreeing that he can. This is what I mean by "say what you mean." Tell me you want to sleep with me only a good couple of times and be out. Don't sugar-coat it with this open-relationship bullshit. If you say open relationship, I'll say, "Oh, you only wanna sex me and be on to the next girl?" I won't let you do that if you come with this open shit. If you say in a smooth way that you find me sexually attractive and you wanna know if we can do this, I'll respect you more for the honesty, and depending on my attraction to you, we may or may not do this. But if you come with the open shit, and I know I'm sexually attracted to you, I won't get with you because you weren't honest. If you're honest, I'll be like, damn, I do like him, but he just said he wants only the sex and that's it. I just may do it because I want you too. I'll get over the feeling that I wished it could have been more, and I'll just be satisfied with the sex. Be for real with your shit. You may just get what you want, and without hurt'n nobody.

Don't ever agree to an open relationship. Whenever you're constantly sexually active with someone, as in an open relationship, you're gonna increase those feelings you already had to start with. You're now sett'n yourself up for the pain. After he's out and it's over, because he's now open with someone else, as was the agreement, you're cry'n yourself to sleep at night. It hurts. But, hey, look at it in the positive. Now, you don't have to put yourself through it again. Now, you know, open relationships, fuck 'em.

I don't know why we don't act within relationships the way we act when we say we're just friends. It's like that one little word "commitment" makes all the difference in the world. When it's like that we start to take each other for granted. Sex becomes the only form of communication and before you know it, it's soon over. When we're "just friends," we make the effort to stay in touch and keep up-to-date with each other. It's like, since we know the person isn't ours, we make the effort to stay in touch. We don't take the other for granted. We act a little jealous about them being with other people, but we don't let it show. When we're friends, we're more laid back and comfortable. When you're friends, it's all conversation because you're not fuck'n. Now, why can't all that be included in a committed relationship? When there's a commitment, all that friend-act'n shit goes right out the window.

I think, for some reason, we're also afraid of serious relationships. We either purposely don't hook up with the person we like, or we get with someone we know we don't really care for. What are we afraid of? If you like the person and the person likes you, we are now adults, we should be mature about it. We should be able to sit down and say "Yo, this is the deal." Fuck the dumb shit. Explore the relationship. If it doesn't work out, it doesn't work out. What are we afraid of? Getting hurt? We need to grow up.

This is college, we should have educational work to do. We should be about the work. We should want to get the bullshit about gett'n with someone out of the way so we can settle into the work. So much time is spent on male-female bullshit that before we know it, we're fuck'n up our grades and we're fuck'n over our parents' money that got our ass here.

This safe little college world, with nothing but young Black men and young Black women, has you oblivious to the real world. This guy-girl atmosphere can have you blinded to what you should really be do'n to prepare yourself for when you get outta here. By your senior year, you realize the real world is two semesters away, you wake up, and you're like, "Let me get serious. Let me get a résumé together." Graduation day and you're formulating a résumé. We need to be serious now. Senior year, you're also like, "Damn, that person I fucked over two years ago, I think that was someone I could have really cared about."

This uneven ratio fucks up things. Guys are about, "I wanna get with that honey and that honey," and the girls are hip to it. It's like, why get serious if I know he's work'n on a ratio? Then we're like, if you can't beat 'em, join 'em. I'll get with that cutie and that cutie. Our shit is just fucked up on so many levels. Date rape. AIDS. STDs. Lying, cheating. I just wanna do my homework and be out.

What is with gett'n with a brother because he's frat? Or because she's a Delta or an AKA. That's another thing, that Greek shit. It looks good on paper but what are they really about? All I know them from are parties and step shows. Yes, the chapters have their scholarships for the unfortunate, but what are the undergraduate individuals do'n? All I hear are hi-pitched squeals and dog barks.

Fraternities and sororities have become something where people go to feel like they belong to something. And our need to belong is so strong that we'll go through extreme bullshit, extreme ridicule, punishment, hazing, sleep deprivation and failing grades, just to join a clique. I don't need it because I have my friends, and they're my friends because they didn't have to pledge me and go through extreme bullshit.

I think Greek organizations were cool in our parents' and grandparents' time because the need for racial unity and organizations were needed. We were denied admission and access to other colleges and fraternities, so we created our own. We copied their shit, and we copied it so well that now we exclude certain types of our own, the same way we *all* were once excluded. Some sororities prefer light skinned sisters only. Some frats, pretty boys. Others, dogs. You get in where you fit in.

I have male friends who tell me they're dissed by sisters at parties because they're not frat. So, now we have people join'n so they can get some play. Check the before and after. I bet a frat member can tell you how things were before he pledged and after.

One thing guys need to know is to cool out with the ego strok'n they give women just to get some play. This is another game of ours. The only thing you can take somebody by is their word. Don't say things you don't mean. Don't be fuck'n with our heads. Don't tell us, "You're my one and only," then go run the same routine to the next female. That shit is dumb. Colleges are closed and close communities. You can know everybody in a year. Why would a brother run the same game to two or more different sisters? Your shit is known after a week. Now you can't get with anyone. Now you can't get with the one girl you really like because your game is seen as fake. What you do will come back to fuck you over.

Girls just need to be more aware. I can't say that enough, because I've seen some dumb shit. If he knows you're a stupid female and he can get over on you he will get over on you. It's a shame we can't trust like we should, and when we do people will take advantage of you. It's a shame that we do this to ourselves. You can say love and respect each other, but in the meantime, you need to be aware. Until this great day when we all can trust and not look at everyone like they're suspect, we need to keep watch'n our backs.

We need to open our mouths and say what we expect, want, like, dislike, need, don't need and everything in between. Have that heart to heart. You can't lose nothing. You just may save yourself the embarrassment, frustration, heartache and tears.

If you don't want to come off with a whole bunch of wants and needs, rules and regulations, at least let it be communicated that you're not someone to be gamed on. If you don't say a word and just smile and look like a silly little dumb bitch because of all the wonderful things he just said, you will be walked on. You may as well start cry'n right after he finishes gas'n your head, because you will be dogged. He'll call you whenever. He'll get with you whenever. He'll get rid of you whenever. But if you open your mouth, let him know that you're not some silly bitch, he'll walk away know'n you're a sister to be dealt with seriously. There will be no times for games. He won't be able to call you whenever he wants, fuck you whenever he wants, think'n you'll be ever so happy to hear from him. Fuck that.

Guys need to know that for women sex is internal. Our pleasure source is on the inside and that's how we view and treat sex, as an internal experience. Our feelings, our emotions, our love comes from the inside. Guys' stuff is on the outside and that's how you treat sex, externally. You don't say anything from deep within. You don't emote from within. You don't internalize the relationship as we do.

We can get pregnant, that's an internal experience. Guys can't get anything. The least you can do is learn to empathize. Try to understand where we're com'n from as women. As internal beings. Then maybe you'd accommodate us a little more, a little better. We've accommodated you enough. Too much, in fact. It's now the man's turn to put forth the effort if the Black man truly wants a positive change for us as Black men and women.

Black women have changed enough. Too many of us are now hard. We'll fuck 'em and leave 'em. We'll dis 'em and dog 'em, and we're do'n this know'n that we're just like him. Enough. Black women need to get back to themselves and Black men need to get back to themselves. Internal, sensitive, feeling beings. Yes, men. Men have only to discover it. Girls, too, because all this hard shit has got to go. Fashion is one thing, state of mind and way of think'n is another. Fuck that. Women, let the men be men, and we'll be women. Men, let yourselves become your original selves. If I can't exactly tell you what that is, I can tell you what it ain't, and it ain't hard, indifferent, cold, silent and be'n disrespectful to me. I guess that means your original self is the opposite of these. We have a lot of work to do, that's why I say we have to be serious now.

Use a fuck'n jim hat and you should be all right. If neither wants to bring a child into this world, both should be up on precautions. She should be on the pill, if not, always be with no less than two condoms. He should always be with no less than four.

If she gets pregnant, don't front. If she wants to keep it, be a man. Be a father. Know that you're half responsible for the child be'n brought into this world, so be half responsible in raising and rearing your child. You don't have to marry the child's mother. That's between you and her. But your responsibility and relationship to your child is on you. A marriage commitment to the mother has nothing to do with your responsibilities as a father. Nothing to do with you being a man.

If she's unsure about want'n to keep it, and you know that you don't want to have a child, then express that shit. Don't wait till the baby is born and then act like you don't have a child. If she wants to have an abortion, be there for her. Even if you know you no longer want to be with her, at least be with her during the abortion. Have that much sensitivity. Be that much of a man.

We need to know every time we fuck over somebody, that makes it that much harder for the next person. That next person is gonna catch hell. Or that next person will not receive the fullest amount of affection. Their partner will be too guarded. They'll be more closed in and less inclined to display their feelings. You've heard it plenty of times before. People in new relationships think, "This time I'm not gonna be the first to say 'I love you,' let him or her say that shit if that's the way they feel." Everybody is think'n, "What if he does me like the last guy? What if she does me like the last girl?" Everybody is deal'n with the "what-ifs," and not deal'n with each other. I believe if we took the time to get to know the person, we'll better be able to see the potential of how the relationship can turn out.

Use that sixth sense and intuition. A lot of times we ignore that shit, and then afterward say, "I knew it! Something told me shit wasn't right." Fuck that, pay attention to those vibes.

Those vibes come because you and the person are not verbally saying shit. That sixth sense kicks in because you're not using the other senses. Within that silence, your body, your vibe, your attitude, all your non-verbals are giving off the truth: Something ain't right about this person. Your intuition picks it up, your vibe picks up the other's silent vibe, but you ignore it. You have to pay attention to that shit. Sometimes it's not even intuition, but common sense.

If the person isn't say'n too much, reveals but so much, sees you only when it's convenient, doesn't go out of their way to do much, common sense should tell you this nigga is dipp'n. Something is happen'n. You don't need intuition to say, "You know, something told me this person wasn't shit."

We need to be more truthful. If we were more truthful, despite being hurt and dissed in the past, but came out all right anyway, I believe those second, third times around could be really beautiful. You both would say, "You know, I was also once hurt. I thought I'd close off my deepest feelings to the next person. But you know. You're no different than I am. We're coming off the same boat. The same pain." You both understand each other. You both can sympathize with the other. You both don't want to be hurt again. You both understand pain and disappointment. You both will be more gentle with the other. You won't take for granted what you have. You'll respect what you have and the only way you can come to this point is to be open and honest. Say where you're com'n from. You both may be com'n from the same place. Don't hold shit in and try a new tactic. Something that's not really you and will only make things worse. Being more cold, more hard, more distant, that's not attaching you to anyone. That relationship is on its way out with a quickness.

Every person is different. You can learn from your last relationship and you can learn from a new relationship, but don't treat the new person as if he or she is the last person. They're not. They're a whole new person. And make sure you've gotten over the last relationship. Don't look to replace what you had by jumping into another. That's a big fault of ours as women. We quickly find someone new and haven't completely gotten over the last person. If they call, we may go back. Now, the new person is like, what the fuck? He's hurt and now he'll get with a new female just to get over you. The dog you went back to dogs you again, you call the old guy you replaced him with, he responds, but now the old guy's new girl is say'n what the fuck? She'll now dog her next new man. It's a vicious cycle. What the fuck? Stop the madness.

Relationships are supposed to be good. If people went into them with total honesty, everything really should work out cool. If everything doesn't work out cool, it shouldn't work out for cool reasons. Not for any of that whack shit that exists.

Relationships don't have to be forever. I don't think anything is forever. Especially at our age. We'll go through many relationships before tie'n a knot. And getting married isn't so much find'n the right person as it is be'n the right time. If it's not the right time, you may go through a couple of relationships. If it wasn't for school, I could marry my next boyfriend, but I plan to first graduate, then get married. I expect to have a couple of relationships until the time is right. Then again, the person you're with can force the time, or have you think'n the time is right now. That's when you have to think and say, "OK, yeah, I feel this way about him, but is it practical right now?" If you two really want to get married, what's the rush? Take your time. Make sure you have your shit together, then do what you feel. If you take your time, you may feel differently much later. You'll be like, "I ain't marry'n this muthafucka. What was I on?" You don't have to rush into anything.

Whatever the case, we really need to check out why we're hav'n so many failed relationships. If we understood relationships are meant to be healthy, positive and be a positive growing experience, we'd then have a different outlook about them. We should still be able to be friends with our former boyfriends and girlfriends. Anything else is some of that totally immature shit. So it's time to grow up and start using our God-given brains. Fuck the dumb shit. I ain't got the time.

Wate**r**

water, 19

beantown

freshman

hobbies: surviving

I love the Black race. I love Black men. I believe we have a lot of positive potential and we are bound for greatness. That is how I feel first and last. That is the first impression I'd like to leave you with. Whatever I say is based on that love. We're bound for greatness, but first we have to become great.

I've been here at Black University for one year and literally from day one I've been shaking my head. I've been shocked, surprised, ashamed, embarrassed and disappointed. Coming from where I'm coming from, I felt very lucky to be here. I expected a whole different behavior from us in a college setting. This is a university and I thought I left a lot of the bullshit I see go'n on here behind me.

During orientation, before classes officially kicked, we're taking a tour of the dorms. While the incoming freshmen are inside with the tour, some upperclassman outside has pulled up on one of our group's freshmen and is hav'n sex with her inside his car. The monitors at the front of the building peeped what was go'n on. I know there's no coed visitation, but damn, give me a break. In front of a dorm, in a car. Welcome to college. That was day one and the embarrassment hasn't let up since.

Since being here and knowing that there's no coed visitation, and knowing that young people are gonna find a way to get busy, there's like a tolerance, or more like a no-surprised attitude for some of the stuff that goes on. Behind the hall there's an area with a bench, not very much secluded from people passing by. I've walked across two different couples getting into it. I've embarrassed couples in classrooms after school, rather, I was embarrassed, they were like oh, well, comes with the territory. I've come across people in the library, you name it, let it be the right time, and it's being done there.

Now, everything is a two-way street. I can't as quickly say brothers have no class, because every time I walked past something, I didn't hear yells of "stop, rape!" Sisters are willingly participating. I can also understand, if this is your man and you want to get busy and you can't go to your dorm room, hey, you make do with what's available. I can appreciate a little danger, excitement and being spontaneous. I'm with going for yours right then and there, but there's a limit. A public bench is a limit.

When brothers don't even consider a hotel, and not because they don't have the money, but because they're a cheap nigga, there's something wrong. In the same respect, sisters need to demand it. It's a two-way street. If I say to one of my girls, "Why don't you and your man go to a hotel," and she says to me she never mentions it to him, I can't say, oh, your man is fucked up. I can't put it all off on him. She has to know that she's worthy of more than being hit up behind a school building. She has to know that the quality spots of her rendezvous needs to be upgraded. There are hundreds of hotels around this place. They're here for the students, they're student priced.

Twenty-nine ninety-five a night is student priced. If your man can't spend $29.95 to make love to you, you need a new man. He has on a hundred-dollar Karl Kani, and he can't pay thirty dollars to spend a whole night with you, in a bed, with sheets, covers and a closed door? Please.

See, where he takes you should tell you something. If a hotel room is just financially impossible, how 'bout getting a couple of blankets, packing a basket full of stuff, romantic things, and create something special. Bring a little something to eat and drink, bring a little music, and you've upgraded the quality of your spot beyond a hotel room. Ain't nothing around this campus but woods and hidden areas. You can get lost out here and die. You can spread the blanket, sit, talk, feed each other and go from there. But do these jerks think of anything like that?

I'm at a small social party. A few friends and that's it. After a while people start coupling off. The guy who was try'n to kick it to me says, "Well, it's about that time." I say, "What time?" He says, "Mak'n-love time." We're in a house with three bedrooms, and three couples already had each bedroom occupied. He says to me, "We can go in the bathroom." So I spend the next five minutes tell'n him about himself. I spend another ten minutes tell'n him about myself. I'm not the type who will fuck you, a stranger, in someone else's bathroom. I consider it offensive that he suggested it, I'm insulted and it's like that. But, hey, I can forgive him. I can forgive him because I understand him as a young brother on a college campus. This doesn't excuse the indecency, it only explains it. I know there are several sisters who would have been in that bathroom on the quick fast. He knows this, and that's what made him suggest it. I only hope he now knows that he can't suggest it to every sister. You have to pay a little more attention to the person you're with.

Not all Black women hold no respect for ourselves. This brother, a prime example of most brothers, needed to know that a woman is something to be respected. Will he ever suggest anything like that again? He probably will, but I hope in a different way. If you're kick'n it to someone, try and feel that person out. Start caress'n the person while the two of you are talk'n. If she says please don't do that, the least you now know is not to suggest the bathroom. If she relaxes into it, move to the next level. A soft, non-aggressive kiss. Give her time to respond. If that's OK, and the kiss becomes heavy, and the two of you are now feel'n it, and you know the bedrooms are occupied, then and only then do you suggest the bathroom. And act embarrassed about ask'n. Brothers are so bold and arrogant, it's a turnoff. Keep things on the smooth tip.

Homecoming weekend. That time of year when other Black colleges and non-students come here. Oh, do we put on a performance? I don't know who's worse. The students or the non-students. That just goes to show you that being a college student does not automatically mean you're a bright person, exercising intelligence, class and restraint. If you'd thought attitudes and behavior toward each other would change, guess again. I think that just shows it's a permanent view and treatment we have of each other on any level. Be it the street, college, or what should be a highly respectable workplace.

This year at Homecoming during the evening, my girls and I are walking toward our dorm. Some signed hype used to go here, and so they came down for the weekend. So we're walking and we hear "Yo, baby, yo." We see this car and one of my girls notice who it is and some other heads with them. We go over after a few "come heres," and one of them, not one of the signed heads, but one of their boys says, "Which one of y'all suck dick?" Now, of course I'm ready to go off, but my girl, the main one who wanted to go over, says, "I don't, but I rap," and she starts freestyl'n. I'm totally through. I just walked off. She there rapp'n after a question like that. I don't know what to say. I don't know if the brother that asked that question was a student, but I do know that my friend who answered him is. What can I say?

Another incident, not to jump on rappers, because I understand they're just taking advantage of their fame, acting like they would, album or no album, but back home in Boston, around the way, Naughty By Nature was on the block, chill'n. No problem. I'm with my cousin and Treach steps to me with "blah, blah, blah." I say, "Well, I think your music is really hype," and he says "Yeah, and I think you look good, so come on, let's go." I'm like, "Where?" He lets me know and I'm like, "No, thank you." Without missing a beat, he turns to my cousin and says, "Well, how 'bout you?" This was more than a year ago, but now in his song he say'n, "I love Black women always / and disrespect ain't the way," so I guess he's been enlightened.

The videos don't help. We don't realize the mixed messages that are sent. Guys watch videos to see female bodies and how hard the artist is. Girls watch the videos to check out the fashion, the dance, the music and the artist. How the women are portrayed and are being treated is of little importance, it's ignored or not taken as seriously as it should be. Girls will go out and buy the same gear they saw on the video because it looks fly, but now the guys are treating us as if we were the actual video hos they saw gett'n dogged. Girls are only try'n to look trendy, sexy and in step. Guys are only respond'n to a type of girl they saw in a video based on looks, and it's an inaccurate depiction. It's not exactly the clothes that make the girl a ho.

I wear some of the things you see in videos because I look good in them. I'm young, my body is in shape and sometimes I like show'n it off. That does not mean it's an invitation for guys to come up and act as if I'm for sale. The clothes shouldn't have to change in the videos, they look good, and the sisters look good wear'n them, what should change is the treatment of the sister. Women want healthy, good-look'n bodies and they want to show them off. Men do the same thing. I love a good-look'n male body, but I respect that it belongs to the owner, not for me to take advantage of. I don't go up to men say'n, "Yo, brother, can I take you behind this building and do you?"

I don't want to have to alter what I wear just because ignorant sisters are wear'n the same thing in videos and are be'n treated like garbage. The bikini swimsuit isn't the problem. Bikinis are to be worn in their proper environment. But when you have bikinis in a video combined with sexism, you have a problem. When you have bikinis and not a drop of ocean or pool is in sight, we have a problem. When you have G-strings and thong bikinis at the stage performance of a Wrecks-N-Effect show, you have a problem. Are you on your way to a pool party or are you up there being exploited? What's the statement be'n made?

Lo-Key's? video *Sweet on You* is a good music video. They go back to the seventies and have a classic red light, basement party. Sisters are in hip-huggers, they look good and they are not act'n like freaks. They're do'n the

Robot, they're do'n the Bump, they got the Soul Train line go'n and everything is balanced. Brothers and sisters are hav'n fun with each other and nobody is be'n embarrassed. I enjoy see'n that type of balanced, non-sexist video. It makes me feel good see'n us like that. It was real. I know there are freaky, wild parties, but every party is not like that. Today women are primarily sex objects. We're always some man's fantasy. The man stands there and we slither up and down and around him. Every video you see, we're look'n and act'n like sluts in love with this one ugly artist. Except for a very, very few of the videos that are out, we are always look'n like we're in heat. I can't name five balanced videos off the top of my head, that's how few there are, but I can run a fifteen-minute list of the unbalanced ones. There's a video, *Hit It from the Back*. The visuals go right along with the title.

What disappoints me most about guys is the things they say. If nothing else, all you have is your word. You may not be able to fly me here or dine me in some fine restaurant, but if through your words you make me feel like I'm the best, can't no amount fine restaurant replace that.

If you're try'n to be the man, be up front with it. It's really bad when you lie, game and just be totally dishonest with what you come with. That's what makes us so mad and so hurt when we find out the real you.

When you're with your boys it's, "That bitch, that ho, blah, blah, blah." Then they'll see the girl coming and they'll push up with, "Yo, can I talk to you for a second? How you do'n? Who you with now? Well, why don't we get together cause I think you're like that?" This is the same female that was just a bitch. Now they're talk'n to her, gas'n her head, making her feel like she's special and special to them, and it's all lies. They want her only for that one thing. They get theirs, then comes the dis, and it's over. They talk about her to their boys and how they got theirs. Now the next guy thinks he can push up the same way. "Excuse me, can I talk to you a second? So you ain't deal'n with that sucker no more?" They don't mean to call their boy a sucker, they just say that to run their game. They follow through with, "So why don't we get together cause that nigga wasn't right. I wanna be your man." She'll trust him because she wants to believe she's worthy of be'n loved. She wants to forget about the last guy, she wants to show him she's not really hurt, and that she's see'n other people, but after the guy gets his, he's out and he disses her too. The shit is sick.

Now the girl is look'n at all men as be'n fucked up. You think she's gonna trust the next guy? The next guy may be for real. He may be totally sincere, but he's gonna catch hell. He can forget it. She's gonna be a cold, out-to-get-hers bitch. She'll be out to dis him before he disses her.

It wouldn't be so bad if we were dogged without all the verbal lies, but guys do unnecessary damage. When you say things after only two months into the relationship like, "When it's time, I want you to have my child," "I want you to name it so-and-so" and "I want it to have your eyes," that shit is a mind trip. We're all gassed. We feel special. We think you want us to have your baby. That shit is deep. We'll fantasize the future. A whole wedd'n and shit, and come to find out you're bullshit'n. We've been totally played. That is so fucked up. It really is. It hurts. It's so painful. We're think'n you're for real, and it's all a joke. Now that's even more incentive for the sister to get herself pregnant when she finds out he wants to be out. Although the guy didn't mean it, the girl will make herself believe he really meant it and when he tries to break out, she'll tell him she's pregnant as if that'll now keep him.

To this day I'm still wondering if this one guy meant what he said. Did he really mean it when he said, "I wanna stay with you, live with you and I want you to have my son." I then later find out he's sleep'n with two other females. Probably tell'n them the same thing. Now, had I been just slightly different, I would have thought, "Let me sex him one good time without any protection and boom, hey, I'm carry'n your son." This is what I was think'n, and just slightly different, I would have been in there. I was like, let's see if he can so easily run to some other female's house when I keep throw'n his son in his face. "Your son needs to eat. You need to take me downtown to buy him some clothes. You need to spend some time with your son." All this because of how he gassed my head up. I wanted to have my cousins shoot his ass, but again I changed my mind.

There's a real big misconception about why young sisters are getting pregnant. A lot of girls get pregnant because when they're in a relationship they want it to mean something to them and their man. If she's been putt'n her heart into the relationship, and the guy is play'n her off, act'n like she really don't mean anything and treat'n her like nothing, the thought is "I'll have his baby and then I'll mean something to him." Or, "If I can't actually have him, I'll have a piece of him. I'll have his baby." Two months ago my girlfriend wanted to have her boyfriend's baby because he was cheat'n on her. "If I have his child then he ain't got time to fuck around." But I knew she was really think'n maybe he'd then see her as someone special to him, someone carry'n his child and that would make her different. This is what I went through so I know where her thoughts were.

And don't let him be the guy in the 'hood that every girl wants. That every girl is sweat'n, and he's committed to no one. He's just boning only two or three females. These competitive bitches will be on him like you wouldn't believe.

Don't let homeboy be a dealer or hustler. The thing is to also have a dealer's baby and then dress the baby in the most expensive, flyest gear you can buy. It's like some fuck'n game.

It's just a given that college and higher education is not a reality. I mean high school was barely finished. So it then becomes all about your neighborhood. What you see around you. What you see happen'n. What you're a product of, mother's thirty and you're fifteen, sixteen.

I have cousins, hard-core cousins, killers, dealers, the whole nine. I mean, they're runn'n the jails. They're known and they stayed on my ass about not fuck'n up. I was gonna be the one person who turned out different. All my younger and older cousins have babies, they're not do'n anything really productive with their lives. Just hang'n out, work'n, gett'n by. I do have one younger cousin that hasn't fucked up, and I'm try'n to stay on her. I got her out of Boston to go stay with her mother in D.C. but that shit didn't work out. Her mother and her don't really know each other and so they're clash'n. It ended fast because the mother is pregnant and she tells my cousin there won't be enough room for her when the new baby comes and so she has to go back to Boston. What kind of shit is that to say to your daughter? She's fourteen and the last time I spoke to her, she told me she just got a boyfriend. She really likes him and they're hav'n sex.

I thought I was pregnant at one time, and my mother asked if I wanted to come home, have the baby and then go back to school? I'm not at all say'n my mother doesn't care, because she does, she loves me and definitely wants the best for me, but she's cool with me com'n home, hav'n the baby and then go'n back to school. Does it really work like that?

My mother taught me about earn'n a man's respect. She taught me about respect'n myself. She does expect much from me. My family in Boston feels that I'm the one person who will turn out to be something in our family.

I think my family will be more surprised if I finish college and have a career than end up pregnant and back home. The mind set is already used to the way things are, so why mess with the routine?

It's not that they don't raise us without any ambition, but between them and the streets, something happens. We can't understand it, or even try to because of what is already real to us. You can talk dreams, but it's easier to accept your real surroundings. But it's OK because there's a lot of love in that surrounding. Hav'n a baby isn't seen as anything bad. It's a happy occasion. If you're not even think'n about, don't know noth'n about college and becoming a career person, you don't feel you're mess'n up your life. You don't see how hav'n a child could be hold'n you back. Hold'n you back from what? It's like a trip for me to be in school. Reality is if I go home, kick back and have a child.

But I can't go home without a degree even if I wanted to because my male cousins would kick my ass. I'd be scared to go home and face them. I'm already scared of them. I've seen these guys stab people. They've kicked me out of parties. They told niggas to stay away from me. Guys were scared to date me dur'n high school. They've manhandled and threatened me not to fuck up. In this terrifying way, they wanna see me succeed. But I see, that's what they had to do. Now, if everybody had cousins like mine, more of us would be chang'n our reality.

The public's perception of these girls hav'n babies is really a joke. All they see is "Teenage pregnancy, why is this happening?" It's on the cover of *Time, Newsweek, Ebony*. It's all over the news. They think the solution is birth control and sex education in schools. That ain't it.

They've totally misdiagnosed the problem. These girls are on a mission. All this birth control, sex education, the vice president visit'n schools, "the proper use of a condom," it's all bullshit. It ain't about sex ed. It's about sisters say'n, "I want this boy and I'll have his baby to keep him." I think all these people from a different social order are applying their thought and way of deal'n with problems to a ghetto Black thang, and that ain't it. You have to know the order of the mind before you can deal with whatever actions the body does. It's the difference in class and ways-of-thinking thing.

It ain't about, "What, I'm pregnant, oh, golly-gee, now I just made my ghetto life even worse." These girls know what they're do'n. Ain't no accidents happen'n. If it's an accident, you either run to the clinic or you'll say, fuck it, I'll have it. Many mothers tell their daughters to have the baby because they're against abortions. They don't care if the girl is sixteen, fifteen or fourteen. It don't matter if the girl and boy ain't together, don't kill that baby is what's said.

These girls ain't ask'n for child support. They don't give a fuck about money he don't have and can't give. What they want is an actual part of the man, that's all. It ain't about hav'n the kid, it's about hav'n the man. I never heard, "Hey, Water, I'm hav'n a baby." What I hear is, "Hey, Water, I'm hav'n *Rashawn's* baby." Said with much pride. Like, "Yeah, girl, I got him." Whole different thought system.

If they even sense a breakup com'n, they'll lie and say, "Well, I think I'm pregnant." It's like this becomes your whole world and nothing else matters. Hav'n his child is decided out of some angry, confused, lonely moment. You just don't care.

All of what your mother tells you about niggas and your need to respect yourself goes out the door.

And your girls don't help. When I was a virgin, my girls were tell'n me, "You better give it up or you're gonna lose him." Your girls may be the ones creat'n the fucked up situation in the first place.

When I think of home, I wonder what's happen'n? It's crazy. I think about my girl Lea. Her mother tell'n her stay by your man. If he's the father of your child, stay with him. He's beat'n Lea's ass, and the mother is preach'n stand by your man. But, you see, Lea's father was slapp'n Lea's mother around, so that's how that goes.

Middle and upper-class women don't have babies to try and keep some man. They involve the Marvin Mitchelsons and sue his ass for all his money. That's how they keep a hold over their man. I think this behavior is just as bad. Just as bad as inner-city behavior, which is to get pregnant. The next class up is to get money. Ivana Trump made sure she had Donald's children, and now she's paid. How long did it take Marla Maples to have his baby? We all have our reasons for hav'n some man's baby. When our reason leads to crime, which threatens the safety of another, there's a problem. This is what others are so worried about. They don't really care about the young mother and her future being messed up. They're worried about "If this child doesn't have a job, will he be putt'n a gun to my head?"

This really depresses me. Sisters who are gett'n with white men for the purpose of hav'n light-skin babies. It's something I'm embarrassed to even say. It's like, I'll go back home and see all these light-skin babies and say who's the father, and I'll get an answer like, "Girl, I don't even want to talk about it." They'll quickly change the subject and avoid any mention of the baby's father. After a minute, you know what's up. A girl will normally tell you who her baby's father is way before you even ask. You don't have to ask. The point of the baby is to proudly say, "I have so-and-so's baby." But when the baby is super light and the mother is dark and you can't get a straight answer about the father, you know what's up. If you can understand our light-skin dark-skin problem, you can see how Black girls are sex'n white men they don't know just to have that light baby. In my own family, I have cousins who have babies only by Puerto Rican men. This is no accident. They have gone out of their way. They want something light and with curly hair. Fuck that, I want a Black baby.

Had it not been for my current boyfriend, I would probably say only one-sided shit against brothers. I would speak on my former experiences and those I know of and it would all be negative. For example, since I've been here I can tell you about rapes. Not rape, but rapes, with an "s."

I can tell you about my scary experience. I can also tell you about my girlfriend do'n two guys in a hotel room. I can tell you about my girl from up top who got pregnant, said she'll keep it, but then changed her mind in her fifth month and had the pregnancy terminated. She's a freshman, this is her chance to live a different life, one that a child might hold back and she was like, I'm gonna keep it. I'm not say'n she couldn't have eventually finished college, but I know it wouldn't have been any easier.

As I said, it's all about background. A sister from Baldwin Hills would have panicked, thought her life over, what the hell has she done, she should have known better, what will her parents think, no way can she have this baby, no way can they find out, no way, no how, and her ass in the clinic.

But back to my man. He's the greatest. He shows me that there are brothers who are about tak'n relationships seriously. He's proof that young brothers are not all about try'n to get some quick ass and then be out to get with the next sister. He's what all sisters should have in a man. He's thoughtful, kind, caring, loving, respectful of me. He's all of that and then some. Yes I'm in love, yes I've been turned out, yes I'm wide open and very vulnerable, but I think I know what I have. It's a matter of knowing what you want and not settling for less. If you don't know what you want, and you find yourself hooked up with Mr. Player time after time, of course you can't ever see me having Mr. Perfect. You don't believe he's out there. You'll know only the players and believe that all men are like that. I know what I want and will not settle.

If I had to be lonely, I'll be lonely. I've gone through the heartache and pain. I now know what's good for me and who I'm good for.

People usually go through some type of experience in order to make a change for the better. I had to go through one, but to my surprise, my boyfriend didn't. I assumed he was out there like the rest, got tired of all the shit and finally wanted something real. But, no, he's always respected women. It's what you're taught. It's how you're raised. It was what he observed. His parents are still together, they respect and truly love each other. He saw his father love and respect his mother. There it is. The same way many brothers see their mother come and go with several men, it's gonna have an effect. Observation is a teacher.

My man naturally feels one man, one woman. Why go through all the bullshit? He's secure in his manhood and doesn't have to prove it through sleep'n with every sister that walks by. He proves his manhood to me. He's attentive; an attentive lover and I have no complaints. My girls are like, "Can I fuck him?" I'm like no, you gotta get your own. Or, just tell your man, "Look, you have to do better."

My boyfriend is very aware. He's politically minded and race proud. We're the best of friends. We love each other and we really like each other. We enjoy talk'n to each other. We have fun with each other and it's like I forget he's my boyfriend, if you can understand what I'm try'n to say, we're just cool together. He'll call me and be like, "What up nigga?" Then he'll call, and be like, "What up Queen?" It's real. It's straight up.

I hate these so-called righteous brothers walk'n around, "peace this" and "peace that," "Black this" and "Black that." Yet, they'll play you in a minute. I knew this brother with the conscientious dreads, deep into Haile Selassie, Lion of Judah, he had a Queen, yet he was sweat'n my boyfriend to ask me about my cousin. He gives this appearance of race pride and unity, up with Black love and commitment, but look deeper. He's all on my cousin's tip. Be one hundred percent or be nothing.

I hope it's some propaganda shit, but why do I have to hear that Martin Luther King was a womanizer? But I wouldn't put it past niggas. King was a brother, he was still a man first. And a preacher, shiiiiit. They're some of the biggest pimps, peep the church. Congregation full of women and it ain't all about God.

My brother totally respects women. My girl from up top, her man is straight up. He wanted to marry her before she got pregnant and still wants to marry her. There are brothers out there who are straight up, you just have to know what to look for. Where and how did y'all meet? Did you take him from some other female? Then how can you think your shit is secure. You yourself have to be straight up. What's up with be'n shocked and hurt when you find out your man ain't your man no more. What goes around comes around. Sisters have to keep company with sisters who have the same positive values as you. If not, you'll be preach'n that "men are dogs" shit. My girls are positive. They have their personal problems due to circumstances, but they're positive. One of my girls is wanted for attempted murder, but she's positive. The heart is good, but sometimes shit is beyond your control and you gotta do what you gotta do. It's about survival and some people really test your will to survive. You can't just roll over. Once others chill, then you can chill like you wanna. You can live and love in peace like your heart wants to.

We hear too much of the negative. I believe the negative shit should be talked about so a change can come about, but balance it with the positive. Let's see and hear those stories that can serve as motivation for all those who believe this Black brother-sister situation isn't totally hopeless. Stories that reinforce brothers like my man. Stuff so that the next sister can draw inspiration.

One day, over the summer, when all day long I was getting, "Yo, come here," along comes this brother with, "Hi, how you do'n?" His whole tone, approach, the way he carried himself, was something you could appreciate. Not hard, not aggressive, not arrogant, nothing to turn you off and say, "Niggas." He didn't push up like all he saw was a piece of ass. The moral of the story, he ended up be'n the one to get it, he's my man. Now I'm in love. After the second date I was wonder'n why he wasn't even try'n to kiss me. I'm think'n maybe something was wrong with me. But I liked him even more for not bum-rush'n me. Then by the time he whispered, "I wanna make love to you," I was like, yes!

So, I believe the individual has to come into his own awareness. We all know right and wrong. If we didn't we wouldn't be sneak'n around, do'n everything on the DL. Do you wanna continue being an ass or do you wanna correct your shit? We choose to be right, or we choose to be wrong.

I think once you gain control of yourself, once you have a sense of control and not follow the crowd with what you think you should be do'n, there will be an overall positive change. Relationships would exist without brothers feel'n that bullshit peer-pressure anxiety of hav'n to have more than one sister. They would focus and put all their energy into what they have. Period. I'm just glad I don't have to deal with the bullshit. I have enough problems as it is. Try'n to stay in and finish school. I'm out this semester due to money. I'll be back next semester, but to have to add a brother to the "problem list," instead of the "be-grateful list" is a bitch. Your mate should be there to help with the problems, not create more.

I can't even say I'm lucky. I believe it's just really know'n what's good for you and be'n patient about it. What you deserve will come and the reward will be so much sweeter.

Lastly, let me give a big up to my man, "What's up, baby, I believe in what we have, I think it's real, it's all of that and let's keep it go'n. I love you. Watch us not be together next week. No, let me not end this on the negative and curse myself. Baby, I love you. Let's make it last. Much love to all those struggl'n and surviving.

VIII
life's favOrite
smile

Vanessa

v a n e s s a ,   2 1

n e w   y o r k

m o t h e r / w o r k e r

The guy I had my baby by wasn't my man. I loved this other guy and we had broken up. I started something with the guy I got pregnant by because he was just there. I had known him awhile. When he found out I was pregnant, he wanted me to keep it. I had already felt it was mine so I was gonna keep it anyway, but I didn't give him that impression. We knew we weren't gonna be together, so he wasn't too sure about what I was gonna do. I keep tell'n him, "I don't know." I wanted to tell him I was gett'n an abortion just to get him away from me, but I knew I was keep'n it.

He didn't know what I was gonna do because he still loved his girl-friend and I still loved my ex-boyfriend. He wanted to have this baby because when he had his first daughter, he was much younger. He was runn'n around, he was into drugs and he wasn't a good father. So this time he was like, have it, he'll take care of it. Like, he'll do everything right this time. So, I finally told him what I already knew, I was gonna have the baby.

Besides him be'n anxious to do it right this time and be a real father, I soon found out he had wanted to get me pregnant. I thought it was an accident, but that wasn't the case, he had gott'n me pregnant on purpose. He meant to take off the condom and *not* pull out in time.

I had a miserable pregnancy, I had an even more fucked-up labor. I know I was depressed and that added to it. Wasn't noth'n cute about my pregnancy. I was in the labor room by myself, I did the push'n by myself, I delivered by myself. While I was pregnant, I told him I'd call him after I had it.

Although I knew we weren't try'n to make it work as a couple, I didn't really doubt him be'n there for his child, and he didn't lie. Everything and

anything she needed, she got. He has been there for his daughter. The two
of us can't sit and have a conversation without arguing, but he's still there
for his child.

I have my mother's support although we don't get along. We're always
argu'n. I'm the youngest in my family and they say the youngest gets
pampered the most, not me, I was never pampered. The last time I was
pampered I was around eight years old. I remember I was the only one
that would say, "I love you momma." I never heard any of my brothers or
sisters say that to my mother. I was the only one. But I didn't do it only to
get attention, I was say'n what I felt. But at some point since then, we've
never gotten along. I guess I grew up too fast for my mother. Her baby
grew up. My daughter isn't my first child. I have a five-year-old son and
she treats him like her baby. I think when I had him, I grew up before she
wanted me to, and now we don't get along because of it. My older sisters
had babies at the same age I did, but she don't argue or fight with them.
She argues and fights with me. I'm her last child and I guess with me it's
different.

I didn't tell her I was pregnant the second time. I didn't feel she needed
to know. She doesn't really help me, so why tell her? I would talk to other
people, not her. One day she asked me if I was pregnant. I said, "Yeah."
She asked why I didn't tell her. I said because I felt I didn't need to tell her.
I used to talk to her when I was pregnant the first time. I'd talk about my
problems and my fears. I'd be try'n to get advice and comfort from her,
and she'll throw it back in my face. I'm think'n I have someone to talk to
and she's throw'n my problems back in my face. I'd end up regretting try'n
to talk to her because she didn't wanna hear it.

That first time I was pregnant I was sixteen and she put me out. I had
broken up with my boyfriend over some other girl, but before we broke up
I was pregnant and didn't know it. When he found out he asked what was
I going to do, was I gonna keep it? I said no, because it was his. He started
break'n and go'n off. We were in the hallway of my building and he started
call'n my mother. He knew I didn't tell her and he was try'n to intimidate
me. But I asked if he wanted me to help him call her. I called her and said,
"Ma, Bo wants you." She said, "What does he want?" I said, "He wants to
tell you I'm pregnant and I'm not keep'n it cause it's his." She was eat'n,
she paused for a second, then went back to eating.

A few days later I was putt'n on a skirt to go to church and I had asked
my mother to zip me up. All my sisters were stand'n around and she said
in front of everybody, "How you gonna put this skirt on and you're
pregnant?" My sisters' mouths dropped and they were on me, "You pregnant? You pregnant, Nes?" My mother said, "Yes, she's pregnant and she's

talk'n about gett'n rid of it, but she ain't gett'n rid of shit, cause if she kill that baby, I'm gonna kill her ass."

I was like, what is she talk'n about, "Ain't nobody here to help me." If I did keep it, I didn't want the baby's father around me. She was like, I don't care what you think, you ain't gett'n rid of that baby. My whole family is like that. My grandmother has seven children and she doesn't believe in abortions. I have six brothers and sisters.

The last thing she said was she'll help me with it. When the time came for her help, she couldn't help me. My baby needed Pampers, she couldn't help me. My baby needed milk, she couldn't help me. I had to give my baby sugar water. I had to ask my sisters for Pampers. Diapers that their own baby needed.

The baby's father did what he could. He had gotten fired from his job, so he couldn't do much. He started do'n what he had to to make money and he would bring things by when he could, but for the most part it was never when the baby needed it. You can't tell your baby to wait two or three days for some baby food. They're cry'n right then and there, they need it then and there.

Bo wanted to have the baby because it was his first child. He was also sixteen and wanted a child. Not think'n that he couldn't provide for him no more than I could.

After my mother said she'll help and I said I was gonna keep it, everything was cool for a while. But eventually we would get into arguments and on Christmas Day we had a fight. She was fight'n me, I was push'n her off. It ended with her tell'n me to leave. I went to stay with Bo. We had broken up and it was final, but I ain't have anywhere else to go. He had gotten a new girlfriend and everything. She would come over but there was no problem.

That was five years ago. Today, he's still involved with his son. He just got released four months ago and he does come around to see his son. He just bought him a pair of sneakers. He bought him some outfits, he and his girlfriend take him to the movies, he takes him to see his grandmother who lives in the next borough and he's really gett'n to know his son.

My daughter's father does the same thing. He makes sure he visits his daughter and he does a lot for her.

If my daughter was to get pregnant at fourteen, fifteen, sixteen, I'd just have to help her with it. If she wanted to get an abortion, she couldn't get one unless she snuck out the house and got it on her own. Although I wanted an abortion when I first got pregnant, I don't feel that way now. I

was young and didn't think anything of kill'n life. Now I couldn't do it.
That's why I had my second child with no hesitation. I don't care that me
and her father aren't together, I couldn't kill her. And although we're not
together, it's good that he does do things for her. He could have been like
most guys and ignore the fact that he has a child. I'm lucky that both my
children's fathers are there for them because I know cases where it's not
like that.

I want my children to be able to talk to me about anything. I don't want
them to feel uncomfortable about com'n to me with anything. The way I
can't talk to my mother, I don't want that for my children. I mean, that
hurts. We argue and fight, but that's my mother. We should be able to say
noth'n but kind words and words of support for each other. I love her
because that's my mother, I'll always love her, but we have a problem. It
shouldn't be like that. Sometimes I'm like, is this my mother or some
enemy off the street?

**I want my daughter to be able to say anything to me. I want her
to say, "Ma, I need some pads, my period has started." I want my
son to be able to say, "Ma, I need some condoms, me and my
girlfriend are think'n about sex." I don't want my daughter and
me to be all the time at each other's throats. I don't want to kick
my daughter out the house on Christmas. I want her to always be
welcome and feel welcome in my home. I don't want her count'n
days, say'n I can't wait to get out this bitch.**

Before, when I would meet a guy, I'll give him all the trust in the world.
People said I was backward for do'n that. You usually make the person
earn your trust, but I would give it to you right off the bat. As soon as you
fucked up, you got no more trust. The first time you fucked up, no more
trust. You then had to win back my trust and that was hard. I'll trust you at
first because I don't know anything about you. Everyone wants to be
trusted at first. We all have good intentions, so I'd give you the trust and
respect, but as soon as you fuck up, that's it.

Now I have a totally different approach to relationships. I've realized
when you're the other woman you get treated better. When a guy has a
girlfriend and he's cheat'n with another girl, that other girl gets treated

better than the girlfriend. So, now I don't fuck with any man unless he has a girlfriend and I become the other girl. I don't want to take possession of no man and I don't want to be taken possession of. If you have a girlfriend you can't claim possession over me. You can't ask me who was that I was walk'n with? You can ask, but it's none of your business, you're not my man. I can say he's just a friend, just like you're a friend. That's how it is. I don't need nobody tell'n me what to do. I already have to answer to my two children. I don't need to answer to anybody else.

I don't let myself get too involved emotionally so that I'm say'n leave your girlfriend for me. If I was his girlfriend, I'd be wonder'n where is he when he's not with me. And this way, I don't let it get to the point where I'm wonder'n where he is and what is he do'n. I know he should be with his woman. I'll see him when I can. The girlfriend is the one be'n dogged. She's be'n played.

I don't want to be the girlfriend because that means he would be cheat'n on me. That means I'm be'n treated like shit. No, I rather be the other girl be'n treated like a queen. You see me when you can. You're happy to get away from your girlfriend and I get the benefits from it. It works for me. That's how I stay happy. I have enough problems without hav'n to add to them the games and lies and cheat'n. This way I know what you are. I don't have to stress myself constantly think'n what's he up to? He says he's hang'n out with his boys, but is he really? Let him tell his girlfriend that and let her worry.

I couldn't trust any guy any longer because every guy I dealt with fucked up. Me and my son's father broke up because of some other girl. The guys I deal with now are cheat'n on their girlfriends. That could be me, so why get a lying boyfriend?

Those I'm dealing with, of course I don't have no business trust'n them. They have a girl and they're with me, how can I trust them? But this way I know not to trust them. When they do something fucked up, it's no surprise. I could expect something fucked up of them. Their girlfriends are the ones that will be surprised, heartbroken, depressed and sour. They're the ones that's be'n lied to. They expect the best of their man, and he's with me.

The guy that I love, since my daughter was born, has tried to start something again, now that he's mak'n a little something for himself he feels he can step to me. But there's a lot of projects around here and these girls are always in his face. He looks like he has something go'n on and they want a part of it. A lot of girls around here like him and he's start'n to speak back. He's stand'n there answering them in length, and I know what they want. The same thing I did. He's there hav'n conversations and I'm like, "are you sure you wanna get back with me?"

I did trust him once. He messed up and I can't trust him ever again. Married men, guys with girlfriends, are always say'n, "Oh, she's just a friend." That's what I started hear'n. "She's just a friend." That's what guys I mess with say about me to their girlfriends. I know the game so what does this guy I love think he's do'n. He's tell'n me these girls are just friends. I'm not that in love where I can't see obvious shit. That's for these other dumb girls. "Oh, I didn't know she was your cousin."

I mean, this one girl used to come knock'n on his door. He didn't tell me in advance that he told her she can come knock'n on his door anytime. I'm like, "Where she get the impression she can do that? She's disrespect'n me." He goes, "No, she's not disrespect'n you. She has to go places and sometimes I take her." "OK, but you didn't tell me that. You didn't tell me whenever she needed someplace to go, you told her come knock on your door." You see, she was gett'n treated better than me and she's not his girlfriend. He's try'n to make me the girlfriend. That means I'm the one gett'n ready to get dogged. Not anymore I'm not. That's out.

It's the man that decides whether the relationship is gonna work out or not. A man will fuck around for as long as forever. The day he gets caught, "Baby, don't leave me. I still love you. I want you. I don't want her. Fuck that bitch." Now the girl is every type of bitch. I'm sure she wasn't that while you were fuck'n her, but now, "She's a nasty bitch" and "I love you."

A woman will forgive him, but these days, if she believes he's at it again, she'll get tired of the neglect and she'll go get her someone. Then if she's caught, the guy is like, "You dirty bitch. You lucky I don't kill you." And "I don't ever want to see your fuck'n face again." They're real harsh. But what is that? Men can cheat every day of the week and expect forgiveness when caught, but when it's the girlfriend, you better get the fuck outta his life, and she's now worse than the bitches he's been fuck'n. He don't want her anymore, although he's been asked to be taken back ten times.

It's the man's fault in the first place and this could have all been avoided. It's always the man's fault. You've cheated so much you've made the girlfriend feel worthless. She thinks nobody wants her and now she goes out to feel wanted. Stop cheat'n and give her all your attention, she doesn't have to do this. But now it's like it's too late and fuck all that. That's why I do what I do.

Yeah, I would like things to work out with the guy I love, but I can't trust him. I think if I was to go back to him, I'd be stupid. After talk'n all my shit about the girlfriend and the other girl, after know'n what I know from do'n what I do, I'd be stupid to think, "OK, we'll have a one-on-one happy relationship. I'm the girlfriend and there's no one else." Even if he says otherwise, I know his record. I can say, I think he's talk'n to other girls because he doesn't know if I'm try'n to get back with my son's father or what? He doesn't even know whether to ask me to be his girl or what. He hates hear'n no and he's not sure if I'm gonna say no. And I'm not gonna tell him I'm not with anyone. I don't want to give him that confidence. He'll have to show me that he's changed and is dead serious before I even give a hint that I still want him.

I remember ask'n him while I was pregnant, and we were semi-involved, what does he do when he gets horny? He said, he works out. I said, "OK, you'll tell me the truth one day." He told me the truth yesterday. We had a long talk. He said he would mess around with some girl he would meet through one of his brothers or his father. I can say at least he told me, but that's all the credit I can give. One of the reasons we had broken up was because I wasn't gett'n any attention. Here he is go'n past me to mess around with someone else. A room with his brothers, his father and some girls. He says, well, what did I expect him to do? I told him don't be ask'n me what I expect him to do. He has to know what to do on his own.

I asked what else did he do? He said he'll bring them to his house and they'd have sex. I said, I thought we agreed we wouldn't bring anybody else into our homes. We go to their house or we go to a hotel until we straightened our shit out. He said, well, what did I expect him to do? Still ask'n me what I expect him to do? I said, "I expect you to come to me." The complaint was I wasn't gett'n any attention while we were together, and he takes it to someone else while we're supposedly try'n to work our shit out. He's giv'n however many minutes or hours to another girl. Those could have been my minutes or hours. But he asks what did I expect him to do?

I should have known better if he's hang'n with his father. His father's a stone ho. He likes young girls. Girls younger than me. He just had a baby by a young girl. He's gotten another young girl pregnant, but she didn't have the baby. She had a miscarriage. He's a dog. His son is hang'n with a dog and he's not gonna bark, come on? That's what I expect him to do.

I'd call him at his father's and hear in the background, "Stop, 'fore I tell your girlfriend." What the fuck is that? He tells me she's there for his brother. Yeah, OK, tell me anything. Later on the girl steps to me and I find out who she is. The girl is sixteen and big as a tree. Now I ask'n my so-called man, "Why are you play'n with this young girl who's now com'n out her face to me?" She don't even know me, or what I can do or have done. Put that shit in check. I'm not a troublemaker. I don't like to fight, but I don't mind fight'n. I'll beat somebody's ass if I have to. I'm one too many bitches and it's on. I'll be two bitches, but after you get carried away, I'm swing'n on you. If I'm not prepared to fight, I'll be back. I'll go put my little fight'n boots on, my fight'n jacket on. I'll pull my hair back in a tight ponytail and we'll be at it.

The guy that I love, if he ever gets it together, because I still love him, despite all the shit we've been through, if he decides I can be his one and only, then I'll take that chance and we'll be together. But right now I just don't see none of that. He'll have to become a new person. If he loves me like I love him, he can change. He'll just have to show me and convince me of that love. Until then I'm not hold'n my breath. I'm handl'n relationships the way I want to and I'm just liv'n for self, my son and my daughter.

tracy

t r a c y ,   1 8

n e w   y o r k

m o t h e r

Brothers just don't treat you right. At the beginning of the relationship everything will be all right. They'll buy you is basically what they do. They'll take you out, do this for you and that for you, and as the relationship goes on, everything starts to die down. That's how it is, and you can't even tell who's honest and who isn't. They all will step to you with what they intend to do, how much they're into you and think you're all that, but after a few weeks you're a memory. That's why I'm now very open. I ask to be told what kind of relationship you want up front. Most will say they just wanna be sex partners, and could we swing it like that? Something like that, I couldn't get with. I'm not the type of person who will call your house before coming over to make sure no one's there. If we're just sex partners, that means you could have someone else there. That means I have to deal with some other girl com'n at me.

Most guys are like, if we can't just get it on in the bed, then forget it. That's OK. That means this heart is not broken. See, guys just don't want to deal with relationships and they really don't want to deal with a relationship if a child is involved, especially a child that's not theirs. But they will think because you have a child, you may want to just have sex with no strings attached, and that's not true. You can still want a relationship. If anything, you don't want to just have sex. You want something more. You're looking out for your child's interest as well as yours.

I met my daughter's father through a friend. Everything was all right in the beginning. It followed the usual pattern. He took me out, brought me things, all the usuals, then after a while, it died down, though there is a relationship that remained. It wasn't like, OK, I got the boots so now I'm out. Ours was different. What happened to make it die down was all the things in the beginning. He had spoiled me in the beginning. And now that I don't get the attention and affection, the sex, as fluent as I once did, I complain.

If I could stay with him and things work out, and we could get married, I would. If things don't work out, if we were to break up, I would just want him to be there for his daughter. He wouldn't have to do anything for me. I'd get over him, but just do something for his daughter. He's already very active in his daughter's life. He buys her things, he takes her out, takes her to his house, his grandmother's, she watches her, baby-sits, and my daughter knows her grandmother.

Some guys, most guys, after you break up, forget everything and act like they don't know you or have a child. They forget about their son, like my son's father, and go on with their life.

At first, with my daughter, I was like no, not again. I tried to have an abortion, but when I went to the doctor, they checked me and said I was too far gone in the pregnancy to have it terminated. Then when I went for my sonogram it showed that I was only five months pregnant, and that was a month after I tried for a termination. So really I was four months pregnant and could have had the abortion, but the doctors gave me the wrong information. I guess God made it where I couldn't have the abortion, and I had her.

It was an accident both times. Back then I was freestyl'n. I was kinda wild, not caring and just running the streets. That's one of the reasons I wanted to have the termination. I didn't think I had time for another baby. I was sixteen and still into the streets and hang'n out. I had a son who my mother and grandmother took a lot of responsibility for, so I really wasn't looking to get caught out there again. My mother knew I was too young to raise my son, my first child, by myself and so they took over my responsibilities. That's also what allowed me to continue to run the streets. I was out there, but I wasn't looking to get pregnant again because I knew this time I would have to take full responsibility. Plus, I would have to start taking full responsibility for my son as well. At thirteen, I could get away, but at sixteen, I knew my mother wasn't hav'n it. She would say you're old enough to raise your own kids now, and things would be different. I wouldn't be able to hang out anymore, do'n the things I was do'n. I mean, I never stayed in the house. Three A.M., four A.M., all night, I would be out. It could be twenty degrees outside, I would be hang'n out somewhere. I would not be home. This time I knew if I had had the baby I wouldn't be able to hang out anymore, and so I didn't tell her I was pregnant. I knew I was gonna have the abortion so I didn't say anything to anybody. I really knew not to tell my boyfriend because I knew he would have wanted me to keep it.

Later on, my boyfriend's best friend sees me and tells my boyfriend, "Yo, I think Tracy's pregnant." He calls me and asks, am I pregnant? I say "No, I'm not," because I had planned on having the termination. In a few weeks I wouldn't be, so he didn't need to know. By this time my mother knew because my grandmother suspected. My grandmother knew because I was sleep'n all the time. I slept all day. I did nothing but sleep. Sleep and eat. I never stopped eating, and she just knew without me say'n a word. She knew how I was the first time, so I didn't have to say anything. Also, I was always out in the street, never home, and now all of a sudden I'm home asleep all the time. My grandmother kept say'n, "I think Tracy is pregnant, I think Tracy is pregnant." She would say to my mother, "You better ask her." They'd ask. I'd say, "No." They'd ask, I'd still say, "No, I'm not pregnant." I'd be steady eat'n, and say'n, "No," falling asleep, and still say'n no to them. They knew, but I wasn't admitting to it. While I was on the phone with my boyfriend, my mother was in the background say'n, "You better tell him, you better tell him you're pregnant."

My mother was like, "You better tell me because if you are, you have to start going to the doctor for prenatal care."

My mother doesn't believe in abortions. She ain't with that. None of the people in my family believe in abortions. My grandmother, my grandfather, my aunts, they don't believe in it. One of my aunts has fourteen kids. The other one has seven.

They feel if you're old enough to get pregnant, you're old enough to have it. If you're too young in the mind to take care of it, they'll help. They had already gone through this before. My grandmother went through this with my aunt. She had her first child when she was thirteen. My mother was young when she had me. They felt I could have the baby just like they did.

When I finally said, "Yeah, I *might* be pregnant," my mother said, "well then we're go'n to the doctor's tomorrow."

When I knew I was keep'n it, I told my boyfriend. He wasn't there too much during my pregnancy, because I had kept it from him so long, he didn't feel a part of what was go'n on. At first, I thought OK, it's gonna be like that again, but after she was born he was there. He was there and she had everything.

I fell behind one year in school. I was suppose to graduate last year, but I graduate this year. I'm so glad I didn't go to high school with most of my girlfriends because they graduated one year before me, and I know I would have been crying like crazy to see them go through the ceremony without me.

I always knew I was gonna finish school and graduate. When I put my mind to do something, I do it. I said I was gonna finish school because I need to. I stayed out a year after my daughter was born and devoted full time to her because she's my responsibility. I always said, I'm gonna make it my business to go back and finish school, and that's what I'm do'n.

Having the baby don't keep the man, that's crazy. Shit, it'll drive them away if anything. He'll leave before the baby is even six months. The buy'n Pampers, buy'n clothes, feed'n him, runn'n to the hospital in the middle of the night, the cry'n and everything is what drives them away. Most of them think they can handle it, but when the baby comes, they can't.

Girls be think'n "his baby," and that's it. His baby, and that's it. They ain't think'n about all the hard work. They think, "he'll be glad that I'm giv'n him a son or daughter," but that's all guys want and that's it. They want to be able to say they have a son and that's it.

The girls that thought, "I'll have his baby, and then he'll love me and the baby" wake up real quick. If you think he'll be there help'n to raise his child, he'll have to come over to visit and see his child, that's how you'll keep some hold over him, let me tell you, if he wants to not ever see his child, he'll not ever see his child. Where is my son's father? He isn't active in his son's life at all. He don't come to see his son. If I was try'n to keep him, keep tabs on him, then I'm the fool cause not for two minutes was he there. To this day, I don't know where he is.

Then, some girls know he won't be there but they have the baby anyway. That's because they love the boy that much. If they can't have him, they'll have his baby. They don't care if they never see him, they'll have a part of him by way of the baby. But they're not think'n either. That's not good. You get stressed, mentally stressed like you don't know. You never get a break. You get stressed, pissed and before you know it, you're tak'n it out on the child. You feed him all this negative shit about his father, "Your father was no good, your father was irresponsible," and before you know it, you raised him to be just like his father. I can't suggest hav'n a baby just because of any man.

If the father's not gonna take the child at any time, then it's you who is the permanent baby-sitter. I wouldn't want to have a baby and know in advance the father won't be there. It's so hard. It is so hard. I mean that. I don't care if you have money from your feet to your head. Money don't cover everything. Not the cry'n, the diaper chang'n, the constant attention. Money don't cover you hav'n to get up early to feed the baby. All your time is taken when you'd rather be out with your friends. You can't come in when you feel like it anymore. Not when you know you have to come in to see about your son and your daughter. You're only at the corner because that's as far as you can go. You're only at the corner because you need to get something from the store for your baby. Babies are not dolls. They're not quiet little do-nothings. It's plenty of mornings I don't want to get up to feed her, but I have to. I have no choice.

These guys out here act too eager. Eager to get your name. Eager to get your number. Eager to get you in the bed. Then if you get pregnant, that's when the eagerness stops. But before that, they are all over you.

Like today, I was on Pitkin Avenue, and a guy in a car was try'n to talk to me. He said, "Hi," I said, "Hi," and I kept walk'n. He's driving and still try'n to ask me all these questions, but after "Hi," I don't have anything else to say. It's rain'n, and he backs the car up so fast, it goes into a skid and does a three-sixty. He's screaming, "You think you all that?" I turned and said, "No, I don't think I'm all that, but you said 'hi' and I said 'hi' back. If I don't wanna say anything else I don't have to." Either I don't wanna be bothered or I have a man. In my case, I have a man, so I kept on walk'n. If we keep talk'n, one thing will lead to another, one of us will get a phone number, and now that brings my daughter's father into the picture and he has a temper. I don't want to involve him in something where another guy is call'n me. This guy didn't have to do all that just because I didn't stop to talk to him. What if he had gotten in an accident? Over a "hi."

Some guys will say, "OK, you have a nice day," and they'll go on about their business. Then you have those who will think they're all that. If you come to me like you're all that, I'm gonna dog you. If you're a dog, I'm gonna do my best to treat you like a dog. I'm gonna dog you out. If you act self-centered and conceited, I'm gonna put you down all the time. I'm gonna dog you because I know how you're liv'n.

I won't try to change you. I'm just lett'n you know you can't get over on me like you think you can. I don't think you can change these guys anyway. They've been brought up this way, and it's like you can't change them.

My cousin has a boyfriend and his little cousin acts the same way he does. The same way that little cousin sees his big cousin act'n, think'n he's the man, talk'n to all the girls, hang'n out, do'n this and that, it's the same way he's grow'n up to be. That little boy will talk to me like he's a grown man, and knows what he's talk'n about.

The worst thing you can do is have a baby from a drug dealer. I've stopped be'n into them because they don't last very long. Either they get locked up or they get shot. I used to talk to drug dealers and it seemed everyone I talked to got locked up. Everybody started say'n I was bad luck, but they bring the bad luck on themselves. I say the worst thing you can do is have their baby, because if someone is after them, and they can't get to them, they'll come after you or the baby. They don't care. I know and talk to a lot of these guys, and they'll do anything without a care just to pay someone back. You fuck over them and their money, forget it.

If you're with some guy, walk'n down the street and you're carry'n your baby, his enemies ain't gonna say, "naw, let's try and get him another time, he's with his girl and baby." The whole sidewalk is be'n lit up.

Dealers are trouble. They're runn'n in and out your house with guns and drugs, around your baby, around you.

You have girls that don't care as long as they get some of the money. But they ain't really gett'n anything. Dealers know these girls are sweat'n them for what they can do for them and give them, but they're like, fuck 'em. I made this money, why am I just gonna give it or spend it on some girl who don't really give a fuck about me? The girls are only think'n about self and what they can have. The guys know this, and this is what they will do. They'll say, she wants some of this money and I want the ass. Let me drop a hundred on her, which ain't nothing when you're mak'n thousands by the weekend, and the ass is had. The girl gets hyped, think'n this is just the beginning, and so much more is in store. She keeps giv'n it up, and just as fast, he's on to the next girl. You've been had for a hundred dollars. That's the going rate for a prostitute.

I'd be at a party with my friends, and they're like, "He was try'n to talk to me, who's he?" They find out he's big-time, and now they're ready to talk. So what he's big-time. That ain't big-time for you. You will find out big-time for who only.

If you're jeopardizing your life so you can get a Fila outfit and some gold, you're stupid.

People just have to learn on their own. People have to learn the hard way. I feel you can have a regular job and you still can live nice. You may not make as much in a day, but you can make enough to keep yourself nice. It'll just take an extra two weeks to buy the gold, the Coach bag, the Fila.

Thousands of dollars and all they buy are clothes and gold, and the phat ride. The 4Runner and the boom'n system. The guy is driving, leaning so far back, he's about to get into an accident, but know'n he's bigtime, but only for a minute. Me and my friends will be on the corner and here comes the ride. Within an hour, six to ten cars have stopped. The guys are big-time and we're supposed to be impressed and want to get in. I'm not gonna get in your car. I don't know who's after you. Your car can even look like someone else's that people are after. They all get the same couple of cars. The Lexus, the Sterling, and the Acura. At night, who knows? It could be a mistake, but now I'm caught in the crossfire.

Stop the pressuring into sex. I had this one boyfriend who all the time asked, "When are we gonna have sex? When you gonna come to my house? You don't wanna have sex at my house, I'll pay for a hotel." If you need it that bad and that quick, go find someone else. When I'm ready, you'll be the first to know. All this pressure is not needed. Take that time to know what you're do'n. When you take your time, you plan, you prepare, you take precautions, you be responsible, you do it the right way.

There are those who take too much time with the foreplay. You'd be in the mood, at the mood and out the mood by time they're ready. I don't like all that foreplay stuff. When I wanna have sex, I'm ready to have sex. They'll still be play'n with your ear, kiss'n your neck, and I've been ready.

Different from foreplay, I don't want only a couple of seconds either. I had this one boyfriend, two minutes, three minutes, maybe. I mean, it was so quick. He'd be finished, gett'n up, go'n to the shower. I'd be like, oh, my God. Oh, my goodness, that's it? I got all worked up for that? And they'd be so macho beforehand. Before they get in the bed, they'll have you think'n they can do something for you. As soon as they get in it, they can't handle it, and it's over. Two-minute brothers. Then they have the nerve to wanna know if they're better than your last boyfriend. They wanna know who was better, who was bigger. It ain't who's bigger, it's how you work it. And you have to say that just to get more out of them. Tell them it's how you work it so they can work it. They can be bigger, smaller or just right, you just want more work out of them. You do want someone you can feel though. If you have a choice, small is not the answer. But I think even if you're small and you can work it, that may make up the smallness. If you're small and all of two minutes, you can forget it.

You have to practice that safe sex. That's the last thing I'd like to say. If not to prevent pregnancy, at least to prevent AIDS, or something. You may think your man is not cheat'n, but think twice. He don't have to be totally out there dogg'n you, it may be just one other girl. That one other girl may have one other guy. That guy may have one other girl and on and on, and before you know it, you have something.

It might be a one-night stand. That one-night stand might lead to something else. Venereal diseases. I'm tell'n you, practice that safe sex. Use a condom. I can show you a drawer full right now. First of all I don't want no diseases, second of all I don't want to get pregnant again. Not by accident or carelessness.

Just as I say for others, I do for myself. My boyfriend might have a one-night stand, I don't know. He may be drunk one night, party'n with his boys, and you never know. All guys know is when their dick get hard, they want pussy. If you ain't around they're gonna get it from the nearest girl that is.

Some girls are the same doggish way. Protect yourself. If you're swing'n, make use of those condoms. You can be out there, catch something, give it to your partner, and then what do you have to say? You're the only one they're sleep'n with, so now you're caught out there.

Some girls are try'n to be just as known as some of these guys, but I don't think it's cute to be hav'n all these different cars pull up in front of your house. You may think it looks good, but it looks like you're a ho. And the guys don't care. As long as they're gett'n theirs, they'll continue to pull up. They'll turn their boys on. That's why so many cars are pull'n up. They don't care. If another car is there, they'll come back later. If they did care about you, they'll pull up, see the other car. Ask who's that nigga? A gun is pulled and somebody is shot.

Most girls are not like that though. Girls get deeper than the guy will. Most girls give their all to one guy. That's why someone is always hav'n someone's baby. But I say you have to be smarter than that.

You have to say, I like my freedom. I love my son, I love my daughter, but to do it again, where's the condom? Don't leave it up to the guy. He don't care. He's not the one gett'n pregnant. He doesn't have to carry it everywhere. He doesn't have to do the two A.M. breastfeeding. If he knows you're out there freestyl'n, he

doesn't even have to own up to it. Would you really know who the father is if you're freestyl'n?

We just have to be smarter than we are, and think about what's in the long run. We think too much in the moment. I'm hot, OK, let's do this. No precautions whatsoever. No nothing, but let's do this. If you have to have one, two children to learn better, then in some cases that's what has to happen. At the same time, I just hope the children can be loved and cared for while you learn your lesson.

nikki

nikki, 16

florida

mother/student/worker

I was like, "I'm pregnant and I'm gonna have an abortion." He was like, "You gonna kill the baby?" He was try'n to go hard with the description because he wanted me to have it, but I said, "Yeah, I'm gonna kill it because I know you ain't gonna help take care of it." He said, "How you know?" I said, "I know because you're a sorry muthafucka." And it turned out be true because he's sorry like a muthafucka. He ain't help for shit. I had the baby all alone and I'm rais'n it all alone.

He was a longtime friend. I knew the type person he was, but we were just friends. We got together, we fucked, one time, boom, I got pregnant. It was the type situation where I knew it was his because I wasn't just out there.

At the time, condoms, safe sex, it just wasn't on my mind. I ain't gonna try and use any excuses, I just didn't care. All I knew was that I wanted to get some dick. I don't use birth control pills because I believe that's another way of kill'n and gett'n rid of our kind. If I wanted safe sex or wanted to prevent a child, I would use a condom, but birth control pills are out.

He didn't want me to have the abortion and I wanted to have it. The only reason I didn't have the abortion was because I didn't have the money. If I had the money, I would have had the abortion. He wasn't gonna give me it because, like I said, he wanted me to have his baby. We're not even in love, haven't been dating, he's just a friend, we fucked one time, I got pregnant and he wants to keep it. Just cause he knows he has a baby on the way, and he's gonna be able to say he has a son or a daughter, he wanted me to have it. He wants me, who he really don't give a shit about, to have his child. I was like nigga, please, I'm ready to have an abortion. Too bad I couldn't get the money from him or anyone in my family. So, OK, I hav'n it.

During my pregnancy he did give me a little money, I ain't gonna deny him that, but after the baby came, he ain't do shit, like I knew he wouldn't. He ain't do shit for my baby since my baby was born. I was fourteen and he was twenty. I'm now sixteen and in two years since the birth, he hasn't done shit for my baby, and I mean *my* baby because he hasn't done noth'n to call my son his son. Other than fuck and get me pregnant, that doesn't make him earn the respect to call himself a father to this boy.

I expect him to be a father to his child like all fathers should be, but I've already written him off. After two years of do'n noth'n, why am I gonna expect someth'n now? He don't deny the fact that it's his baby, but he might as well deny the fact it's his because he sure does denies his responsibilities to the baby.

I not gonna tell or hound him about what his responsibilities should be to his child, he should know. He knows diapers ain't free, milk ain't free, food ain't free. But all niggas know is just because they got a baby, they're a man. That's all they want to become. Ain't do'n shit for the baby, but now they think they're a man. I just wanna tell them all, they ain't shit. If you ain't do'n shit for your baby, then you ain't shit and you certainly ain't a man.

I wanted the abortion, but I didn't realize how much better off I would have been had I not had the baby. I dropped out of school. I'm now in and out. It's now hard to get a job career started. With a child you have to go a step at a time. Without a child you can just go without a care. Pick up and move. You can job-search every minute. How am I gonna job-search without a job and without money for a baby-sitter? The grandparents get tired, and he's my responsibility.

Three and four o'clock in the morn'n the baby wakes up cry'n and you have to get up. You also have to get up at 6:00 A.M. to go to school. You're feel'n like, damn, I'm tired, this baby. You always want to complain about the baby. The baby did this. The baby needs that. I couldn't make it because I had to baby-sit. It's always someth'n about the baby. If the father was a man, the problems wouldn't seem as much. But I laid down, I opened my legs, I had it, he's mine, he's my responsibility.

Before the baby I really wanted to tour the world. I can still do it and I'm gonna do it with my son, but now I have to make a way for the two of us to tour the world. Before it was just me. Now it's me and my son. Now I have to save, work harder for two and make sure what I want to do doesn't interfere with his school. It can be done, it's gonna be done, and I know it's gonna be hard like a muthafucka. But that's on me. I made my bed, I'll lie in it.

When I was pregnant my mother didn't approve of it at all. She felt I was too young and I agreed. But although I wanted to have an abortion and didn't have the money, my mother wasn't gonna give me the money because my family don't believe in abortions. They're against it.

During my pregnancy my mother didn't bother me and I didn't bother her. She was satisfied with me hav'n it because she didn't want to see me end the pregnancy in the first place.

I'm sorry, but if I got pregnant again, I would have the abortion. It's hard with one child, let alone two. It's hard to feed your mouth and then feed an extra mouth.

Even if the man said he'd be there for his child, I still wouldn't have one. Even if he said he wanted to marry me, I wouldn't have it because I'm insecure. Marriage is not forever. There is a such thing as divorce. And niggas cheat. I don't care if you're his girlfriend, fiancée or wife, he'll have his dick in some other pussy.

Brothers in general cannot be true. They cannot stay faithful. For me, in a relationship, it's not about be'n in love, feel'n this way and say'n you feel that way, it's about be'n able to look me in the face and tell me the truth. It ain't about loyalty because it's in a man's nature to cheat. I ain't gonna say, "Well, baby, don't go cheat," I'll never say that to a man because I know better. I know he's gonna cheat. I don't want to put him in a position to lie. So, all I do is ask in advance, tell me what's up. If you're gonna go get some extra ass, let me know. Just tell me the truth. Don't say, "I love you, you're the only one," say the truth, nigga. If you're always tell'n the truth, then sooner or later I can fall in love, because I'll know you're truthful. Then I can have your child because I'll know whatever you tell me will be the truth. Do you or don't you wanna have this child? Do you think you can be a father to your child, or if you can't be a father because you really don't want this child. If you're used to tell'n me the truth, you'll tell me the truth about this or anything. That's what I want to hear, the truth.

I ain't seen too many brothers out here that are truthful. If you tell me you cheated, I'm not gonna say well you gotta get your shit and get the fuck up out of here. I'm gonna ask you some questions. I wanna know what is it about her that you had to have her? I wanna know what is it that I'm lack'n that made you go somewhere else? If it's just a man thing, a dick thing, it's not the girl in particular, I wanna know are you gonna try to get with every girl you see? Is this gonna be a constant problem? Were you fucked up, were you in heat and I wasn't there, am I hold'n back too much, or did you just want to fuck the girl? There's a reason to everything. Is it me or is it you? Just let me know.

I'll ask questions to try and understand the situation. Most girls will pitch a bitch, end it and go through the same shit with the next guy. Again and again, over and over. If I ask questions instead of cutt'n you off, I'll know what the reasons are, and if it could be worked out. Why throw away one bad apple only to get the same thing again?

Guys say it's just an attraction thing. Well, I can be attracted to more than one brother, but I don't drop my drawers and say here goes some pussy. I see plenty of niggas that look good and I'll approach them and say can I get your number? But when I get home, I'll look at my man and say naw, this number ain't needed.

I believe by nature all men are dogs, but not all men act on that nature. There are those that say, no, let me not do this to my woman. And there are those that say fuck that, I'm gonna get mine, what she don't know, she don't need to know. All men have that dog in them, but not all men let it come out. You know the difference between right and wrong, but you consciously choose the wrong. This is what brothers are do'n. Not giv'n a fuck. Choos'n wrong. Lett'n the dog in them come out at the expense of a girl that really cares about them, is truthful and is faithful to them. But those niggas will get theirs. Believe that.

I feel what's the use of hav'n a woman if you're all the time out in the streets cheat'n? If your woman ain't fulfilling your every need, fantasy and want, then let her go. Don't play her. Ain't no need to say, "Oh, I love you," and you just got out of some pussy, fitt'n to go get in some more pussy.

I don't believe it's a phase thing, a certain-age thing that you outgrow. It's what's in your head. It's the head not the heart that I believe in. The head leads in all your actions. It tells you what to do. It tells you if it's right or wrong and you make a decision. If we were all led by our hearts, without lett'n our brain tell us better, we'd all have AIDS. It's know'n right from wrong, and a child learns that immediately. It's not some pass'n phase because boys are cheat'n dogs and old men are cheat'n dogs. When is the phase outgrown if it's a phase thing? It's know'n right from wrong, and you know what you're do'n.

Young Black couples, me for example, never take the time out to talk, communicate and have their differences worked out. It's always, "I like her," "I like him." Why? Because you're fuck'n each other and the dick is good and the pussy is good. But if you think you like me, get to know me. Don't just want to up and jump in the bed with me. You don't know what I got. I could have HIV all up the ass, and you don't want to use a condom? Shit, you can have HIV, I don't know, so I'm using the condom, like it or not. Until I get to know you and see some test results, a condom will be worn.

If it's just a fling, and I don't know you, are you gonna tell me the truth and say, "By the way, I'm HIV positive." If you don't know me and you don't wanna use a condom, I'm gonna figure you must don't have shit to live for and you already got AIDS.

Most girls out here don't want noth'n out of life, and men like girls like that. Guys like girls like that. They can use these bitches to become men. The men can use these bitches to get their dick wet every now and then. They'll know that she'll always be home with your kids, struggl'n, not do'n shit, and yet satisfied. Happy with you com'n over, fuck'n her, mak'n her come, say'n hi to your kids so they'll remember your face and not be a problem for when you come get the pussy the next time.

Black men in particular play this masculine role. "Oh, fuck her." While he could have said, "I don't like what you did. It hurt." Instead, Black men will break it down into "fuck you." Women don't say fuck you. We're straight to the point, and that's every woman I ever met. You try to call it emotional, but I call it be'n direct and strong. Say'n what we mean, when we mean it and why we mean it. Then if you don't get it, then we'll say fuck you. We'll put it in a language you understand. Something you can relate to, but that's not us.

Mostly all men get what they do from right out the home. If I was a man and however I saw my father's display of love to my mother, I would pick up on that and it would make a last'n impression. If I see him show'n that he don't give a fuck about her, but every time he turns around she has food on the table for him, I'll feel I can treat a bitch like shit and she'll still have food on the table for me. It ain't in your genes or your class, it's in what you see. You'll pick up something quicker with your eye than if you're told something. I can say respect women, but you already saw your father treat your mother like shit and still have his dinner, pussy and anything else he wanted. Tell'n you to respect women is a joke. A woman ain't noth'n but a dumb bitch as far as you're concerned. Why respect her? Did your father respect your mother? And who do you wanna be like? That whole visual makes a bigger impression than me tell'n you words. My words versus your big visual picture can't compete.

I'll break the cycle by teach'n my son how to be a man, because I know there isn't a man in the street today who is capable of show'n my son how to be a man. Me, a woman, is gonna teach him how to be a man. Be'n a man ain't call'n a woman a bitch, a ho or a slut. Be'n a man ain't hav'n babies because that's what everybody else is do'n. Be'n a man is go'n to school, graduating and do'n someth'n with your Black ass, because the world is too hard out here to be all about bullshit. Be'n a man is, if you love a woman, tell her. No bullshit. You don't lead her on. Be'n a man ain't sell'n drugs, hang'n out and fuck'n just to be fuck'n, and fuck'n irresponsibly.

I'm gonna teach my son how to be a man because if it was left up to his father he'd be a pussy just like him. He be just like most boys today. Fuck'n this girl because she's fine, she has a body, or because your boy got some. No, you have sex with her cause of what's in her mind and because of what she does to your mind, not just because she makes your dick hard.

I'm not the type that's gonna tell my son, "You ain't gonna be shit, just like your daddy." That's what these angry bitches do, keep'n this fucked-up shit go'n. Just yesterday I heard, "You ain't gonna be shit, just like your father." The boy was about eighteen and the mother was scream'n this at him. If anything, I'm gonna say his daddy was a lawyer, a good man and he died in an accident. Never he wasn't shit. My son ain't gonna hear that.

I want my son to be a part of, and bring in the next good generation. Black children who'll grow up know'n better than what's now out here. Better than songs that talk about girls being bitches, hos, and tricks. And the girls are sing'n it louder than the guys.

There are many sisters who wanna be treated like what you hear in so many rap songs. A man ain't gonna do no more than what you allow him. If you know your man is out there cheat'n and you don't like it, you're supposed to cut him off right then and there. Let him know, you're nobody's toy. You can't be played with like that. If you have a man and he insists on fuck'n up and fuck'n up and fuck'n up, and you insist on tak'n him back and tak'n him back, then you deserve whatever you get. Whatever shit happens, you have no one to blame but your own dumb self. If you get pregnant, someone else gets pregnant, you get a disease, you deserved it.

If every time I see you, and some bitch is pag'n you, or you're always in some bitch's face, but she's always just a friend, then you forget about me. You can keep your bitch and so-called friend.

Even if I believed that that one brother who knows he's a man is out there for me, my main priority is still not to get with him. A man has never been my main priority. When I got pregnant, I knew the father wasn't shit. Whether he was shit or not was not a priority. I just wanted to fuck. That fuck blew up and I got pregnant. I didn't sweat him for anything. I didn't ask or demand this or that because I knew he couldn't or wouldn't do it. I just assumed, and he proved me right. He proved not to be that one man that knows he's a man, and how to be a responsible father, and I didn't fuck with him anymore. I'm just a pregnant sister about to have a baby. Don't ask shit about the father because I don't know. He's not a priority in my life, my son is. This man to be is. I'll take the negative and make a positive.

Don't come around say'n you love me when I know you don't. Don't jeopardize my life any more than you already have. I know the difference between lust, love and like. I know you got me pregnant out of lust. I don't love you, I don't even like you, so don't fuck with my head. If you want to take responsibility for your son, fine, but don't fuck with me. If he was a good man, he would have made it his business to find out when I had to go to the hospital, when the baby needed something, but he didn't, so he proved what kind of boy he is.

You can want a man, but only a lazy bitch would need a man. Any girl in her right mind, with a good head on her shoulders, wouldn't need a man. The man would really want her. He shouldn't need her, but because she's better than the rest of these dumb bitches, he would want her.

I don't need no man. I want to see what man wants me. And then I want to know exactly why you want me? I'll know why you should, but I want to make sure you know why you want me. If from your answer I get the sense that it's basically because the pussy is good, I'll know I don't need to be with you. If all you know is pussy, pussy, pussy, you ain't think'n about what's in my mind, you're think'n only about what's in this hole.

Sisters that's all about the brother with the most money, the drug dealers, they're just lazy bitches. The same bitches that stay on welfare. They need to get a job. Like they say, "No cash, get a job, lazy ass."

As for me, fuck welfare. I work. I bust my ass for my son. If didn't have him, I'd probably be somewhere hav'n a good time. But as I think about it, I'd probably be somewhere gett'n pregnant. Hav'n had the baby makes you see what the fuck you were do'n wrong. Kids slow you down so you can see the shit you were into and where you were go'n. If not pregnant, maybe worse.

When I wasn't pregnant, somebody would call me up, "Nikki you go'n out, you go'n to this party?" I'm go'n, "Oh, yeah, be there in a minute." After the pregnancy, when you have a child, you're like, "No, I ain't go'n cause my baby ain't old enough to get in the club." Once you have to sit home every day with that baby, you notice shit. You want to go back to school. You wanna get more involved. But now you also know you need a good job to feed yourself and your child. You ain't think'n that shit while you're out runn'n, hav'n a good time. You're like, fuck school. It's all about the parties and hav'n fun. Hav'n a baby and be'n qualified to only work at McDonald's, you'll see how much your ass should have been in class. You're sixteen with a child to support, work'n with thirteen-year-olds, flipp'n burgers. Mommy let them out to have their first job, and you're stand'n next to them because that's all you're qualified to do. Is that a bitch or what?

I really wouldn't know what to say to anybody out there. Had someone said to me at thirteen, I'm go'n too fast, slow down, this is what can happen to me, I still wouldn't have listened. I would have been like they don't know what they're talk'n about. They're just old and jealous. Shut the fuck up. You can't do this shit I'm do'n, and you just wanna fuck up my fun. I know, when you're hav'n fun, can't nobody tell you shit. You couldn't tell me shit. So, what can I say? I can only raise my child the way I wasn't raised. I can only tell others what I was told, and that's "You'll learn." You will learn on your own. The greatest lesson you can learn is the lesson you give yourself. Look at me now. This is my punishment. And I call it a punishment. I love my son, but I have no choice but to love him, let's be realistic. He's still a punishment because now it's harder to do what I want to do when I want to do it. Had I listened to my parents, I would be home study'n and that's it. I wouldn't be hold'n this boy. I would accomplish what I want to in life, then I would have my son, and love him the same then. But because I didn't listen, I've been punished. I've been punished with hav'n to love him this soon.

I can also look at it as a bless'n, because so many of my friends have been shot and killed by just hang'n out or party'n somewhere and shots rang out. Sometimes I think that could have been me, but because I have to stay home with my son, it's been one of my friends. It just as easy could have been me. So, I can look at my situation a number of ways. That's one of them. I can also say, had I listened to my parents, I'd be home study'n and not out gett'n shot at or gett'n pregnant.

You're affected in so many small ways like you wouldn't imagine. School football games are meant to be enjoyed. Take your baby, it cries, screams, hollers, you can't enjoy the football game if you're try'n to concentrate on your son. Ain't no need in go'n. Just tell me who won. It's like that. If I got pregnant again, today, God forgives all, but I'd have to have an abortion. What I wanted to do has been put on hold. I don't want to start over again from zero by hav'n another child. You'll end up constantly putt'n your shit on hold and you'll never do it.

I'm a responsible mother. If my son can't go somewhere and you want to date me, then I can't go. I had an opportunity to go to the movies at three o'clock in the afternoon this past Friday. My idea was to take my son, too. The nigga was like, "You need some time to yourself." I was like, a two-hour movie ain't no big deal. That ain't no vacation. What we gonna do in the movie that my son can't be there? What movie we're gonna see that he can't see? What we're gonna discuss that he can't hear? That's the way I was feel'n about it. I know it's hard to get a man if you already have a child. That's why I ain't try'n to press up on nobody. They're say'n they just wanna be with you. But if I can't bring my son along, fuck it. I am a mother, there is a child, you have to put up with him if you wanna put up with me. I don't care how damn bad he is, if you want to deal with the mother, you have to deal with the child.

See, a weak bitch would have hurried up and found a baby-sitter and, boom, she's outta there. Me, no, I'm responsible. If I wasn't before, I am now. My son can't go, I can't go. It's like that.

Step to me like a man with interest in me *and* my son. My son

is a part of me. You wanna know all about me, you're gonna know all about my son. If I'm with my son and you step to me ask'n only about me, that shows me you have a one-track mind. You ask about my son, you work'n the correct way, on two tracks.

The nigga will do for you when you ain't got that baby, but when the baby comes, he don't even want to look at you. Before you got pregnant he just wanted to hear let's go to that room, or let's go out, let's go club'n. When that baby comes it's a whole different conversation. Ain't no room, ain't no club. Let's go to the supermarket and get some Pampers. Let's go downtown to get some clothes, but they don't wanna hear noth'n about spend'n no money. Niggas nowadays wanna look fly for themselves. They wanna keep that green paper for self. They need that money to catch more and more bitches. By you want'n them to be there for their baby is slow'n them down. They don't want that. And when you sweat them, they're think'n, oh, that bitch needs me. She ain't got no money. I can fuck her and do what the fuck I want because she ain't got shit. That's why I say make your own money, bust your ass, it ain't gonna hurt. Don't ever let someone feel they have you like that. Like you can't do shit for yourself, and you need them.

Once you're a lazy bitch and want noth'n out of life, you're through. Get a job. The money is the same. It all spends the same. Fuck she needs me because I can buy her clothes. No, I can buy my own clothes. I can make my clothes. Too many girls today don't know how to do shit for themselves.

When you have a baby, you have to grow up. Ain't no two ways about it. You have to assume responsibility and get your shit together. If all women thought like me, they would be lonely. LONE-LY. No sex, no man, no kisses, no noth'n. The way niggas come at you with "I just wanna fuck, that's all." Well, go fuck yourself. Fuck your mama is the way I feel. The way they come off, think'n it's attractive because that's what they hear and see on videos is bullshit. That's what they hear rappers say, but it's just a show. They're gett'n paid to talk shit. In reality they probably have good girls. Why would they be serious with the dumb bitches they're rapp'n about? Look at Ice Cube's wife. Look at who he marries and look at who he talks about at concerts. Your dumb-act'n ass. If all women were like me, they'd be lonely because I don't settle for that bullshit.

All niggas know is pussy. "Man, that was some good pussy." But how can pussy be good if you don't know me? How can pussy be good if you don't know how the girl emotionally feels before you fuck her? That's some weak shit that brothers do. How could it be good if there's no foreplay? And foreplay are the words you say before you even do anything. Don't stop at "Let's go in the room." You get in the room and ain't another word said. All you do is go for the clothes and that's it.

Niggas need to learn. Learn they don't know shit. First they need to learn that they don't know shit, then they need to find out what it is they need to learn. Learn it and start be'n men. Stop be'n ignorant niggas. Don't know noth'n, just like their daddies. But if you're smart enough, you'll know, OK, my father wasn't about shit, so do I want to be the same, or do I want to be better than that nigga?

As for sisters, do you wanna be a lazy bitch or don't you? I'll just mind my business and raise my son, much better. Much better than the answer to those questions will probably be.

Serita

serita, 25

718 area

hairstylist

e are in trouble. We are in trouble as Black women and Black men. Unity and foundation within relationships does not exist, and it seems to the point where we do not even care. Black women who may know that they deserve better from relationships are being content and going along with all the disrespect that occurs. They feel, why bother? Is it really worth it? Who out there is really trying to fight this so-called "struggle"? They feel, "It's not being fought in my neighborhood. Is there a fight? All I see are Black boys fighting each other."

Brothers who may, at one time, have wanted a so-called "good girl" are finding contentment with the video hos they sees on Video Box. They support all the exploitation of us and Black women especially, by their willing participation. Black women are so used to seeing themselves as hos, they starts presenting themselves as hos. This helps justify what brothers are doing. We are both ignorantly helping each other. We respond to each other in terms of minimal dress and optimum body parts. We then wonder why we can't communicate. We can't communicate because no one upholds any values that requires us to communicate. We respond to each other based only on what we see.

We've forgotten about the inner self. Black men have sold out, and Black women have sold out. Black women are not look'n for men of substance. We have stopped look'n because of the obvious. We feel there aren't any Black men of substance to look for and they are not being cultivated. We generally feel Black men aren't looking for anything stable, so what are we left to do but lower our expectations and standards.

We're not look'n for men who can complement us in a positive way. We only look for the man who can satisfy our external needs instead of our interior, the material instead of the spiritual. We allow ourselves to be called out our names, in casual conversation. We now refer to each other in derogatory terms, in casual conversation, that no one deems derogatory. "Hey, bitch, what's up?" "Nothing, bitch, just try'n to make it."

I believe we do have the potential to better ourselves, but we have to decide that's what we want to do, but no one wants to take the initiative. We seem perfectly content with the way things are. We're all right with the way things are going. We know we should have someone who is healthy for us, but we've sold ourselves out. We know we should have someone who'll be beneficial to us and us to them, but we've sold out for someone who'll just do. And just do what? Pay the rent, put some food on the table. It would be nice if he could buy my son some new toys. I know the boy ain't his, but, like, I am sleeping with him. He should do that much.

We use the excuse that there are no good men left, and I personally feel it's just that, an excuse. It's an excuse so we can justify our improper lifestyle. All of how we generally feel, I personally beg to differ. All of this substandard behavior and expectations are due to limited and limiting experiences. According to those you listen to, according to the type of men Black women are conditioned to associate with, there just may be no good men out there. According to them, this is true, but I say where are you look'n? Are we allowing these good people to come into our lives? Are we be'n productive with ourselves so we have productive people in our lives? Are we goal oriented with a positive purpose, and are we seriously try'n to socialize with the person who will be an asset to our goals? Or do we hang out at the five-and-ten-dollar clubs, with the three-dollar drinks, getting hit on all night with obscene propositions, taking the best one, and then complaining that there are no good men out there?

I'm upset because although there are those out there who are try'n to do something positive, they are for the most part be'n ignored by sisters. We feel we don't want that type of person. The exact type of person we should know should be in our lives, we view them as boring, different, not down, they don't like to party every Friday and Saturday night, they don't smoke ses, they don't like spending money on the things we like to buy, and we just don't want to be with them. We just don't know any better. There's your possible good man right there, but we continue to say ain't a good man out there. I hear it all day while I'm do'n hair. We believe the good man likes hang'n out every weekend, spending money on us like it's going out of style, gett'n high with us and remain'n truthful to us. We need to realize our values are all messed up.

We need to realize that the real good person is right under our nose. He or she lives on our very same block. He's go'n to work every day. She goes to work every day. They don't have time to be hang'n out on the corner do'n nothing because they're busy do'n something productive, but you'll never know because you can't see this person. He or she doesn't look like the freaks from the videos so you'll walk right by them and not even see them, as if they weren't there. We pass him every early weekend and Sunday morning. He's on his way to work or going to church and we're coming from the Underground or Nells or the Shelter.

We hope and pray the man we're with, the one we met at the club, the one whose attention was pulled from that other girl, will be loving and caring. We hope he'll be true to us. We hope the man we're with, the one we met on the corner, do'n nothing, will be sincere and dedicated.

How many times have we dissed the nerd in school because he wasn't popular enough, he wasn't the class clown, he wasn't the flyest dresser, he wasn't always in trouble? But how many times did we run to the nerd because he did his homework and we didn't, and we needed to copy it? Then during lunch and recess we ran to the popular boy? How many times have we dissed the nerd because he was studious and preferred the boy who always had to be disciplined? Well, what are the boys doing now? *What* is the nerd doing and *where* is the other boy?

The brothers who are about nothing need to realize when a sister is about something. Let that sink in. When you're about noth'n and the sister's about something, don't project your nothing on me. Don't assume I accept substandard. I am not a street person who doesn't have any respect for herself, who doesn't have any morals, who'll accept be'n talked to in a disrespectful manner. I am not someone who stands for nothing and will fall for anything.

I carry myself with dignity and respect; I demand respect. I have a name and I wish to be called by it. My name isn't "Yo, baby." If you don't know my name, ask. I mean what I say, and I say what I mean. I don't want to be whistled at, jumped in front of, grabbed or felt and you don't even know me.

When I want to be intimate, that's when I want to be intimate. My mother told me when you want to be intimate, be intimate in the bed. Not in some building's hallway. Not in the alley. Not on a roof. Not in the school's auditorium. Be intimate in the home. Have some respect for your body. The easiest thing in the world to do is respect your body, and it doesn't cost you nothing.

My advice is to the sisters. Explore who you are and what you like. Have the self-awareness to explore what you want, where you want to go and make yourself the center of everything. Make yourself the center of everything. Your goals and your self-awareness will fill the void of any man who is not healthy for you. Know'n who you are and what you are about will carry you far. If you don't know who you are and what you're about you will end up no farther than the corner. If you don't know yourself, others will surely be quick to define you. Your avenue boyfriend will use you and be like, "Dee, my ex, that slut." So, now you're defined. You didn't have a definition for yourself, so there's one. "Dee the slut."

If you know who you are and have all the right elements for what you want, you're moving toward it and you're determined, you'll meet the person along the way. He'll see that you have already defined yourself, and now you're "Dee the scholar, Dee the success story, Dee the determined one, Dee the focused one, Dee the role model." You will be who you truly want to be and obtain those things you truly want to have, and you will deserve it. You'll know better than to want a brother who is all about nothing. You'll start to expect more for yourself and more from your Black man.

Sisters need to know if she's wish'n for her man to change, she'll be all her life wish'n. She needs to know this person isn't for her because he's not what she's about. Once you have set in your mind on what you want and know what is good for you, then you'll find yourself settling for nothing less. Less should not even come your way because less will not even be where your mind state is.

Don't worry about try'n to change the man. The advice is, **worry about chang'n yourself. Change doesn't come from try'n to change others, it comes from changing yourself. Once you change who you are and what you're about, once you change your way of think'n, can't no one step to you with anything but other than what you're about. You won't be hav'n it. The person will be dismissed.**

You will have a tolerance only for those who are like minded as you.

They will either come into your life because you know that's what you will accept only. Those who are about nothing but are try'n to get with you will have to change their ways. That's how you change someone. You change yourself. Once you change how you think, how you act, what you do, what you'll accept and what you're about, if that man really wants to be with you, he'll have to adjust in order to have you. He'll know he can't call you bitch because you're not one. He'll know not to call you bitch because you won't tolerate it. He'll know he doesn't have that type of woman. He'll know he can't run around here and there see'n this girl and that girl because you won't tolerate it. He'll know he has to act like a man. And act like one in the proper, positive, respectful sense of the word. He'll act like a man because he'll have a woman. Brothers today will openly get with another sister—you can't even call it cheat'n—because they know all they have to say is "well, if you want me to leave you for her, I will," and all is forgiven. It's gotten to the point where he can tell you exactly where he's go'n so you don't have to worry. You'll know to reach him at his other woman's house if you need him.

If you change, he'll have to change. It's not about accommodating him. It's about him accommodating you and being the best you're striv'n to be. If he wants to be a part of your world, he'll have to change. He won't do it because you made him. You can't make anyone do anything they don't want. If you do, they'll automatically rebel. They'll do the exact opposite. They'll go in the opposite direction. If you change self, and know self, there won't be any room for any manipulation of what you don't want. There's no room for any compromise. There's no room for noth'n other than mutual respect. It's that plain and simple. This is how I feel and this is the way it is for *me*. You can either be a part of it, or you can move out of the way and make room for the brother who will.

The reverse holds true, too. If you're a sister about noth'n, and you want to get with this positive, about something brother, then you have to change to accommodate his best. You hold'n a brew is not going to hold his attention. Get rid of it. Clean yourself up. Change your diet, change your bad habits. You'll have to find some direction and purpose. That way when the two of you are together, it won't be about what can you do for me? It'll automatically and mutually be positive. You'd feel an automatic sense of purpose of doing for each other, our children and our people. He'll be about positive and you'll be about positive, and that's the right track toward building a strong, unified, positive Black family. Do we think we're gonna be immature young people runn'n around party'n all our lives? At one point, whether you like it or not, you grow up. Then what do you have? How have you prepared yourself for independence? How have

you prepared yourself for bettering your community? How have you prepared yourself for meeting that good man?

We seem to talk as if we're on the right track, but we don't act like it.
And we don't act like it because we feel no one is serious about try'n to
change. We sit around like a commercial, "I'm not gonna try it, are you
gonna try it?" "I'm not gonna try it, are you gonna try it?" We can't wait for
the next man to change. We have to be the one to change. If everybody did
that, then we'll start to see a positive difference. A difference in thought,
perception and outlook. We're always wait'n for the next man, and noth'n
gets done. We talk and talk and talk about the problem, and then we go
home. We'll meet again same time next year and talk, talk, talk, talk, talk,
talk about the problem, and once again, we'll go home. Nothing is accomplished. We have only a hoarse voice to show for it. What we need to do is
go home, go in the streets, go in the community, go in the schools and
apply the talk. All these Black churches meet once a week to talk. Talk
about God and getting to heaven and how we as an individual must live in
order to get to heaven. How about saving your brother and your sister here
on earth? There are very good people in the church, but we need to get out
of the building. I've never seen a picture of Jesus in a building. He's always
out in the street making a change. Doing the Lord's work, as our preachers
like to say. Well, how much work can you do from behind a pulpit in a
building? The abuse, neglect, drug dealers and violence are outside. Ain't
nobody deal'n crack in the church. They're deal'n it outside. So go outside
and meet it head-on. The preacher will deliver an hour-long sermon about
the horrors of crack and leave drugs alone, and the entire congregation is
already drug-free. The congregation is occupied with heaven. The
crackhead, the basehead, the hard-core addict, the dealers, are outside.
    How can *everyone,* sisters and brothers both, feel that there are no good
mates out there for them? *Everyone* feels this way. A man is stand'n there
talk'n about there are no good women. Two feet away, a woman is stand'n
there talk'n about there are no good men. Now, something is wrong.
Strange how all these positive people, do'n all this jaw'n, can't turn toward
each other and say, "Oh, here you are right next to me." That's another
problem of ours. We all like to be heard and not listen to the other person.
If we did, we'll see that they're say'n the same thing we are, and they must
be or should be as positive as we are, because when *we* say there are no
positive people out there, that automatically excludes us. So how come
when we hear that coming from others, we can't turn two feet and hook
up? Because no one really listens, we all like to talk, talk, talk. We like to

hear ourselves talk. Bitch, moan and complain, then go home until the next time. We need constructive solutions that we can concretely apply. Mere words never changed anything. It's in the application. It's in the thing. Now, what thing do we have? Nothing. We have only the talk.

Once you change who you are and know self, if he messes up and leaves you for another, there should be no cause for you to get hysterical. If you're centered in self and know what's good for you, you'll realize that this person wasn't the person you thought he or she was. They weren't for your benefit and it's only right that they're out of your life. You won't need to worry about what you did wrong, what could you have done better or differently? You'll know that it wasn't you, it was him. He lost out. He wasn't about try'n to establish anything. He's not worth the energy of you call'n, plead'n for the two of you to talk things out. You don't need to know what you could have done differently because you'll then find yourself go'n backward. He's not worth your constantly think'n, worry'n about and cry'n your eyes out. What were you do'n before he entered the picture? Go back to it. He didn't make you. He damn sure shouldn't break you. You weren't a nothing before he entered your world, you shouldn't feel like you're a nothing after he leaves it.

Our mind set needs to be different. We need to have more self-worth. Realize the person wasn't what you thought they were and move on. You can be hurt and saddened by the thought of what could have been, had he or she been the right person, but since they're not, be smart about your pain. You can mourn the loss of the idea, but not the actual person if that person proves not to be the person for you. In fact, you should celebrate that you've escaped something that could have been much worse.

I can feel sad about not hav'n a positive Black man in my life, but I don't cry and beg that Black man who isn't positive to come back into my life; to come back and not contribute to my personal growth. I should be stronger than that. I know I'll meet the person who will contribute to my positive growth, and once that happens, I'll know that I made the right decision. I would then thank the former for making way for the latter.

Right now I don't have a man. It would be nice to have one to complement me and to complement my son and be a positive influence in both our lives, but if it never happens, I can be a positive influence for myself and my son. I don't let one non-positive brother who can't be a father to his son cloud how I view all brothers. That's how sisters get this "no good" view, they overgeneralize. From one or two bad experiences, they make this sweeping generalization. And those experiences could very well be more the sister's fault than anyone else's. How did he end up be'n a no-good father to your child? Did you have protection? Did you make sure he had protection? Were you both in love? What exactly were the circumstances? That's when you need to change your thought. That's when you need to see what keeps you go'n in a circle of negative and unhealthy relationships. That's when you should realize it's the quality of brothers you're choosing and allowing to come into your life. That's when you ask yourself, "Did I ever really know Fred?" Sisters are out here thinking they have a man, when they don't. If you ask them where is Fred? "I don't know." Where does Fred live? "I don't know." What does Fred do for a living? "I don't know." What does Fred think about his future, your future? "I don't know." Have you ever meet Fred's mother? "No." And yet he's your man. You'll see how much you have Fred when you never hear from Fred again. What happened to Fred? "I don't know." Now you're upset over something you lost but never had.

That's why we need to take self-inventory. That's when you develop a tolerance level. That's when you become centered in self, know self and know what and who works well with yourself. Then if this wrong person tried to come back into your life, you can say, "I'm sorry, but no, you are not for me." If he really changed, you'd be able to tell because you have changed. You'll actually be able to see if the person is for you. Your vision will be clear and your decision will be based on a mature, non-compromising basis. Not based on feeling you need a man. If he's not for you, you can remain manless for however long you need to be manless. But also know that you won't totally be alone. That's when you should be able to turn inward to self, loving yourself. Be centered in self and know that you will always be there for you. You'll be able to survive. You have friends. You have a mother. You have yourself. You have your child.

It's all about change of self. It's not about everyone accusing everyone else of be'n a good-for-noth'n. It's not about everyone talk'n and just talk'n about the problem. We all agree there is a problem. That's not arguable. So now what do we do? What do we do to help ourselves and others?

One day we should be able to all say, "What problem?" I'm with someone good, you're *not* with someone good? Well, that's odd. Negative, non-progressive people are such a rarity. Well, let me introduce you to one of my ten positive friends. You and this guy I have in mind seem to have the best matching personalities. Now I'm with someone positive, you're with someone positive, "What problem?"

IX
mrs. right

Iamide

lamide, 19

motherland

artist

I was born in Lagos, Nigeria. I was raised in Lagos and grew up in London. I have both cultural perspectives. I came to the United States to go to college, therefore I really have three different cultural perspectives on Black men and relationships. Many people think there's little difference. They think Black men are all the same wherever, but there is a difference. There is a cultural difference.

I'll talk about Africa first. The African man, specifically West Africans, have a definite polygamous attitude. This is a part of the culture and how the African male has been brought up. To have many different women at the same time is normal on the part of the man and woman. This is the culture, yet I must add there is a tremendous amount of respect shown to the African woman. Polygamy is not perceived as a disrespectful act, as others may incite. There is a tremendous amount of respect shown the African woman, especially in comparison to what I've seen here. I didn't realize how much the African woman was respected until I came here and saw how much she's disrespected. Here the practice may be the same, but the attitude isn't. Here it's not socially accepted, and many more problems are created. I guess it would be lessened if Black men and women here knew and properly practiced their original culture, but they don't.

In traditional Africa, true polygamy has the man providing for and maintaining the family. You take on more than one wife for the benefit of posterity. Continuing your lineage is very important in Africa. Where there is peasant farming, polygamy makes it more economically beneficial for African families to manage and cultivate the land, and therefore provide more income.

When the men run around after their girlfriends, this too is part of what's culturally accepted. It's not viewed as a bad thing or dogging the wife. The girlfriends are just a social hobby, like a drink after work. In Yoraba they call her *Ashewo*. Men go to the *Ashewo* for pleasure and it's understood. Everyone knows their place. The wife is the one all the meaningful attention, love, respect, honor and praise is given. The wife is the queen. Anyone else is a hobby.

Traditionally the women walk behind the man or in front of the man, it depends. Again, this can be viewed as a submissive role, but it's only tradition. It's not really a reflection of a lower attitude toward the woman. Low in a disrespectful way. This is just order of tradition.

Today in Africa, as far as some women are concerned about polygamy, there is a lot of jealousy. Black magic and hexes between the wives are even practiced because of this jealousy. And if you know anything about cultural religions, you do not usually hex people. That is not usually done or accepted, so you can see how strong the jealousy is. This jealousy is new and it's instigated. Jealousy isn't a part of traditional polygamy.

There's a lot of divisiveness among African women about the role the woman should play in society. There is a large number that believe the "stay-at-home walk-behind-the-man" structure should be followed. They feel it's traditional and cultural. They don't feel inferior to the man because they are secure women, and they would like to preserve their traditions.

Then there are the career women who are providing for their own independence. They believe the tradition is outdated and holds no significance today, only to elevate the man and lower the woman. They believe this tradition lowers her self-worth, self-interest, identity and independence. This African woman has been heavily influenced by the Western woman, the suffrage, the 1960's and the changes going on in the rest of the world. So, there is this large division. There is a huge tug-of-war between the traditional culture and the Western influence. That's what accounts for all the confusion and coups within many African countries.

Personally, I don't like to see polygamy losing much of its original purpose. I don't like when it's abused and used for pleasure rather than to benefit the survival of the family. When today's wives are only displayed as showpieces, that speaks of Western materialism. They're shown off like cars or expensive art in their mansion homes.

Those who want change are facing a lot of resistance. The African tradition is being challenged, and with many African traditions, you just don't do that. But the argument is if there is no longer a need for the survival of family, that means there is no longer a need for polygamy. If you don't feel degraded, it's because you've been conditioned to be used to it, and are so blinded by tradition that you don't know any better, as you should, because it's an unequal partnership with one man and several women. European and American influence has helped bring this out. At first you say how can you blame Europe, African women would have come to feel this way naturally. But this was going on for hundreds of years in peace, without jealousy or opposition, the woman was praised and respected, but since European influence and instigation, you do now have this opposition. Women are now believing they were never respected, when in fact they were, and still very much are. After hundreds of years in peace, and now this.

In Africa you have a large number of interracial marriages, especially Black men marrying white women, having mixed kids and telling their kids that they are half caste. This is a British term used widely in Africa for children who are products of biracial couples. The term "half" disturbs me because it makes you sound as if you're not a "whole" person. Like I was called half caste. It disturbs me because it's supposed to instill a sense of superiority over full-blooded Africans, but in reality when you go out into white society you realize you're still Black. And because you think you're "half," you don't really belong to either side, or you feel either side doesn't want you. I had to come to terms that I was Black because my appearance is Black, I'm viewed and treated as Black, and although half white, white comes from Black, so I'm Black. You can say a "whole" white person is really Black because his ancestors are Black. We're all Africans. Africa is the birthplace of mankind, and then you had evolution. White people, or *white Africans,* are due only to evolution.

But African men do like light-skin women. Again, British influence. The same as the European influence in the United States upon African American men.

The African countries that are deeply influenced with this condition are Zaire, Kenya, Sierra Leone, Gabon, and a few more. Ghana is not very much into that. Nigeria, which is their neighbor, as well as Togo, and Benin in the middle, are.

In certain African countries, you'd walk down the street and you see so many interracial couples you'd think it was the law.

A funny thing though, with the younger Nigerian men, they say they would marry a light-skin girl or a mixed girl but never take a white woman home in marriage. Their view is "You fuck a white woman, you play with a white woman, and that's it." You don't marry one. You see, African women don't sleep with you just like that. The white women that go to Africa are more promiscuous, and the Black men will take it. Many of the white women act as if their only purpose for going to Africa is to bed an African man.

There is a slow change among the younger generation of African men. It's moving from the obsession of wanting and bedding white women to feeling a stronger tie with their African women. There is becoming a high appreciation for the black African woman because she doesn't look European.

England. Now, that's a whole different matter. I'm gonna talk about London. Today, as of late, there has been a major positive movement of pride in being Black. Way more than in Africa. In fact, Africa, again, is taking their cue from the outside, but in this instance it's a good cue to take because it's from ourselves. It's from Blacks in other countries. The African American movement of Black pride greatly influenced Blacks in Africa and even more so in London.

Blacks are beginning to realize that they are not inferior. That they don't have to be bus drivers, and we don't all have to be singers and dancers or athletes. We are realizing our sole purpose here on earth was not to entertain the white man for his leisure. We recognize that we have more choice, and we want to exercise that choice. We realize we don't have to date white people to feel better about ourselves, and that was a vicious lie to begin with.

England is a very fashionable, fashion-conscious place, and it's very fashionable to mix. It's fashionable to have friends of color. I have a lot of white friends there because the attitude is "there is no color," and everyone wants to befriend you to prove there is no color.

The political system is different, it's all white, but this no-color attitude is solely the social fashion. On the social level you'll find a lot of interracial relationships. It's more common to see an interracial relationship than to see two of the same race walking down the street. There was a stage, 1986–1989, every street you went down you'd see an interracial couple, if you weren't one yourself. There'd be a Black guy and a white girl, that was the pattern. You'd even see in magazines, "the dos and don'ts of fashion: Do date a Black man."

Today, there's a difference, and that difference grew when white men started to date Black women. The white men started to put the Black woman on a pedestal and really worship her. The Black men saw this and felt, "Yeah, our women are special, they are to be worshipped. Hey, we have to get with the sisters." They felt, "We have to get back together,

Black on Black love is the thing, it's beautiful." People got into *Soul to Soul* and Jazzy B., and people started voicing us in their songs and speeches and their dramas and TV. In the shops you'd see posters expressing Black beauty. The attitude was you have to be conscious. You have to go back to your roots. You don't have to go back to Africa but you could create a little Africa in your own communities. Not be confined by your Blackness but appreciate your Blackness and openly express it.

Now, mind you, all this was triggered from the Black man seeing the white man take his woman. Then all of a sudden the Black man woke up.

There's not very much sexism in England within the Black culture. There is in the white structure, but with the Blacks, they're very much nu-wave. The new kids coming from Jamaica are not ingrained with that European sexism. They're already ingrained with a deep respect for Black women. Similar to Africa, Jamaica's culture is very much matriarchal, and the kids coming to England are largely from Jamaica, so the catching on of Black pride is understood. Jamaica already has its own history of Black pride and unity. The Black woman is very strong. She's worshipped and greatly respected for her wisdom. The men listen to what the women tell them.

Now, these niggas here in the States, I'll tell you. They do not have any respect for the Black woman at all. It's a whole new world. I mean, I learned about slavery in school. The physical slavery Africans went through here in America. But the whole mental and psychological aspect has been totally left out. You don't know anything about the psychological aspect until you come here and witness how Black men and women relate to each other. It's hard to believe these are African people.

There is no trace of the African spirit left in Blacks here. If I enslave an African and then free him, he's still an African. In thought, beliefs and in practice. In America he was freed, but he was no longer African. His African mind was totally destroyed. I can see that since being here.

This preoccupation with sex is one of the biggest things that confuses me. It's so big, you disrespect women over it. You do not do that. Even the younger, changing African men, in their most disrespecting manner, when dealing with a white woman, he's still respectful. Respect is just a natural way of behaving. Even to your enemies. You hex someone, but you don't hex or curse them to their face. Not casually. There's a respectable way of doing all things, and especially when relating to someone for their sex. In America you can walk down the street and the guy will think of you only as a sex object. I'm sorry, I don't mean to generalize, but since being here it seems every Black man is like, "Hey, baby." I'd say, "Good day," and go on about my business. But I've been grabbed and asked, "Yo, bitch, what's up with you?" After two minutes I realize they're swearing at me because I don't want to have sex with them, AND! they're disrespecting you in the middle of the street. I can see how this creates two types of sisters. One type that's very angry with Black men, she will curse you back, and the two of you fight. The second type conforms. She feels the way to get a man is to wear the hoochie shorts and be the bitch she's so often called. I can see she's told this so often she believes this about herself. She becomes manipulative and talks the way she's spoken to. She feels the type of Black woman the Black man wants is loud, loose and bitchy.

I found men here to be so possessive. They're possessive to the point of beating you, and the woman will stay and tolerate it. When I first came to the States I went to this club up in New York, called the Red Zone. I was dating this rap star. I was mingling, because I'm very social. He grabbed me to a corner and was like, "So what's up?" He wouldn't let me go and I said, "What's up with you, let me go." He said, "You're my bitch." I was like, "Excuse me," and he repeated it. "You're my bitch." I said, "Who are you talking to?" I told him I was not his bitch and don't talk to me like that. We almost had a scene right there in the club. I couldn't believe he called me a bitch. He said, "That's how we are in America. We call our girls bitches, don't take it personal." I couldn't believe it. Guys will treat you as if you're here for their own personal pleasure. Never mind what you think and how you feel.

Now I have a really nice boyfriend. He's really, really cool. He's very sensitive to me, which I think is normal, but he was so hard to find. The majority that I've met have not been respectful, not by how I know it. Not from an African to an African. It's so sad. For a while I was like, I want to go home. I was like, what's wrong with the Blacks here? They're crazy. They've really lost their minds. Then I had to realize it was the mental slavery, and I'm sympathetic. I know it wasn't until recently that you started calling yourselves African. You used to accept the term Negro. But I see things are changing.

In early tribal African cultures the woman was treated with the utmost respect. She was the mother who ran the house. Once the man stepped inside that house you gave her all due respect. That still goes on, but once colonizing came and did its thing, we're now in debates and wars over our traditions. Despite all that, the one thing that was not lost was the respect due the Black woman. Polygamy or not, respect for the Black African woman is maintained.

Blacks here in the United States have to realize, if they're serious about the term African American, they have to first learn the African part. What it means to be African, the history, beliefs, values and culture. It begins with the woman. It ends with her being the last one you disrespect.

And the other thing is Blacks here in the States have become the ones to follow. Your talent excels. You're the best in music and sports, fashion and style. The Blacks here are the cream of the crop. But before you stick your chest out. You're the cream because Africa was raped of its best during the slave trade. You come from a line of the bravest warriors. The poor conditions that exist in Africa today are because she was raped of her best. If she weren't, Africa would be twice as powerful as America is today, but she was looted of her people and materials. The rest of the world will never acknowledge this, because the rest of the world is guilty. I don't expect this. I expect us to know this and overcome the devastation.

So think again about how you feel being the best. Think and take on some responsibilities, because as being the best to follow, I understand why certain countries in Africa are so torn. Africa wants to copy you. We know you're Africans. We know you're the best that was stolen from us, so you have a lot of influence on us. But at the same time you have to realize this influence and exercise more responsibility. The rest of the Black world is watching. But if we see all the disrespect you carry out among one another, we'll look and say maybe we shouldn't look to Black America. They've trespassed the very thing we hold most dear. So how much longer should we pay attention?

If you think about it, I guess if you have the bravest, strongest and best here as slaves, you'd really have to do a lot to break them. Break their will, spirit and knowledge of Africa. This is what happened and now you have some of the bravest and strongest mindless puppets here in America. You have the bravest and strongest killing and disrespecting each other. And I really like what you've done to the number one entertainer in the world. But I don't believe they broke the spirit of every last slave that was brought here.

When it comes to sex, England and America are very much the same because we're still living under a white-dominated attitude. So whatever the white attitude is there, it's the same here, and we as Blacks follow that attitude. Here it's like, "let's see how many women we can bone this week." Same in England, especially with this new "love the Black woman" awareness. Maybe 30 percent are into sleeping with just one woman at one time. And that's a big rise because of the black awareness.

The same with women in this country. In this country and in England women think that sex is just fun. It's like sex is a pastime. It's not anything spiritual. It's nothing that's given on a spiritual level. It's nothing and emotionally giving and taking with your partner.

After moving to England and being there awhile, I started to have promiscuous sex. Then I started thinking more. I started thinking how I didn't enjoy sex anymore, it just became a hobby. I came to the point where I didn't have sex for a year because I didn't get any personal enjoyment out of it. Now that I'm in a relationship, sex is very much sacred to me. It's gotten back to being an African experience. I view sex as very special and very intimate. A very beautiful thing. I became aware of the relevance of sex from a spiritual standpoint that is very African. It became deeper. The act became more meaningful, and it was like I had returned home.

In Africa sex is very spiritual. It's very spiritual. Even if you're promiscuous it's very spiritual. It's like you're becoming one with another person. In Africa many men may date many women, but they don't necessarily sleep with all these women. A man will speak of a woman he's dating as pretty, smart, beautiful figure, but he won't have sex with her because he wants her to remain in that image. This is another level of the respect an African man will have for the woman he seriously cares for. He's not so quick to try and bed her. He'll go to the *Ashewo* for sex until he and the one he's serious with deepen their relationship.

All men have this ego when it comes to sex. You worry about, "Did I rise enough, did I come too quickly? Did I come too late?"

I've found that American and English Black men love to please women in bed because of their ego. African men love to please women because that's what sex is for. The sex is to please each other, enjoy each other. Here in the States it's like, well, I'm gonna please myself, and if it turns you on while I please myself, lucky you. I love to see you scream, and call out *my* name.

A lot of women, just as a joke go, "Yes, yes, ohh-ahhh," and fake orgasms just because we know the man will get turned on and feel good about himself. Women are too conditioned to be sexually submissive to men. Women should speak openly about sex. If you're gonna give a part of yourself, give it right.

Women tend to give themselves to their man even when they don't want to. They say, "It's just to please him." They go through the motions like they're enjoying it, and now you have all these men who think they're doing something right when they're not. That should stop. We need to say sex needs to be done better.

We give in too soon, and again it's because we want to please him, get him and keep him. That's not the way. We must be earned, not bought. Not bought again, this time from each other.

The first thing I feel Blacks here need to do is get in touch with their heritage. That doesn't mean you have to walk around wearing kinte every day, but you need to respect your heritage. We should turn all this around. All that we see keeping us down, keeping us disrespecting each other, keeping us hurting and killing each other, we need to turn around. We need to see we're really like little dogs following the master's plan. We need to dwell within our heritage and just know the fundamental things. It's all about treating ourselves and other people—women, men, children, homosexuals, straight, whatever—with respect. Treating even the white people with respect. You'll never forget but you can forgive. You treat them with respect as individuals, until they prove otherwise. Until they prove unworthy. Until someone shows that they're not worthy of your respect, you should automatically give it to them.

We need to have pride and believe that our race is the best. That's what others do, and I can't blame them for that. That's what the Jews do, that's what the Asians do, the Spanish countries, every race except us, and we need to do that also. We have to think and travel within before we can help the next person. We need to travel within and find out what's wrong within ourselves. We need to listen to preachers, even if it's Christian, Muslim, Tribal religion, anything. We have to think more, use our brain. The brain is the most powerful thing on this earth and we neglect our brain. We don't use 90 percent of our brain, and that's for some of us who are thinking. Those who aren't thinking neglect 99 percent of their brain. We need to open our eyes and see what's going on around us.

The first thing that needs to be done is to treat the Black woman with respect. If you don't treat Black women with respect, then we will go to men of another race, and you won't be able to get us back, even if you wake up. It'll be too late. We'll ignore the Black man and we won't have a culture or race left. We don't have much of a pure breed left anyway. It's beautiful that we have all these complexions, but it has to stop being at the sacrifice of our culture.

Through it all I think there's a lot of change happening. I think there's a lot of positivity coming in. I think there's a lot of good energy coming forth, and an increase of pride going on. I think more of us are getting back to our roots, and I know it's gonna take a while before we all grab hold of that root, but I do see the change coming. *Umoja,* as we say.

She**r**yl

sheryl, 27

yard

med student

Black women as a whole don't respect Black men because they are wrongly basing their definition of *man* on what we've learned from the ruling white society. We are judging our culture, a culture that has a whole different set of emotions and spirituality, by one that hasn't any. Not the same. Not our emotions. We're looking at a race whose whole history can be summed up by greed. Power-hungry, land-hungry exploiters. They couldn't leave other cultures at peace. They had to upset and destroy. So here we are, judging our Black men by these standards of greed, power, destruction. We indirectly ask, how greedy and power hungry are they? We directly ask, "How much is he making? Is he a doctor, lawyer or engineer, drug dealer, hustler?" The occupation doesn't matter. It's not that he's a doctor, saving lives; a lawyer putting criminals behind bars, he could be a defender for all we care. What matters is a doctor makes money. A lawyer makes money. A politician is powerful, he's above the law, it's not that he's making a profound difference for society. Politicians can give a damn about the average working Joe.

This value has permeated on all levels. All economic, social and racial backgrounds. If I'm in the ghetto, I have to be king of the ghetto. I mock, with whatever means available within the ghetto, the lifestyle and value of the ruling class. In the ghetto, what's available is what the ruling class supplies. Drugs. So, I have to be drug hustler. I'm liv'n large for a short while before I'm gunned down, but I'll mimic the ruling class by obtaining the Lexus, the Fendi and all the promiscuous, illicit relations my money will allow me to have. We become the Ivan Boesky, Leona Helmsley of the projects.

Black men define themselves in these terms and Black women define themselves in these terms. We've become so materialistic. It's become, what can this man do for me? "What have you done for me lately?" "Ain't noth'n go'n on but the rent." We're about due for another song along these lines, to help remind us of just how materialistic we are. It's, what can he do for me? Not, what is he about? What does he stand for, his concern for humanity? We believe what we've seen and see in the media. We believe in Blake Carrington and J. R. Ewing. I don't know who the contemporary Ewings are, I don't watch TV anymore.

We believe Rambo and Terminator, once they've killed and maimed half a country, are viewed as real men. Similar to our Native American brothers and sisters, mowed down by western cowboy heroes, real men.

This country is not unified by any moral code, practice of belief. We try to have one. You hear them every major election. Good, clean American values. We're told what they should be, not what they are. America is turning out *Terminator I, II* and *III. RoboCop I* and *II. Friday the 13th, I* through *XIII.* This seems to be the prevailing ethical code. This is what's produced more and has more weight than any once-every-four-year political rhetoric on ethics. Where are the sequels to the moral movies? This isn't what America wants. The top-grossing box office receipts will tell you where America's standards are, and sadly enough we African Americans have bought into it. Why do you think they make sequels? Then they wonder why crime is the outlet for all the ghetto conditions that are politically created? Hollywood doesn't care about Capitol Hill. Capitol Hill don't care about Hollywood. And they both don't care about your average American. They both care about staying on top and mak'n themselves capital, and that means exploiting the majority, and that's about as common a denominator as you'll get between the two.

The reality is that our good men, the ones we should pay attention to, are bus drivers, garbage men, train conductors, mailmen, blue-collar workers. They're work'n an honest job and that's an important beginning to all you need to know. Pay attention to the Black men on unemployment. Not the ones on unemployment who sell drugs for the government to their own people as an alternative, but those who refuse to be made a puppet and are struggl'n to stay a man.

You find out what his views are, his passion, his soul. We've internalized the important things to be how much do you make? If we're told six figures, we want to marry him. That's not the way we should be, nor originally are. We shouldn't know anything about these ridiculous divorce

settlements that occur day in and day out. Materialism. That's why everyone wants to get with or get into a Fortune 500.

I'd marry a garbage man. If he's the type of person I'd marry in morals and spirit, his occupation doesn't matter. As long as it's an honest one, it doesn't matter. My requirements do not include his job, it requires him as a person.

His blue collar, if that's the case, is not a reflection of his ambition. Not in this country. Especially if you're a minority. There's a lot more to it than lacking the ambition to succeed. I'll pass on the details. It'll only upset me, and I'm in a good mood. But if you don't know, read any Black history book not written by a white man.

My numerous experiences in medical school have confirmed many times over that we are just not wished to succeed. Why is the only Black med student, as part of a general medicine team, during medicine rotation, the only student not paged to participate and observe X-ray photos? If not for the sympathy of an Asian student, who paged me when he and everyone else were paged, I would be assed out. "Another Black who wasn't smart enough. Who lacked the mental faculties." No, just a victim of racism. If not for this Asian, another minority who understood the racist games they were playing at Temple University, I'd be behind and frustrated, fed up and possibly another minority student dropout. And then for the record it would appear that I couldn't cut it. But for reality it would have been that I couldn't cut through the racism. And I say Temple University because this was not an isolated incident. I'm not being overly sensitive as a woman or overly sensitive as a Black person. Racism is racism. And subtle, sneaky racist tactics is the standard practice and general atmosphere at Temple University as far as I'm concerned. The saying, "We have to be twice as good" is no joke. But, really, we just have to have twice the patience, tough skin and tenacity of the average person for all the bullshit you'll go through if you're Black. It's not so much being smarter. I can be as smart as my white colleague, but I'm facing subtle and effective bullshit that my white colleague isn't. My white colleague can dedicate full attention to his studies, while I'm interrupting mine by having to think how pissed off I am at this last act of bullshit. I'm constantly under suspicion and second-guessed. How did I get in and make it through an Ivy League? Was it because of affirmative action? I'm not asked was it because I was in the top two percent at my previous school? It's not so much being brain smart as it is street smart when you're up against racist behavior and practices. You just have to know how to anticipate and play their little games.

But my point was, your blue-collar job is not a reflection of your ambition. As long as you're ambitious enough to provide a comfortable and moral living for you and your family, I feel that's enough. If you can help someone else along the way, that's even better.

Black women simply need to reevaluate what they look for in a man. Evaluate it through the eyes of a Black woman, not through the eyes of a Black woman looking through the eyes of white America. Show me a Black man who's committed, has redeemable values and morals, loves his Black woman and Black race, and I'll show you an available woman.

These little racist episodes are what build solidarity for me and the Black community. Better than ever, I know I need to hold on to and love my Black man that much more. When we really know what we were up against, we would bond that much closer. That's the up side of racism. The down side is as long as we don't know, and we continue to operate only within the four walls of our ghettos, we'll continue to turn on each other, fight among ourselves and continue to bring each other down.

I really don't want to exhaust myself on why Black men don't respect Black women. I know why. I've seen the bigger picture. It makes me love Black men that much more. So if I hear the Black man's a dog, I say I love him that much more. I have to. Why bring him down any further? We have to build. I know that there are beautiful Black men out there. I know he loves and cherishes his Black woman. He too knows we have to build. We'll find each other. And we'll help the next person and generation.

There are healthy Black relationships out there. I've been a part of them. I feel once we learn how much we really do need each other in order to survive, physically and psychologically, we will generally love and respect one another. There are those of us who already know this and it's just a slow grind until we are all aware. Until we all love and respect ourselves and one another.

A change will come. Change is natural. Everything changes. Even the dismal state of Black folks. I'll meet my positive mate. Preferably someone from Yard, like me, a fellow Jamaican, that's the only request. It's not a must, but the cultural match is ideal. Like my sister and her new husband. My brother Dwight and his girlfriend. Like my parents, married over thirty years and still going. If he's not from Jamaica, my second request is that he be of African descent. We can bridge any cultural differences. It won't be that much anyway, if he's a Black man.

More of us only have to continue to become aware, know what's up and we'll be on schedule. Now, excuse me. I gotta go back to study'n. Despite what some might wish and conspire against, I am going to be a doctor.

Much love to all Black men and women.

X

Wisdom

some are wise, some are otherwise

- proverb

eunice

eunice, 34

brooklyn

I don't think my generation's state is critical. But that's only my personal viewpoint. We have our problems, but I should say we're not *as* critical. My age group is not out there shooting each other over clothes and shoes, and making babies to prove manhood and womanhood. My generation has come to the point of understanding each other a little better. It comes with age and it comes from our difference in upbringing. The way I and many of my friends were raised is not the norm for how many children are raised today. In terms of communication with my generation, being up front and forward is the way to go. There is no more time for being unsure of what and who you want. And things do seem to work out better once we know from the very beginning what we want and can communicate that. One big help is that I find men have gotten to the point of expressing themselves better than when they were younger. Although I knew what I wanted, the guys were still running around unsure of themselves. As you get older you see the truth behind girls mature faster than boys.

My relationship, personally, I'm working it out. I have a mate that is still kind of selfish. His most famous words are "my, I and mine." He's not willing to sacrifice. I try to explain to him that he has to learn to share. You cannot be in a relationship and continue to think and do only for self. He has a good heart, but sometimes that good heart is doing only him the good. You have to share that goodness. This is what creates the problems. I understand that your things are yours, but can you expect not to share what's yours if you're in a relationship? Or, other than sharing, shouldn't you consider how your belongings may be interfering with another person. I can respect what's yours and your personal enjoyment, but I feel you should be thinking whether your personal enjoyment is a joy for someone else or is it a inconvenience. It's a two-way street.

The apartment is but so big. He has enough music and DJ equipment to open a music store. I ask if it can be turned down. He says no, there are no knobs. This is what he tells me. It's permanently set at a certain level. It's so loud you can't hear the lyrics. All you hear are the walls vibrating. But he does not like to compromise. He says this is his job, this is his enjoyment, he's not out there running around with other women, this is his other woman, and I should be glad. I do take that into consideration. I respect that. I do consider his feelings, but he has to consider mine. Of course I would rather him be into his music than running behind other women. I would love to allow him to have his equipment in the house if we can have the sound at a decent level, but his equipment is made for a dance hall, not an apartment. I tell him, "Rob, you should get a space where you can practice." Rent a studio or some space where he can go and practice, not an apartment building where I'm not the only one who lives here. I'm not against music, but I have to respect my neighbors. I have to consider them. They may not respect me, but I have to respect them. My neighbor above, she's moved, but while she was here, partied all the time, all night. She was young, and every weekend and many weekdays it was party time. But I'm not gonna allow my man to play his music to get back at her at times she might be trying to rest. My neighbor on this floor is my buddy. So I want to respect her privacy and not have loud music from my apartment going to hers. Everything is about working together. Next-door neighbors, boyfriends, anything.

One day Rob asked if he should take on a DJ job with a person that more than once treated him bad. I said he should not take the job and leave the man alone. I said this person has a whole lot of heart for asking in the first place, and if you ask me, no you shouldn't take the job. He didn't like my answer. He says my answer is based on not liking his music. I'm trying to tell him the man is trying to shit on him once again and he should leave him alone, but Rob is not taking my answer for what it is. He's wondering if I'm saying it just because he feels I'm against his equipment. You asked me, I told you my answer. If you don't like it, you shouldn't have asked. Don't take my answer and then twist its meaning. The answer is based on what I know about this other person, not because I won't let loud dance-hall music be played in my home.

Living with a man has its ups and downs. We're used to each other and of course that helps. He has a ten-year-old daughter from another relationship and he has a good relationship with his daughter. I encourage that. There were some stressful moments where he was caught between trying to settle down with his daughter's mother and be a family. He feels that the right thing, but their relationship wasn't working out. I told Rob I feel a family should be together if they can be together and he's a good man for feeling that way, but I told him don't be blind to the fact that he and the mother have their differences. It seems to be the same differences that they can't get over because of who they are, and if it can't be worked out, don't try to force it. You can't force it. I do love him enough to let him go be a family to his daughter if that's what could be, but I also love him enough to point out the problems. I'm not using the excuse that I love him and I'm saying this because I don't want them to be together, I'm way past that. I'm also his friend and I'm saying what a friend should say if that's what they saw and knew. Just like with his music being played here and his taking certain jobs, I'm gonna give you the truth.

Rob and I met at the Casablanca. He was the DJ. It was my birthday and my girlfriends took me there. One of my girlfriends knew Rob. She brought me there with the idea of introducing me to him. She had told Rob about me and he was ready to talk to me before even meeting me, but when he was brought over and we were introduced, I was not into him. I wasn't listening to what he was saying and I was out of the conversation. He told me no matter how hard I tried to run from him, sooner or later he was gonna catch up with me. Two days later he was at my door. My girlfriend gave him my address. She told me she did, but I didn't believe her, not until he showed up. We talked for quite a while and he left saying that he'd come back the next day or the day after. He was telling me he wasn't gonna stop pursuing me. He didn't and he made me a believer. At this particular time I wasn't believing much of what men were saying. That was the frame of mind I was in. From one bad relationship before Rob, I was feeling that I just didn't want to be bothered with men, but he made me a believer. By being consistent with what he said he'd do, I was made into a believer. I was putting faith and trust in him because I had to say to myself not all men are the same. Whoever was before him is not him.

It took a year until I felt this way and that this is the beginning of a relationship. He asked, the same as he was asking all along the way, if I finally felt ready to be in a committed relationship. I took a couple of more days and then gave him the answer yes. Past relationship or not, you have to take your time and know what you want and what you're getting into. Also, you see, if a man wants you, he'll go out of his way for you. If you

need a year and he's serious about you, he'll be there. That's one year
dedicated to the many y'all can have. No need to rush. You really have to
be careful and patient and know what you're getting into.

Example, my neighbor above me, that moved, she's been with this man
for three years. She has a child by him, but she didn't take her time getting
to know what she was getting into. Now, to this day, he beats her down.
They had to go to court. She had to call victim services because of him. He
kicked her door in. He beats her in front of their child. Do you know when
she moved, she took him with her.

She once asked me how to get rid of him. I told her to sit him down and
talk. I said she would have to tell him that he can't treat her the way he's
been treating her. It's not good for her and it's certainly not good for their
children. He doesn't hit the child, but you know the child is being affected
watching him beat their mother. Either sit him down and talk this out or
just up and leave. But she was too afraid of him. She was so afraid of him
she would leave her own apartment and hide because of him going off on
her. This is her apartment, not his. You don't let anyone run you out of
your own house, having to call the police to have him removed. Then she
lets him back in later on. That's not solving anything. After giving her my
answer she became annoyed with me. I think she expected me to be a fool
like her. She wanted me to say something like, well if *you* do this for him
and *you* do that, things will be different. But she wasn't the problem. It
wasn't what she could do for him. She didn't have the problem, but she
wants me to tell her what she can do with herself to make things better. I
told her all right. I told her exactly what she needed to do, but she didn't
want to hear it. So now she has an attitude with me. One day she tried to
call me out by saying, "I see your man is back in your life." Like, I couldn't
take my own advice and get rid of him. I said yes, he's back but he's not
beating my brains out. We have a different kind of problem. We can work
out our differences, but can she stop her man from beating her every other
day? I didn't make any changes to make things better. We made changes
for the better.

I told her one day he could kill her, and to this day she hasn't said a
word to me. I saw her last week across the street. I asked, how's the new
apartment? Do you know she didn't open her mouth. And this is someone
who has come running to my apartment to hide from her man. I'm now
risking my health by him coming to my apartment. I'm protecting her,
trying to help her and now she can't say one word. She feels I'm trying to
break them up and not help them. She wants an answer, but she don't
want the answer to be that she has to leave him. She says he says he loves
her. OK. You know, what can you do? She says he says he loves her.

I was taught you try and work things out. I was taught you have to sometimes stand back and let that person breathe. You have to take time apart to get yourself together and at the same time the other person is getting himself together. You then come together, talk about what you think and how things can be worked out. You have to be able to be patient, leave the person alone and let them think on their own. I know how emotional and quick women react because of emotions, but those reactions are not always the best. If you take the time to pull back and think on what's going on, how you both can work things out, consider his views, respect his views, consider your views and then see if you can work together, that's better than reacting on just emotions and thinking a problem is being solved.

My mother told me you do not get involved with a man that doesn't respect his parents. You must pay attention to how he relates to his mother. Do you ever hear him say, "I love you" to his mother? I know men have a problem with expressing themselves that way, but does he do or say anything that says he respects and loves his mother, a woman. How he relates to his mother can be how he sees women.

I was taught if a man is abusive while you're courting him, you immediately get out. Don't excuse anything. Don't say we're just starting out and things will get better. Don't feel you need to change yourself to make him better. You should go in the exact opposite direction. If he's abusive while you're courting, you should say, "Things will only get worse if I continue seeing him. If I let him feel he owns me because of a relationship, he'll really flip." Don't think things will change for the better. We have this problem of excusing what we know and later cursing ourselves because we should have known better. When you continue to turn things around, it can cause some serious problems. You then have someone like my neighbor.

My mother taught me you have to love a person enough to leave them alone if they're no good for you. You have to be that strong. No matter how lonely you'll be, don't get involved if you can see the relationship will not be any good for you.

It was me and two more sisters growing up in my parents' home. I'm the oldest. Both sisters are married and in good marriages, and I'm so sick of them teasing me about being the oldest and not married. I haven't been that lucky. I tell them Lotto hasn't come in yet. And I'm not settling for less. They know this is what we were taught. One sister and her husband were together since high school and then they got married. The other sister was engaged for two years before she got married. You take your time make sure you know what you have and what you're getting into.

This is what we were taught and they have the good results from it. Plus, because of my son I've had to be more cautious. When you have a child, men are also cautious. There's more than one reason why I'm still unmarried.

I can't say whether or not I see myself marrying Rob. I have to leave that up to God. If He feels that Rob is for me, then that's who I'll be with. But first we have to work on our differences. Our moments of bickering have to be solved. I can't excuse the fact that we do bicker or play that fact down. If I do that, I'll have no one to blame but myself if things blow up and become worse down the line. I'll be saying I should have known better, but I'm not going to do that. I'm too old. At this age I should know something.

I love peace in my life and I want to be able to take care of any problems, no matter how small they are, now. If we can find peace and come to an understanding now, then I'm willing to take things to that next level. I understand there will always be problems, but I want to make sure I'm with someone who's willing to meet in the middle, be cooperative and work things out. As of now, Rob is not totally meeting me in the middle. Once I see he can meet me in the middle to work out any problems, I'll be ready to take our relationship to the next level. And he is coming around. So, I know he can change. There were some bad habits he had, I expressed my feelings and he changed. He's told me he's willing to cooperate with me about the music. He said he'll take some of this equipment that's here now out of here. But I don't get happy behind what someone says. As of now the equipment is still here. I know he's the type to follow through on what he says, but this time he may drag his feet about it.

My mother also taught me when you're in a relationship and there is love, you have to constantly be aware of the other's feelings. You have to ask yourself how would they think about this or that? I know how I would feel from a woman's point of view about something, but you have to also consider how the man may feel about things. There's always a difference. If there isn't, then at least you considered that there may be. This helps tremendously. You must think for two when you're in a relationship. There are two people with two different sets of feelings and thoughts on anything. You must consider those and not assume his is the same as yours. You can avoid many problems that way. I was taught you should treat people the way you want to be treated.

My mother is from North Carolina. She passed away two years ago, but her words and advice are still with me. My father is still alive and they were together until her death. My father's biggest thing was he'd like to warn his daughters about avoiding married men. His number-one concern was not to get involved with a married man. Today, I can now spot a married man a mile away. My girlfriends would say, Robin, you didn't even give him a chance to say two words, and I'll say because he's married.

The things my mother taught me are not being taught today. Especially mothers to daughters. If I was to go into a boy's house as a teen and young woman, it would be in his living room, the kitchen, and the bathroom if I had to go. Certainly not his bedroom.

I'm a grown woman and I still respect and address people as Mr., Miss or Mrs. Even if I'm on friendly terms with them, I'll address them like I'm supposed to. People I've known since I was younger would say I don't have to call them the way I do, but I'd feel funny otherwise. I feel more comfortable saying Mr. or Mrs. Jones. If I'm calling their first name, I'll say Miss Bernice or Mr. Henry. I don't care how grown I get, I'll still show you that sign of respect. And this is a respect that I just don't see out there anymore. Parents let their children call them and other adults anything they want. I hear what they call each other, so I fear what I may be called.

I have a son and he feels, "Mommy is too strict. Mommy is too old-fashioned. Mommy is mean." But it's all for his best. Of course he doesn't see it that way, but one day he'll come to know that it couldn't have been any other way. Especially if he lives to be an old man. In his day and time he'll look back and thank God I raised him the way I did.

I was a mother at sixteen. I had to learn the hard way. As I got older, I realized I was being taught and raised a certain way for a reason. I wised up very quickly and then took everything to heart. I sure didn't continue to do wrong after my son. My grandmother would say there's a difference between making a mistake, learning from it and making a mistake and not learning anything. You make the same mistake over and over again. It's no longer a mistake, it's stupidity.

My son's father is still somewhat involved in his upbringing. I say somewhat because I'm not too sure about his type of upbringing. My son is now eighteen and he tells me he's going to hang out with his father. I tell his father, if he wants his son to respect him, partying, and *only* partying, with him is not the way to go. He's thirty-three and is taking his son to parties where older women are asking my son to come live with them. I have to call his father, raising hell. You do not do these things. My son says, "Daddy says to tell the women we're brothers." They do look closer to being brothers and anybody can believe it. So now I have to worry about my son being taken for his father's running buddy, his homeboy and not his son. I don't want to not let his father be involved in his son's life, but I don't want him involved in a negative way. I have enough trouble with negative influences without him. If this is all it's gonna be, I can't be hav'n it.

My son has a girlfriend. She's a beautiful girl. I tell my son, you see how your mother struggled for us to live decently. For us to have a roof over our heads and food in the house. Don't go mess this girl's life up. His and hers. I tell him over and over again about not mistreating women. He says, "But Ma, I love her." I say, well what about these other girls and the phone ringing? "Oh, they're just friends." They'll call when his girlfriend is here and I have to tell him to tell these girls his woman is here, tell them he'll have to talk to them later. I have to lecture him about this. One day he came home upset. I asked him, what's wrong? He says he was at his girlfriend's house and she was on the phone with some other nigga while he's there. I say, see, what did I tell you? What goes around comes around. If he shows her the respect while she's here, she'll show him the same. It upsets him when it happens to him, so now he sees how it feels. You have to think for two. Like I've been taught, that's what I teach him.

I jokingly tell him I'm too young to be a grandmother. If they're out there catting around, as my father used to call it, he has to be smart. Use what's available to be used. I let him know that she is not allowed to sleep over. That was a big issue last month. "But Ma, you do it." Wait, wait, wait. I'm grown and independent. This is my house. I ask him, what is he? Besides his mama's boy. What does he do? He says her mother says if it's too late, he can sleep in the basement. I said get the girl's mother on the phone. I told her mother the only way to let my son stay at her house is if her daughter and her are sleeping in the same room for the entire night. The mother says to me, "I trust my baby, I know she won't do wrong. I talk to her all the time." Yeah, I talk to my son till I'm blue in the face, too. Are these young people listening? Don't get me wrong, the girl is a beautiful child, but I know she and my son have a mind and feelings of their own. Despite what I and the mother say, they gonna do as young people do. Not listen or think. I can only hope they half listen. And if I can half cut into the opportunities they have, then maybe as time goes on they'll get smart and be smart on their own. I can only believe without my help they would have been parents by now. I don't know, but I'm gonna do my job as a responsible mother.

I had to call the girlfriend out one time. I was home and she came over and went straight to my son's bedroom, where he was. I said I'll sit here and see how long she stays back there. I thought I give them a chance to come out on their own. Now, if this mother talks to her daughter, what is she saying? I see it's not anything about going into a boy's bedroom. Now, what if I weren't home?

So, I'm waiting for them to come out of the bedroom. I look down the hall and I see that she made herself comfortable. She's sitting on his bed. I had to tell her to come out. I had to explain to her that you do not disrespect me like that. I told her you're a young lady and to me you present yourself as one. No one sees what's wrong with going into a boy's bedroom. And when they walk out pregnant, no one still sees the wrong. My son goes, "But Ma, let me ask you something. Why can't I do what you're doing? I'm grown." But no, you're not grown. You don't have a job. You live with your mama. If you get this girl pregnant, I'm the one who has to raise it. The baby will either be here or at the other grandmother's house.

I tell him about the streets and not doing what everybody else is doing. I tell him if he's out there and gets in trouble, even if he's standing there watching something go down, and he gets caught up and goes to jail, don't bother calling me. "But that's wrong, Ma. I'm your only child." Yes, and I taught you better. You know right from wrong. And if you choose to do wrong, I choose not to try and help you. You made your choice, I'll make mine. You help yourself. If you're grown enough to choose to do wrong, you'll be grown enough to help yourself out of what you created. I can see if I neglected my part as a mother and didn't teach him any better. I'll feel it's my fault and maybe I'll try to help. But if I know I'm every day telling you right from wrong and you go and do wrong, what do you want me to do? I wash my hands of you. "That's cold, Ma." And that's cold what you've done to me. Don't dis me and I won't dis you.

There was a day when you saw kids fighting. You'd break it up and send the kids on their way. Today, you try to stop the fight, they'll curse you out, fight you, go home, tell their parent and the parent wants to fight you. I'm going OK, OK, I just thought I'd try to help your child. I know if my child was getting jumped by five people I'd want somebody to help and break it up.

I know the streets will raise my son, too. He once tried to talk back to me and he lost his front teeth because of it. This was only last year. He got out of hand, he let his mouth get out of hand and he got knocked in it because of it. He mumbles now. He'll go in his room mumbling, thinking I don't hear him, but mumble too loud and he'll lose some more.

He wants to come in 6:00 A.M. in the morning. I want to know what job will he be coming from at this time of morning? I tell him I hope there's a paycheck at the end of the week. "Well, then I going to stay with my father." I tell him to go ahead, I'll help pack. He wanted to stay with his father and stayed for all of two weeks. His father calls saying he's bringing him back. This is after two weeks. I've raised him his whole life.

He tells me, "Ma, I could be selling drugs, you don't know, you have to let me make my own mistakes." This is how a young person says let them do what they wanna do. I tell him I would be a terrible parent to let him make those mistakes. To do wrong while I just sit back and say he'll learn from his mistakes. No, it's my job as a person who has brought life into this world to not let him make mistakes that I know he can avoid. I'm not the parent to let him snatch a purse and then split the profits with him. I know a parent in this building who is encouraging her son in his dealing drugs. She accepts all the things he buys her, so, to me, that's encouraging him. She ain't saying no, son, that's wrong.

It's other things to do other than deal drugs. I did factory work to put food in his stomach. You relocate if you have to. Selling drugs is not a last resort. It's really more of a chance to live the lifestyle they want to live. Driving Maximas, wearing the latest and most expensive everything. If many of these young people have the choice between a legitimate job and selling drugs, they'll sell the drugs. No jobs out there ain't the reason. That's the excuse. They're out there so at sixteen they can have a Maxima or an SL500. I was in the emergency room two months ago. This little fool, that's what I call him, he was in there with his leg shot up. He's carrying on, "I ain't got time to be in here. I'm losing money. I ain't got time for X-rays. I need to be out. Let me go." This boy didn't care. He's got bullets in him and he wants to be back out there selling drugs, making money and getting shot at again. All he knows is I have to live this lifestyle.

The system has everything to do with the state of things. If my son does something wrong, and I get on my child, the BCW tells me I'm doing wrong. They wanna tell you how to raise your child. My child does something wrong and I get on him, but the courts dismiss his case for a number of reasons. If they do get to jail it's like a country club. They go to jail and get three meals a day and law degrees. If I want a degree I have a problem with loans and grants. I'm supposed to pay the loan back immediately. But if I do a crime and go to jail, forget a loan. Forget rent, bills, where your next meal is coming from and I can get a degree.

Things are set up so after jail we can't deal with the outside. We want to go back. I've heard men say they can't function out here and they're so used to being in jail that when they get out they don't know what to do with themselves. The jails are not preparing them to function out here. So they'll do something to go back.

I met a lady downtown at family court. She's pregnant and she has a six-year-old daughter. Her sixteen-year-old son was selling drugs and bringing all these bad elements around her home and she put him out. The courts tell her she has to take him back in. He's physically fighting her and she's pregnant. They told her if she couldn't control her son, they were gonna take all her children from her. The unborn baby and her six-year-old daughter. They're telling her she's an unfit parent. Her daughter is not the problem. Her unborn child is not the problem, yet this is what they're telling her. Her son now knows he can do anything he wants. She's at her son's mercy. The parent's at the child's mercy and the system sets it up this way. She asking for help with her son and they tell her she's an unfit mother. They're gonna tell her she's not doing her job. She sends him to school. If he don't go, what can she do? He's fighting her back and she's pregnant. Instead of killing him, she asks for help, they threaten to take two children who are not the problem from her. Children who it seems are turning out to be the best they can be, but now, if they're taken from their mother they're gonna be the worst they can be. They're now labeling three more Black children as failed and substandard and inferior. Another destroyed Black family.

They wanted me to take my child to a psychiatrist. He's a straight A-B student. He always finishes his classwork first and then he gets bored. He starts talking to his friends. The school calls me and says with my permission they want to take him to the psychiatrist. They're so quick to label a Black child a socially dysfunctional and a problem child. They'll do anything but give him more work to do. It seems to me the problem is he's smart, he finishes first and gets bored. And they want to take him to a psychiatrist. They're the one that needs the doctor. I told them did anyone think to give him more work? He's an A student and they talking about putting my son in special ed because of what they see as a behavior problem. They want to put an A student in a class with C and D and straight F students. They think I'm a mother, like many, who don't know their child is a bright student, I'm a single parent too busy to know my child and so when they say he needs to go to special ed I go OK. I told them if they put this A student into a class where he doesn't belong, I will own the Board of Education.

If you can't bring a child in this world and be there for him or her every step of the way, making sure that they grow up to be the very best they can be, then don't have one. I was told by my grandmother that it takes more energy to do wrong than do right. If we want to better ourselves and our lives, stop wasting all this energy doing the wrong thing and then taking more energy to try and correct that wrong. Taking more energy to cry and worry and go crazy over the wrong we create. Things only become worse. If we do right from the start, everything will fall into place with no effort. It's less energy, pain and discomfort to do what's right. Some things are on us and some things are on the system. Let's correct our thing. We shouldn't have the system and ourselves against us. If we straighten ourselves out, we then can straighten out the system. As long as we're our worst enemy, we'll continue to be taken advantage of. We need to begin with doing the right thing for ourselves first. I pray for us all the time because I sometimes feel no one else does.

lucille

lucille, 84

saluda, south carolina

retired

I first came to New York in 1935. I came like many Black folks came north, for better opportunities and better living conditions. I was twenty-five years old. Before I left Saluda, I worked on the plantation. The plantation was called Henry Ellis plantation. I was a cook. I washed, ironed and cleaned. This is also where my husband worked. M. L. Coleman was his name and he worked as a farmer and a cook. He became a cook once I got pregnant. He took over my job when I couldn't perform my duties.

We grew up together. We went to the same school, church and we worked on the same plantation, working for the same white folks. We started courting in 1926.

We went to church. Mount Enon Church was my church. One day out the month we would visit different churches around the local areas. Lock Heart was one. That's where I got married. Saint Paul's was another. This was how we dated. This is what we would look forward to. We ain't have no movies to go to. We'd go off to places for walks.

You were allowed to be alone?

Yes.

Was that because you knew better not to do anything?

I did. I didn't have sex, if that's what you mean. I was a virgin. I was a virgin until the day I got married. Of course he wanted some. He did like everyone else, but it wasn't really like be'n pressured. He'd ask and I'd say my piece and that was that. We did kiss though. French-kissed. He wasn't the first man I kissed like that though. There was another man who I really loved. I was so in love with this one particular person.

Now, that's who was supposed to be my husband. He had to leave with his sister for Philadelphia to seek work. He wrote me a couple letters and I wrote him back. He didn't promise anything in the letters and that was the thing. I didn't know what his intentions were, and when he came home in August I had just gotten married in July. I had put him out of my mind once the letters stopped, but he came home to marry to me. He was saving to come back and get me and marry me, but I didn't know that was his plans. He wasn't the type to express himself, he just did things. He assumed he would come back and marry me, but it was too late. That really hurt. To this day I haven't gotten over it. I don't know where he is today. Probably dead and gone on to glory. Patrick Bouknight was his name.

I got married to M. L. Coleman July 26, 1931. My husband soon left for Philadelphia to find work and then on to New York. He wrote that he was going to send for me once he found us both work.

At that time it was very normal for a husband to go to another state or city to find work and then send for his wife and family if there was one. No one thought they were being left. Up north was where everyone was heading. It was a new place and you'd want your family with you. Husbands couldn't get their wives with them fast enough. It was different times. If nothing else, the family was all you had.

I was still at home with my mother until I got married and until I was ready to join my husband in New York. My mother was a cook for the same Ellis plantation until she couldn't do it anymore. She got arthritis and then I took over. My grandmother, I remember, was a slave for a different family. I can't remember the name, Williams something or another. John Williams was her master's name if I'm not mistaken. She was sold to him. My grandmother would tell me how she was sold to him on the block because, excuse the expression, she was a hell raiser. She would talk about the times they had to beat her to discipline her and make her do right. She died soon after I got married. She didn't die a slave though.

My sister Carrie was a fast girl. So it wasn't all that a surprise when we found out she was gonna have a baby. She was fifteen. She didn't marry the father. He went his way and so did she. He married someone else and she married someone else.

How was having children out of wedlock viewed?

The mothers would be heartbroken when their daughters would get pregnant and not married. If they got married, I guess it was OK. My mother was heartbroken when my sister became pregnant but didn't get married. She didn't beat her or anything like that. She was just heart- broken.

At that time my mother made a root tea to try and bring my sister's menstrual on, but noth'n happened. She was already pregnant.

I remember the night she got pregnant. The moon was shining like day.

We were at home. My mother had gone off to visit a sick person a little after suppertime. After dark, along comes Coot on this mule. He lived on another plantation. James Sims was his real name, but we called him Coot. I don't know why we called him Coot, but that what he was called from the time we met him and his family.

That night we were suppose to go and stay at my cousin's for the night since my mother had gone to visit, but my sister didn't listen. She must have known Coot was coming by. They must have planned the meeting.

We were all on the porch until I got sleepy. I was put to bed and Carrie was suppose to join me. She did at first and that's how I went to sleep. When I soon woke up she wasn't there. I went to the porch and she was sitting there with James. They weren't doing anything and I went back to bed.

My mother knew Carrie was pregnant soon as she noticed her gaining all this weight. I really don't know if Coot would have married Carrie or not because soon after she became pregnant she wouldn't see him. He would come by and she would hide and tell us to tell him she's not there. She didn't want to have anything to do with him so he went on and married someone else.

I was also born out of wedlock. My mother's husband was not my father. My father was Charlie Gary. My mother's husband was Josh Coleman. I took on his name instead of my father. My father married somebody else and I would see him from time to time at church and different places, so I did know him. He would give me things. Material to make dresses, but I didn't take on his name. Josh Coleman was who I knew to be more my father.

I came to New York once my husband said he had jobs for us. This was in Hamilton, New York, upstate. I worked for the Keer family. M.L. was working for the Littlefields. We were working for different families but we were together. We stayed at a house that Mrs. Keer provided for us. That was a nice, quiet short time. I had two of my children up there in Hamilton.

We left Hamilton because we got tired of it. It wasn't no Blacks up there. Noth'n but whites. You went to church, it was white. You went to the movies, it was white. We just got tired and homesick and we moved to New York in 1939. We went back down to South Carolina for a month's visit then we came on up to New York that spring. By this time I was pregnant with my third child.

Soon after we got to New York, M.L. found work, but then soon after that he had lost his job. And at that time I was near to delivery. We went down to the welfare office and tried to get assistance. They told us they couldn't give us any help because we hadn't lived and worked in New York long enough. We told them we'd take any little amount but they said there was nothing they could do. M.L. told them if they didn't help us he would leave me and then they would have to give me assistance. They still said they wouldn't. He didn't believe them. He left, and they didn't give me shit. This was a time. I'll tell you, it was something.

How I did get welfare, much later, was due to this Jewish woman. Along Eastern Parkway, from Utica to Rochester, you'd sit out on the benches and the Jewish women would come up and ask, "Ya vanna verk?" That was called day's work. It wasn't no steady work, it was just for that day. You'd go every day to see who had work for you. At first I didn't know what they were say'n. Their accent was so heavy. My girlfriend had to tell me what they were saying, "Do you want work?" So that's how I'd work. Twenty-five cents an hour. Some would pay thirty, but twenty-five was what was normal. Two dollars for eight hours. They'd also give you carfare and a boiled egg. That was good in them days. Coffee and a boiled egg for lunch, or a bagel.

I found work with a Mrs. Lavine, something like that. A very nice lady. This was the time when everybody had measles. It was go'n 'round something awful. At that time they said measles was very dangerous. They could take a turn for the worst, and it can kill you. My children had them and Mrs. Lavine asked shouldn't I be home with them. I told her yes, but said they have to eat, too. I have to pay rent. Keep a roof over our heads. She then gave me a letter to take down to welfare, and when I did, they gave me assistance, just like that. I don't know what was in that letter. It couldn't have been much, it was more like a note, but I received assistance because of it.

I found out where M.L. had gone through his cousin, Daisy Bates. She came and told me he went to Jamaica, Queens, and had met some girl. Gene was her name. He told her he wasn't married, he was single and didn't have no children. He died in 1967. I met Gene at his funeral. She was pleasant.

With him in Queens, I got to meet Harry Hall. He owned a corner grocery store in my neighborhood. Corner of Fulton and Utica. It's apartments over there now, but that's where his store was. From shopping there, I got to know him. He's the reason I'm still in New York today. He really helped me and my children. He was more of a father and husband than the man I was married to.

It never got to the point where you wanted to marry him?

He was already married. He had a nice wife who worked in the store. I wouldn't say we were friends. She knew me from shopping in the store. Her name was Alice. Alice Hall. I'll tell you, I've prayed so hard and asked God to forgive me for all the wrong I've done. But before that I was praying for Him to help me out any way He can. I don't know if He sent me Mr. Hall, but I sure did need the help and God knew it. The way I was praying He couldn't not know how bad I needed help. There were plenty times I wouldn't eat myself and give the food to my children. My stomach would be just as empty, but I'd rather me than my children go hungry. Those were some hard times. Back in 1939, during the Depression, things were bad. When I met Mr. Hall it was hard not to accept his help. God forgive me. I hope He looked past my faults and saw my needs. He knew my children had to eat. Mr. Hall didn't have any children and he helped mine like they were his. We started seeing each other and just naturally became closer.

I can't say I was looking to get pregnant, but when I did, he helped even better. And I'd tell you, this man was so old, I didn't think he could make a baby. I was in my twenties, he wouldn't tell me his exact age, but I just knew he was too old to be making babies. Well, it didn't work out like that. I had to have it.

No thoughts of termination?

I'll tell you, I didn't even know to think anything of getting rid of babies. All I knew was you'd get pregnant and have a baby. Back then you have that baby. That's taking a life. The sixth commandment is "Thou shall not kill." As far as I'm concerned, an abortion is killing. It's wrong. If any of my daughters had gotten pregnant at any young age, I would have to advise them to have the baby.

Last night on the news I heard this man say he heard this crying sound and he looked in a garbage bag and there was this new baby boy. That's terrible. Why would someone do something like that? That baby would have frozen to death. You have that baby and keep it. You do the best you can or people shouldn't have sex.

I was in the hospital delivering Mr. Hall's baby, when my husband M.L. found out. He would still come around to visit the children from time to time, and this time when he came 'round, Marie, who was minding the children, told him I was at Saint Mary's Hospital. When he got there, oh, was it something. He let everybody in that hospital know that I was having another man's baby. He was yell'n and scream'n, "This is my wife, but this ain't my baby. This is some other man's baby." I told him, yes and I wish all the rest were someone else's. Oh, we made a scene.

Do you know years later that sucker told me I was the only one he ever loved. The only one.

Do you think he left only because he couldn't support you, not because he didn't love you?

No, I think he left because he didn't want to be responsible for his family. I believe had he found a job, he still would have soon left. He may have loved me more than anyone, but he wouldn't work for nobody. He had a car he could have sold, but he didn't want to sell. When we were at the welfare office they asked if he had anything he could sell and we could live off until they could help. He told them yes, he had a car his brother left him after death, but he wasn't going to sell it for nothing. That man didn't want to work. When he left, that was it.

When I had the baby the nurses went crazy about this little girl. All of them. They would usually bring the mothers the baby in a basket during their feeding time, but they would carry my baby to me. The other mothers would get so mad, but this was one pretty baby. And an old man's baby at that.

All my children turned out well. I tried to teach them right from wrong, but I know it's not all me. You can tell someone something, but you can't make them do it. You can give them good sound advice and be satisfied that you gave it to them. If they follow it, you're happy, but if they don't follow, I wouldn't blame myself. Their adult decisions are up to them.

One of my granddaughters is a doctor and one of my granddaughters fell into drugs. It's not the fault of the parents, because both of their mothers are my daughters. I raised their mothers. I raised them both the same. They both taught their daughters the same values I taught them, but it's up to the individual to take those values to heart. Depending on how God makes that person out, it's up to them whether they'll listen or not.

Can you help shape that makeup?

You can try, but who they are is up to God. I can give two different people the same advice and guidance from birth, but depending on how God made them, they will either listen or not. How do you explain what some people will do and what some people won't do? I think once the children become adults and go out in the world, it's out of your hands. You can only pray that they took the best of what you had to give them and will turn out all right.

Since young

there's nothi

have

people are having sex, and I see they're gonna have sex,
ng you can do about that, but since they're gonna do it, you
vise them to use some protection. The worst thing is to tell them
ey will and they'll do it with no responsibility. But nowadays I
children say they wanna have the baby. You'd have to tell me why
If there are those who don't want to get pregnant, I guess they're
doing the right thing not to get pregnant.

ortion, you know, is out of the question. I wouldn't suggest that in
circumstance. I'm eighty-four years old. I guess my beliefs are not for
today. You have your own ideas today, your own beliefs. I was a twenty-year-old virgin until my wedding night. My husband had to get some Blue Seal Vaseline for me.

You're not supposed to use that.

You are so. If you've never had sex and you needed something, we knew to use Blue Seal Vaseline. It's good for everything.

But not sex. You go to the drugstore and get what's appropriate.

We ain't have no drugstore.

You had a grocery store. Wasn't everything combined? Food, clothes and whatever?

Yeah, and Blue Seal was the whatever.

But now we've found out that's no good.

Good or not, it helped. Well, what are you suppose to use? What do you use?

Nothing.

Nothing?

I've never had sex with a virgin.

No?

No.

Well, if you did, what would you use?

There's something called K-Y jelly.

Seem like y'all really don't need anything anyway. You're born ready. And sex used to be sacred, but today it's so open. It wasn't like that when I was growing up. The Bible say it's better to marry than to burn, but are parents teaching that? Parents today are busy doing their own thing. They don't have time to raise their children the right way. It seems even if the child wanted to make a choice with the parent's help, the parent is not there. They're not being taught proper from the start.

I believe it's up to the women to say how things are gonna be. If you let a man do what he wants to do, he's gonna do it. We're the ones carry'n what you men want, so we should be in control of how we use it. It's ours, that's the way it should be.

I see how the men don't respect the women, and th̶... ̶y̶ both don't
respect themselves, I don't know who to blame first. I guess ... ̶he parents if
they're not giving them any guidance at all. After that, it's up to ... ̶nts if
that person, but you at least have to start them off with proper gu...

I would like to say getting an education is very important. You ...
much more opportunities than I had growing up, I think if you knew ho...
hard it was, you'd run to school every day.

I'm ashamed to tell you. I went up to the fifth grade. We went three
months out the year. January through March, and then school was closed
for the rest of the year. I believe I was twelve when I first started. Vestine
Clark was my teacher. But I've learned a whole lot since. It seems young
people should want to go as far as they can in school. Even if you can't
afford college, you should still want to go. Anybody's college. As long as
books and teachers are there, you can better yourself. It don't matter
where you go. They all got teachers with something to teach. A lot of
Blacks got noth'n, so they should wanna learn someth'n.

The first time I voted was in 1944. I was thirty-four years old. I ain't
know noth'n about voting in the South. Not until I came up to New York
did I know about voting. We had to take a literacy test in order to vote. I
took it and passed and I voted for Roosevelt. Today you don't have to take
a test. Our children need to know about King and the 1965 voting rights
campaign. You have to take advantage of these things because your people
died for it. You owe it to your forefathers.

You ever wonder about Africa?

No, I don't know noth'n about Africa. I never heard my parents
or grandparents ever mention anything about Africa. The only thing I
know of Africa is from *Roots*. But if learning about Africa is a way for
Blacks to better ourselves, then I'm all for us learning more about
Africa.

Thank you, Nana. Nuthin but love.

etc.

After all is said and done, send in the clowns. Traditionally, I would be obliged to end on an optimistic note, leave with all the good-time feelings and pink and green emotions. But true to its title, LOVE AWAITS remains unresolved.

The word "love" by definition expresses affection. It's positive, esteem, spiritual depth, passionate and deep feeling. *dearest brothers,* LOVE AWAITS, *much peace, your sisters* is sincerely that. As obvious as the word love is, however, the tense word "awaits" is also prominent. It conditions the love, which becomes something smoldering, just around the corner. It's calming, waiting, while we're somewhere up the street stuck in the middle of the block just chill'n, languishing.

Joyous unions and celebrations are experienced by many, but they are so far out of reach for so many more. And look at what's keeping our feet on this broken conveyor belt. Victimization is one thing, but to self-victimize on a continuous and indifferent, dare I say enjoyable, basis is a special kind of pathology. To slur and profane each other physically, to defile and butcher, to add pejorative layer on top of disparaging layer to our own, yes, first man-made, but now self-maintained oppression, is worse than any kind of real or fictional sickness I know. The key, answers, solutions and remedies are in our hands. But how much longer until we realize this? How much longer until we *do* blame ourselves? How many more lives until *we* do begin to share responsibility? How much longer until this *love* no longer *awaits*? If I'm told for as long as it takes, well then, God, do I admire its patience.

Traditionally, sighs of relief and salvation-on-the-horizon are endings peculiar to most concerns about African Americans. But realistically, historically what has this optimism meant? Historically, complacent sighs of relief in the face of constant adversity have been a part of our stubborn problem. Adapting to the most comfortable position while undergoing the most inhumane indignities until we no longer feel the pain, ultimately believing we are no longer in pain has become something of a selfish custom peculiar to us. The ever vigilant, "Yes, things are bad, but they can always be worse," be it infidelity, pregnancy, disloyalty, drugs, rape, murder, racism, _____, fill in your own blank, is continued only due to this peculiar enduring tolerance we have for it. No, "fuck all this bullshit" outcry and be done with it. I simply fail to see any up endings until this is the scream heard round the world.

How does optimism remedy my pain and suffering for today? How are poverty, lack of education, recognition, and love today made any easier? How much longer should I hold out?

I could tell of my boy's recent wedding to his long-time lady. Congratulations to the new Mr. and Mrs. Niles. I've said there are numerous accounts of Black love getting off the conveyor belt and turning that corner. But does that allow everyone to say, "Yeah, that's me," as mostly everyone believes their defecation is gold, even with more than half of all marriages failing and with relationships checking in even more dismally. LOVE AWAITS; I'm told it most certainly does, but for how long? How much longer? I'll question its patience if no one else will.

Vanessa and Tracy are still home with the untimely new life they've brought forth. Nikki, Serita, Freda, Lisa, Coco, Hannan and Assata are still surviving doing a deadman's float in the middle of the ocean with no land in sight, but still surviving. Mia, one of the many whom you may never know, is still home with Evenflow in one hand, reasons and motives and a firm grasp of escape in the other.

In LOVE AWAITS you may find your own personal truth. If not, you must soul search and find it wherever it lives and, if need be, make the necessary adjustment in your life. May your truth be positive, life-affirming and progressive, causing no harm, pain or injury to anyone.

Communicate at every level. Even if it's with your grandmother. For anyone to state, "You spoke with your grandmother about what? I couldn't go there," speaks of the problem. If parents and grandparents cannot speak to their young about life and all its intimacies, then this art of living life will remain as naive, instinctive and as self-destructive as it is now.

If we don't change, our relationship to our personal selves, which is where we must start, will continue as in "You Don't Know Me" by Ray Charles. Our relationship as Black men and women to the rest of the world, with all its fears, stereotypes and misconceptions is in "You Don't

Know Me." Our relationship as Black men and Black women to one another will remain "You Don't Know Me."

This awaiting love cannot be embraced until we correctly focus, not on what we have said, but on what we have felt. Why do we feel the way we do? What motivates our language and actions? Through mere words, what frustrations are we expressing? This is the heart of the matter, not how many references to bitch a song has, as if one isn't enough and why is that one felt? What is it that has been internalized to produce and uphold such decency?

True pain is repulsive. It's ugly, vulgar and offensive. Its tone is reflective of that. Nigga, nigga, nigga, bitch, bitch, bitch comes as no surprise if we are referring to a people despising themselves. Once attitudes, spirits and beliefs are changed and dealt with, our choice of word expression becomes automatic. Just as we always have, we'll find we can create the words to reflect our sentiment, sisters and brothers, Kings and Queens. Elders, Griots and Sages, Africans and Gods.

As of today, I look in the mirror, repulsed, not by a physical reflection but by spiritual deformities and malformations. LOVE AWAITS, so I guess I too must find the patience, as I continue learning the Watusi.

—Courtney

acknowledgments

Honor to the Supreme Being, Goddess and her son, God, no ifs, ands or buts. The primaries, Joe, Betty and Paige. The Long and Coleman families. The family at Birdy's Records and The Gospel Den, James, Stan, Greg, Isiah, Isaac, Donald, Ricky. The universities of the 117, number one in particular, Vera, Selmon, Kelsey, Doc, Henri, Janet, Claudia, George, Peter, Renee, Walker, Irma, Dr. Donaldson and Frank Smith. Bucky, Eric, Dennis and Everett. Good looking out, Phil and the family at Saint Paul Community Baptist.

Honor to Al Kubulan. My brothers and sisters of the lost children of Israel, soon 'nuff. Peace to my surrogate home of birth and nurture, Brooklyn, USA, Bed-Sty, Crown Heights and East Flatbush. Much love and continued unity to the 32 Family.

Honor to all Queens who know it, in particular Diana Mills, Guinea Benett, Kamala Gordon, Lissa Jean, Shellie Carter, a little something. Tracy Blair, top five. Michelle Clouden, Kat, Leatha Remington, Felicia Robinson, Charm, Shaunna, Sheila, Brigette Moore, Dina Fortson, Mlysses Newson, Namusa Smith, Dulcea, Audrey Batts, Beverly Jenkins, April Jones, Corina Prados, Jenese, Ada and Karen Babino, Sydney Boone, Dawn Nock, Cheryl Taylor, Debbie Williams, Inonge, Alvina Stewart, Natlie Bullock, Julie Brussard, Wendy Robinson, Wendy Davis, Melissa Taylor, Sydney Whitten, Marlow Wyatt, Clezel Sewell, Dree Calloway, Libra Riley, Saleena Mohammed, Malaika Finney, Nina Lane, Regina Johnson, Courtney, Tori, Deloris Laws, Grandma Funk, Celeste A-Re, Beverly Smith-Dawson, Saba, Jai and the Mo'Dels, and Walidah.

Erinn White stands alone.

The twenty-six represent'n all those who want change.

My brothers on offensive, Adrian, Laudwin, Kevin, Alex, Ed, Auddie,

Julian, Vamp, Skeeze, Qkawan, Dwight, Lewis, Horace, Bill, Larry, Bert, Mike Scott, Tim Harris, Tracy Whitney, Freddie-Air-Graf-X and Gary Alexander. Koye, Malik Sayeed, Joe Gibson, Mark Seabrooks, Mark McClendon, Mike Stevens, Shahid Mustafa, Everett Edwards, Tim Byrd, Ricardo Solomon, Vincent Siders, Vincent Miller, Jason Carmichael, Morris Beasley, Steve Benson, David Calloway, Eric Ruffian, Isiah Washington, Anthony Lamont, Johnnie Fairfax, Alphonse McCullough, G. Stubbs, Adrian Nurse, Joe Myrick, Mike Jones, Dwight Birmingham, Maurice Dixon, Rodney Stratchan, Rodney Stewart and Anthony Anderson, Dana, Cory and Kyle.

Deep appreciation to Mitch Rose, Leslie Meredith, Brian Tart, and Lauren Field.

Brothers on defense, Nationalist, Naturalist and Field Niggas, I got your back. Peace to sons and daughters developments inc., grow up and be somebody.

about the author

COURTNEY LONG is a filmmaker and writer. He is developing a film that will be based on *Love Awaits*. He is a member of sons and daughters productions, an African American artists' organization, and is at work on a book of interviews with African American men that will be the sequel to *Love Awaits*.